The Visitor's Guide
to
TURKEY

GW00566514

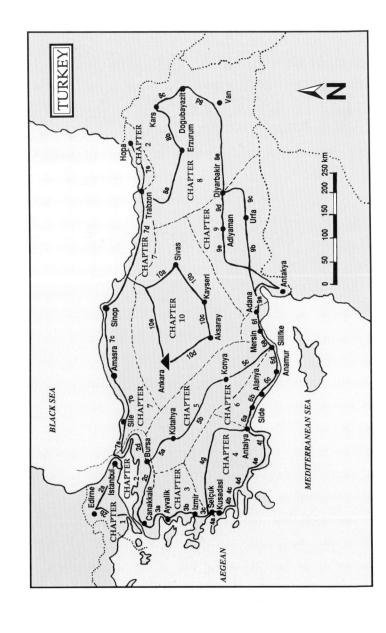

THE
VISITOR'S GUIDE TO
TURKEY

AMANDA HINTON

MPC
HUNTER
PUBLISHING INC

Published by:
Moorland Publishing Co Ltd,
Moor Farm Road,
Airfield Estate,
Ashbourne,
Derbyshire DE6 1HD
England

British Library Cataloguing in
Publication Data:
Hinton, Amanda
   The visitor's guide to Turkey.
   1. Turkey - Visitor's guides
   I. Title
   915.61'0438

ISBN 0 86190 334 X (paperback)
ISBN 0 86190 333 1 (hardback)

Published in the USA by:
Hunter Publishing Inc,
300 Raritan Centre Parkway,
CN 94, Edison, NJ 08818

ISBN 1 55650 234 6 (USA)

Colour and black & white
origination by:
Scantrans, Singapore

Printed in the UK by:
Richard Clay Ltd, Bungay, Suffolk

Cover photograph: *Sherbet seller,
Kahramanmaras* (A. Hinton).

Illustrations have been supplied as
follows: S. Greenwood pp 11, 14,
15, 19, 90, 98, 99, 102, 103, 110,
127, 147, 151, 154, 171, 183, 186
(bottom), 190; A. Mudford pp 51
(both), 106, 107, 167.

All other illustrations are from the
author.

CONTENTS

Key to Symbols Used in Text Margin and on Maps

 Recommended walk

 Parkland

 Archaeological site

 Nature reserve/Animal interest

 Birdlife

 Garden

 Building of interest

 Castle/Fortification

 Museum/Art gallery

 Beautiful view/Scenery, Natural phenomenon

 Other place of interest

Key to Symbols Used on Maps

 Road

 River

 Town/City

 Town/Village

 Reservoir/Lake

.... International Boundary

– – – – – Ferry Route

Note on the maps
The maps drawn for each chapter, while comprehensive, are not designed to be used as route maps, but rather to locate the main towns, villages and places of interest.

INTRODUCTION

Turkey has recently experienced a boom in its tourism industry and many holidaymakers from the west who once went to the Greek Islands now favour the Turkish Mediterranean shores. Beaches, boat trips, scenic ruins and natural countryside are just some of the attractions; good food, low budget accommodation and generous hospitality follow closely behind. The country has a high rural population and travelling around remote villages is like stepping back in time: farming methods rely on the wooden plough and the hand scythe, and many of the old traditions and crafts such as carpet-making and weaving are still a way of life. In tourist centres and major cities the atmosphere is more Western and the regular cry of the *müezzin* is one of the few reminders that Turkey is an Islamic country with a 99 per cent Moslem faith.

This book is divided into ten interconnecting routes which cover the chief places of interest as well as lesser known attractions. Each route is subdivided into stages; each stage can usually be covered in a day, and ends in a place where overnight accommodation is available. It requires at least 6 weeks to get around the entire country. Most visitors on a short holiday break limit their travel to the beaches and classical ruins along the south coast but an increasing number of people are also exploring the central and eastern areas as they slowly become more developed.

The Weather and Seasons

Turkey has four distinct seasons dispelling the common myth that it is a land of sun and sand 52 weeks of the year. Winters are as long and bleak as in any other part of Europe, and in the central and eastern regions entire villages are cut off by snow for up to 3 months of the year, which limits winter-time travel for the visitor to the east.

The coasts remain snow-free and the warmest winters are along the Mediterranean where the temperature rarely drops below 6°C (43°F). In spring the weather is variable and there is often a deal of rain interspersed with warm sunny days. The countryside passes through a brief spell of being lush and green before the long hot summer droughts set in.

Sun screen protection is essential for visitors travelling to Turkey in the summer and care should be taken to avoid dehydration as temperatures can reach up to 45°C (113°F). Along the coast, evenings are often uncomfortably hot and humid. The air is cooler inland on the high altitude plateaux and a long-sleeved shirt or a light jacket are recommended for the evenings. In early autumn it is still warm enough to swim on the south coast. In October the Mediterranean Sea has an average temperature of 25°C (77°F).

The Terrain

Turkey is composed of a number of high plateaux surrounded by mountain ranges. The Black Sea coast mountains known as the Pontic Alps drop steeply into the sea leaving a very narrow coastal strip. The Mediterranean coast is dominated by the Taurus mountains which swing inland and meet up with the Pontic Alps to form the mountainous eastern region. The two coasts offer contrastingly different landscapes, the Black Sea coast is covered with verdant forest, the south coast has a typically Mediterranean vegetation with olives, oleander and dry herb shrubs.

As the major mountain ranges have an east-west orientation, travel from the north to the south is difficult. A number of passes cross the mountains but most roads keep to the plateaux or follow the coasts. Off the main roads rough tracks, suitable for jeeps, lead to the more remote villages. Unfortunately there are no maps showing tracks or paths but the countryside is ideal walking terrain and the only hazards to look out for are the occasional guard dog or snake.

Agriculture is as varied as the landscape with banana plantations in the deep sheltered bays along the eastern Mediterranean shore, vast fields of cotton in the rich alluvial plains surrounding Adana and Mersin, endless fields of cereal crops on the central plateau, and abundant olive groves along the Aegean. The land in the east is poor and degraded and is only suitable for grazing sheep and goats.

History and Monuments

Turkey has a long and illustrious history well marked by historical monuments and ancient remains. The earliest traces of humans are found in the neolithic caves along the south coast. The oldest civilised settlements are in the south-east close to the Tigris and Euphrates rivers on the fringes of Mesopotamia and date from the seventh millennium BC. The best remains of early civilisation are from the time of the Hittites, an influential people whose capital city was at *Hattusas*, east of Ankara. The well-preserved city ruins and temple complexes date from the second millennium BC.

At the start of the first millennium BC the Aegean and Mediterranean coast was colonised by a wave of Greek migrants who built cities and established small kingdoms. In 546BC the colonies fell into the hands of the Persians who retained power up until 334BC when Alexander the Great conquered Anatolia and freed the Greek cities from Persian rule. After Alexander's death in 323BC his kingdom was divided between his generals. Lysimachus took Anatolia and founded one of the most powerful dynasties in the classical world. The capital city was at *Pergamum* which remains one of the most impressive ancient sites on the Aegean coast.

When the Romans took power in the first century BC they generally enlarged or built on top of the already existing Hellenistic cities so that most of the classical sites in Turkey have a mixture of Greek and Roman architecture. Between AD47-57 St Paul brought Christianity to the Roman province of Asia as he wandered through the region spreading the gospel. The simple rock-hewn churches carved at this time still remain, as do many of the later Byzantine monastic centres. Cappadocia has a particularly rich collection of churches, many of which are decorated with outstanding frescoes.

Although the Byzantine empire lasted for over 1,000 years surprisingly little is left. Most of the buildings were destroyed during the Turkish invasion, and Aya Sofia in Istanbul stands as one of the few examples of Byzantine architecture. The decline of the Byzantine empire began in 1071 with their military defeat at the hands of the Seljuk Turks at Manzikert. The Turks gradually seized more and more Byzantine territory in the east, at the same time the Latin church threatened from the west. Crusaders en route for Jerusalem were drawn into the conflict sacking *Constantinople* in 1204.

One of the many tribes encouraged by the Seljuk Turks to expand their territory at Byzantine expense became so powerful that they took over from their former rulers. These were the Osmanli, known to the west as the Ottomans, so named after their leader Osman. Bursa became the first capital of the Ottoman empire in 1326, from there it moved to Edirne and finally to Istanbul in 1453. The empire expanded quickly reaching its height in the sixteenth century under the rule of Suleyman the Magnificent, and some of the finest Ottoman monuments date from this era. After the sixteenth century the Ottoman empire slowly started to decline, so that by 1909 a political

A field of poppies growing beside Beysehir Lake

group known as the Young Turks were able to wrest control from the sultanate. After World War I, during which Turkey allied itself with Germany, the country was occupied by France, Britain, Italy and Greece. Turkey gained its independence in 1923 after Kemal Atatürk waged a military campaign against the occupying Allied forces.

Mustafa Kemal Atatürk was born in Ottoman Greece in 1881, and he was the moving force behind the struggle for independence after World War 1, leading the republic until his death in 1938. Throughout this period he introduced numerous reforms intended to transform the country into a modern Western society. Atatürk died before he had completed reforming the country, but his principles and ideals have been adhered to ever since and he is regarded as the great national hero. There is a statue of him in every town and his memory is held in great respect; it is an official offence to make any derogatory comment about him.

People

Before 1923 the population of Turkey included large numbers of Greeks, Armenians, Jews and Venetians, and many of the most

Collecting water at Aygir Lake

influential figures in business, trade and the arts were non-Turkish citizens. After the War of Independence in 1923 there was an exchange of populations between Turkey and Greece, and most Greeks were re-settled in Greece. Small communities of Greeks and Jews remain in Istanbul, but the only significant non-Turkish ethnic group in Turkey today are the Kurds. Kurdish is widely spoken in the east and Arabic is common in the south-east, but the official language is Turkish. English is taught as a second language in schools and German is fairly widespread as a great number of guest-workers are employed in Germany. In centres of tourism and main cities the touts and shop-sellers seem to speak any language that may bring them business and most people have no difficulty in communicating.

In more rural areas it is rare to find anyone who speaks a foreign language and a few words of Turkish can get the visitor a long way. People in the country are generally very friendly and it is not unusual to be offered drinks and refreshments. The Turkish people generally pride themselves on their hospitality but in some of the more developed tourist centres this attitude has started to wear thin and hospitality has taken on more mercenary motives.

Religion

Ninety-nine per cent of Turkey's population is Moslem, but Islam plays no part in the running of the country; Turkey is a secular state. The degree to which Islamic principles effect people's lives varies a great deal. However, even those who do not observe the religion very strictly would still claim to be Moslem, and the *Koran* sets a moral foundation which is the basis of the Turkish sense of honesty, kindness and generosity.

The Islamic way of life is most closely adhered to in the rural parts of the country and amongst elderly people. Men and women live segregated lives outside of the family, prayer is an integral part of daily life and the fast is strictly observed with restaurants, and shops selling alcoholic drinks, shut for the duration of Ramazan. The cities are more lax in their attitude and people follow their own lifestyle. The mosques are attended by less people and alcohol is widely available. Women have freedom outside the home and many have professional careers, wear fashionable clothes and mix in society with men.

Islam is a tolerant religion and it is generally accepted that foreigners need not follow the Islamic codes of behaviour, although visitors should be careful not to give offence when visiting mosques or other religious places by wearing unsuitable clothing. The normal dress-code for Moslem women is a head-scarf, a long skirt or the traditional *salvar* baggy pants, and a shirt with sleeves; men usually wear trousers and jackets.

Travelling to Turkey

BY AIR

Atatürk Havaalani, the international airport in Istanbul, receives most of the flights to Turkey. The airport is modern and efficient and has a good reputation for security. Flights call here from most of the world, including all major European cities, the USA, China, India and the Middle East. There is another international airport at Ankara, although this is less used, and a third on the south coast at Dalaman. During the summer Dalaman receives most of the charter flights from Europe, some also go to Izmir and Antalya. A budget charter flight to Dalaman is probably the cheapest way of travelling by air to Turkey. Details can be obtained from local travel agents.

Regular non-charter flights are more expensive, although the price is lower if the flight stops off at another city en route. Non-direct flights from New York call at either Amsterdam or Frankfurt, while from London they call in at Zagreb or Amsterdam. Direct flights from London take about $3^1/_2$ hours and from New York about 12 hours. (For addresses see Useful Information.)

BY CAR

It is over 3,000km (1,860 miles) by road from London to Istanbul. The most direct route is through Germany, Austria, Yugoslavia and Bulgaria. The journey takes about 4 days with driving conditions deteriorating the nearer one gets to Turkey. It is advisable to check on current visa requirements before travelling. US citizens need to obtain transit visas for Yugoslavia and Bulgaria; the Yugoslavian visa is available at the border. Both US and UK citizens should obtain 30-hour Bulgarian transit visas before arriving in the country. Visitors should apply to their local Bulgarian Embassy. Visitors are allowed to bring cars into Turkey for up to 3 months at a time. When travelling in Turkey, cars are frequently stopped by police and drivers are required to produce a current driving licence, a green card and ownership papers. It is worth checking whether travel insurance covers the car for Asia as well as Europe.

Vehicles are registered in passports on entering the country and crossed out when leaving. Once a vehicle is registered in a passport it is impossible to leave the country without it. If the vehicle is stolen or written off in an accident, statements from the police and the customs must be obtained in order to leave.

Visitors who wish to stay for longer than 3 months can either apply for an extension, which is a bureaucratic nightmare, or simply leave the country for 24 hours and re-register the vehicle on entering again.

BY BUS

There is a regular coach service from Paris to Istanbul which calls at Lyon, Milan, Venice, Ljubljana and Belgrade. The journey takes between 3 and 4 days and is barely cost effective when compared to the cheap apex and charter flights on offer from London.

BY RAIL

There are direct rail services from Ostend and Munich to Istanbul. The journey takes between $1\frac{1}{2}$ and 2 days and fares are quite competitive. Visitors should book well in advance as the route is heavily used by Turkish guest-workers in Germany.

BY SEA

The Orient Express cruise liner which runs weekly between Venice and Istanbul is the most comfortable, but also the most expensive, way of making the journey. The Turkish state-run ferries, Turkish Maritime Lines, are much cheaper. They operate a weekly ferry between Ancona and Izmir, and the Greek ferry line, Libra Maritime, has a regular service between Brindisi and Izmir. British Sealink is the agent for the various services that run from Italy to Greece and

Moving house by camel, western Turkey

Yugoslavia. During the summer small ferries ply back and forth between the Greek Islands of Kos, Chios, Rodos, Samos and Lesvos to the Turkish coast. (For addresses see Useful Information.)

BORDER FORMALITIES

Visitors from Europe and the United States need only a valid passport to visit Turkey. A tourist visa for 3 months is automatically stamped in the passport at the border. For periods exceeding 3 months it is necessary to apply for a resident's permit from the Turkish Embassy or leave the country to obtain a new tourist visa.

The restrictions on what visitors can bring into the country are quite strict, although items for personal use are rarely questioned. Electrical goods and valuable items such as fur coats are registered in visitors' passports and must be taken out of the country when leaving. Knives, narcotic drugs and pornography are strictly forbidden.

Visitors who have purchased antiques or old carpets while in Turkey should obtain a certificate of export from the directorate of the local museum. Generally however, there are very few problems when leaving the country.

Drying grapes in the sun to make raisins

Visiting Turkey

ACCOMMODATION

Hotels are classified by the Turkish Ministry of Culture and Tourism and are priced according to their facilities and standards. This varies from region to region, but most hotels have their official price list displayed in the reception. Quite often hoteliers are willing to accept a lower price, particularly out of season.

The international hotel chains, Hilton and Sheraton, have branches in Istanbul and Ankara, but luxury-class Turkish hotels also meet international standards. Hotels classified by the ministry as *turistik* are given star ratings, a one-star hotel is simple, but clean and comfortable. Lower quality hotels are graded into *sinif* (class). The first *sinif* are usually good value for money while the third *sinif*, although very cheap, are often dirty and lack any facilities. *Pansiyon*, only to be found in tourist resorts and not in cities, range from being small hotels to a room in someone's home. They are usually well priced, clean and friendly, and may have cooking facilities available. Youth hostels also provide cheap accommodation in Istanbul and Marmaris, and there are student residences in other parts of the country which are also used as youth hostels.

There are numerous camp-sites along the coast, but even the best are not as well equipped as their European equivalents. Mocamp Kervansaray is one of the best and most reputable chains. Camping on open ground without permission is against the law, but hoteliers often allow visitors to camp in their gardens.

FOOD AND DRINK

Istanbul and the south coast have the best selection of restaurants, but simple and appetising food is served all over Turkey. The Turks pride themselves on their cuisine and the food served in restaurants is fresh and attractively presented. Fish is very popular and is usually served grilled with an array of tempting salads and side dishes, known as *meze*. Some typical *meze* include: *dolma*, stuffed vine leaves; *börek*, cheese-filled pastries; *midiye dolmasi*, stuffed mussels; *patlican ezmesi*, aubergine and yoghurt purée; *çacik,* yoghurt, garlic and cucumber; *haydariye,* yoghurt mixed with herbs and white cheese. Many different types of fish are caught along Turkey's long coastline, amongst the most common are: *lufer*, blue-fish; *kalkan*, a turbot local to the Black Sea, Bosphorus and Marmara; *barbunya*, red mullet; *kefal*, grey mullet caught in the Marmara, Aegean and Mediterranean.

Kebabs are the national food and can be found, in one form or another, almost anywhere. The meat used is generally beef, although lamb is used in some regions of Turkey. The *sis* kebab — cubes of beef on a skewer, is the most common. Adana and Urfa kebab, skewers of minced beef and onion, the first with red pepper the other without, are also widely served. The best kebabs are grilled over charcoal and served with fresh salad and bread. The *döner* kebab, however, is perhaps the most popular type. A vertical spit of marinaded meat is grilled in front of charcoal and sliced into thin slivers while still cooking. The Iskender kebab is a tasty variation on the basic bread and meat, and is topped with melted butter, yoghurt and tomato sauce.

The cheapest restaurants, *lokanta*, serve ready-cooked food and cater mainly for the lunchtime trade. *Lokanta* food is excellent value for money and is usually fresh and hot. *Kuru fasulye*, white beans in tomato sauce; and *nohut*, stewed chick peas, are amongst the most common dishes. There is always a choice of home-made soups and a variety of meat casseroles. Simple pizza, which are more akin to bread and cheese, are served in *pideci* restaurants. There is only a limited range of toppings: *peynir*, white cheese, *kiymali*, minced meat, and *kasar peynir*, yellow cheese, are the most common.

Turkish sweets and pastries are a meal in themselves and although most restaurants offer a choice of two or three desserts, the best selection is found in a *pastane*. *Baklava*, a light, flaky pastry drenched in syrup, is layered with a variety of fillings ranging from pistachio nuts and walnuts to cream and semolina. *Kadayif* is similar to *baklava* but the pastry is shredded into fine strands. Oven-baked milk puddings and caramels are also good; *tavuk gögsu* is a special pudding made with cream of chicken breast, and *asure* is a nourishing pudding made with raisins, walnuts, whole wheat, chick peas and apricots.

For a country where alcohol is not very widely drunk there is a surprisingly good selection of alcoholic drinks at moderate prices. The Turkish word for wine, *sarap*, is derived from an Arabic word which, literally translated, means bad water. The cheapest wines constitute little better than this, but a quite drinkable bottle can be bought for about £1.50 ($2.40). Raki, an aniseed flavoured spirit, is more popular than wine. It is drunk with ice and plenty of water, often accompanied by *leblebi*, roasted chick peas, or other snacks. By far the most popular drinks are cola and *çay*, tea. There is also a good selection of bottled fruit juices and freshly pressed juices are available from juice bars.

TRANSPORT
Public Transport in Towns and Cities
Every town and city has a bus service run by the local council. Services are frequent and cheap, and very widely used. Tickets must be bought before getting on a bus and are available from ticket offices at the main bus-stops, or from small shops. Tickets are all one price regardless of distance, and are valid for as long as one stays on the bus.

Dolmus, a type of shared taxi, are another cheap method of getting around. The fares are calculated by distance, but the cost is minimal. Every *dolmus* has a fixed route, but the driver picks up and puts down passengers at any point along the way. The vehicles range from regular taxis to rusting mini-buses and dilapidated chevrolets.

Taxis are also cheap by Western standards as the meter turns according to distance and does not account for time. There are two charge rates indicated on the meter: *gündüz* is the day rate, shown by a single red light, and *gece* is the night rate, shown by two red lights. It is quite a common trick for taxi drivers to turn on the night rate for unsuspecting tourists, so it is just as well to check the meter before setting off.

Coaches
Coaches are the most widely used form of transport for getting from one city to another. They are operated by dozens of individual

companies so that there are frequent services linking all the major towns and cities, 24 hours a day. It is quite usual for ticket sellers to shout out the destinations of coaches about to leave. This is a useful way of getting onto a coach quickly and saves the trouble of searching around all the ticket offices. The coaches vary in standard but the fares are all fixed by the local council and are posted on a large board near the ticket offices. The best coaches have air conditioning, a free supply of bottled water and regular dousings of eau-de-cologne. For long journeys it is worth shopping around for a reputable company.

Trains

The railway network in Turkey is rather limited and some of the trains in use date back to the age of steam. Consequently, travel by rail is usually slow and it is really only convenient for travelling long distances overnight in a sleeper.

Boats

Turkish Maritime Lines operate ferry services along both the north and south coasts. The ferries carry cars and have cabins, but the services are usually well booked in the summer and reservations should be made well in advance. Turkish Maritime Lines addresses can be found in the Useful Information section.

There are three different services from Istanbul. A 10-day cruise travels along the south coast and calls at Dikili, Izmir, Marmaris, Alanya, Antalya, Fethiye, Datça, Bodrum and Kusadasi. This operates twice a month, during the summer only. However, there is also a ferry twice a week to Izmir, taking about 17 hours. The Black Sea ferries run regularly during the summer along two routes: to Giresun, calling at Zonguldak, Sinop and Ordu; and to Trabzon, calling at Samsun. It takes about 40 hours to travel from one end of the Black Sea to the other.

Domestic Airline

The state-run airline, THY (Türk Hava Yollari) operates flights between all the major cities in Turkey. There are 50 per cent reductions for children aged 2-12, 90 per cent for infants under 2, and 10 per cent is marked off one ticket for a married couple. Timetables can be obtained from THY offices or local travel agents. The flights are usually efficient and run to schedule, and are a convenient way of covering long distances in a short time.

Driving and Car Rental

Driving in Turkey can be either a pleasure or a nightmare. The

Traditional basket making, near Manisa

pleasure is in driving along deserted roads across beautiful, unspoilt countryside. The nightmare is in dodging the people who rush out into the road, finding buses coming round blind corners on the opposite side, and dealing with drivers who have little concept of the highway code.

Drivers should be extremely cautious when passing through towns and villages, as people have little awareness of danger and allow their children to play unsupervised on busy roads. Drivers should also be very careful at night when tractors, trucks and trailers are almost invisible as they rarely have lights. At junctions and roundabouts the general rule is to give way to vehicles coming from the right. However, it is advisable to make liberal use of both horn and lights and to give way as much as possible. Fuel, *benzin*, comes in two grades: normal and super. Super is often hard to come by in remote rural areas and the octane is lower than in Europe. Safety belts are a legal requirement, but the law is very loosely enforced and most people do not bother. The maximum speed limit in a built-up area is 50km/h (31mph) and on main roads 90km/h (56mph). Driving is on the right.

In the case of a road accident the police must be notified and a report obtained. Members of the AA or RAC can present insurance claims to the Turkish Touring and Automobile Association provided they have had the necessary extension made on their policy before leaving.

International car-rental companies have branches in all major cities and at international airports. Cars are a luxury convenience in Turkey and car hire is quite costly even by western standards. The charges range from about £225-300 ($350-470) a week. See Useful Information for car hire companies.

VISITING PLACES OF INTEREST
Museums
All museums in Turkey are in the care of the Kültür ve Türizm Bakanligi, the Ministry of Culture and Tourism. The ministry publishes a yearly list of entrance prices which is available from the major tourist information offices. Museum charges are operated on a two-tier system, one for Turkish nationals and the other for tourists. Entry prices are usually reduced on *halk günü*, Sundays and public holidays, although this is not always applicable to tourists.

Photography is generally forbidden inside museums although this does not apply to exhibits displayed outside the museum building. In some cases there are no restrictions except on the use of flashes and tripods, but a camera fee is often charged. Visitors should always check the regulations beforehand. People who wish to photograph particular exhibits must apply for permission from the Ministry of Culture and Tourism in Ankara.

Museums are well staffed, but the attendants do not usually speak English and may only have a limited knowledge about the exhibits. However, every museum has a *müdür*, a curator, who is usually well informed and will help where possible.

Archaeological Sites
The Ministry of Culture and Tourism also controls all archaeological sites and the regulations and prices are the same as for museums. In most cases there are no restrictions on photography, although there may be a charge for the use of video cameras.

The law regarding illegal excavations and the smuggling of antiquities is very strict in Turkey. Many sites are littered with interesting fragments of pottery and local children often try to sell old coins they have found, but visitors should be careful not to infringe the law. The sea bed along the south coast is equally rich in ancient remains and scuba diving is only allowed with permission from the Ministry of Culture and Tourism and when accompanied by an approved guide.

Mosques

Mosques are active centres of worship and should not be regarded as museums. Many mosques are only open during prayer times, but visitors should wait until the end of the service before entering. Care should be taken not to walk in front of people who are praying or to disturb them.

Shoes are always removed outside the mosque and left on the shelves provided. Men and women should cover their arms and legs, and women should also cover their hair. In some mosques these coverings are provided at the door.

HEALTH

There are no formal inoculation requirements for Turkey, but it is wise to protect against cholera, typhoid and polio if travelling in the eastern and more remote areas. There is very little risk in the western regions where the water supply is all treated and chlorinated and levels of sanitation are quite good. As a general rule the best form of protection is to check that food is clean before eating it, wash all food and avoid drinking water in small villages. The only other health hazards visitors may possibly encounter are rabies and malaria. Rabies is fairly widespread and stray animals should be given a wide berth. Malaria is rare, following the Turkish government's campaign to eradicate it.

Chemists offer drugs to treat most minor illnesses, and anti-biotics can be bought over the counter without prescription. State hospitals provide the services of a general practitioner, while private doctors generally specialise in a particular field. Private hospitals have better facilities than those run by the state and a few foreign private hospitals can be found in Istanbul and Ankara.

MONEY

The first thing to learn about money in Turkey is that inflation has been a problem for many years with the annual rate hovering about the 100 per cent mark. The exchange rate of the Turkish lira changes daily, making it better to change foreign currency as it is needed, rather than buying it before setting out. Traveller's Cheques and Euro-cheques are widely recognised, but Visa and credit cards are only accepted in the major centres. Foreign currency can be changed at banks or change bureaux, but more competitive rates are offered on the free market in the covered bazaar in Istanbul. Banks are open from 8.30am to 12noon and 1.30 to 5pm Monday to Friday, but are closed on national holidays.

CLOTHING

Most Turkish people keep within a restricted dress code. Men wear suits and jackets and women long-sleeved tops, long skirts and usually something to cover their legs. In the tourist resorts beachwear, shorts and T-shirts are perfectly normal. In other areas it is regarded as slightly offensive, or at least strange, for women or men to show their legs and arms.

Light cotton clothing is all that is needed in the summer. In the higher altitude regions it may be necessary to take a jacket for the evenings. Sturdy shoes are essential as the terrain is rough, especially walking around historical sites or hiking in the countryside.

SOUVENIRS

Although purchasing a carpet is outside most people's souvenir budget, visitors to Turkey cannot usually resist the temptation to buy one. There are literally thousands of carpet shops in all cities and centres of tourism, and buying a carpet can be something of an evening's entertainment. No carpet has a fixed price and the carpet salesman, having made his customers comfortable and supplied them with tea, will probably start at a price roughly twice the amount he would realistically accept. Over the course of the evening it is the visitor's job to bring the price down, bearing in mind that the average carpet costs the dealer around £75 ($100).

Leather clothing is also popularly bought in Turkey and is considerably cheaper than in the west. Smaller souvenir items include onyx and copper, silver jewellery and decorative ceramics. It is advisable to shop around as the prices vary enormously and it is quite acceptable to bargain if something seems unreasonably over-priced.

Many of the larger carpet, leather and souvenir shops employ touts to bring tourists in off the streets. Visitors who are brought to a shop in this way should be aware that the tout's commission, at least 10 per cent, will be included in their final bill. Shops are generally open from 9am to 6pm and do not close for lunch. Small local stores open from 8am to 9pm.

1
ISTANBUL

A nkara is the official capital of Turkey but Istanbul is the country's historic centre and commercial heart. It is the largest city in Turkey with a rapidly growing population that has already reached 7,000,000. The city has a long and cosmopolitan past and it is one of the few places which still harbours ethnic minorities, namely Greeks, Jews and Armenians. With half of the city in Europe and the other half in Asia the familiar reference to Istanbul as a bridging point between east and west is more than a romantic image. Contrasts between east and west, rich and poor are in evidence all over the city. The *geceköndü* shanties stand next to grand Ottoman *yali* along the shores of the Bosphorus; veiled women walk side by side with young girls dressed in European fashions. The city is as fascinating for its contrasts and conflicts as it is for its wealth of historical monuments.

Istanbul is divided into three main areas: the old city referred to as Stamboul in the area around Sultanahmet; the commercial city on the opposite side of the Golden Horn; and the wealthy suburbs of Kadikoy and Üsküdar on the Asian shore of the Bosphorus. Frequent ferry services and small *dolmus* boats cross the Golden Horn and Bosphorus in all directions and provide one of the pleasantest ways of getting about the city. Public transport is cheap but overcrowded. Yellow taxis, which all have official meters, are the most convenient means of travelling about the city, although much of the sightseeing can be done on foot.

Most visitors stay in the old part of the city within easy access of the main historical sites. There are a few select hotels in converted Ottoman mansions around Topkapi Palace, but the majority of hotels are in Aksaray along Divan Yolu. The big international chains, such as the Hilton and Sheraton, are centred around Taksim. The best restaurants are found along the Bosphorus where fresh fish is served with *meze*, fish restaurants can also be found in Kumkapi along the shores of the Sea of Marmara. There are a number of international restaurants around Taksim serving Chinese, Japanese, Russian and Italian cuisine.

The four itineraries in this chapter require about a week to cover in detail. Itinerary 1a can be spread over 3 days, the others require a day each.

Itinerary 1a — Old Istanbul

Istanbul's chief historical monuments are located within walking distance of Sultanahmet, the Blue Mosque district, stretching from Sarayburnu, the seraglio point, to the covered bazaar.

 Sultanahmet Cami, known to the west as the Blue Mosque, stands next to the ancient hippodrome on the site of the Byzantine palace. It was built in 1609-17 by the architect Mehmet Aga, and was the last and largest of the imperial mosques to be built during the Ottoman era. It is one of the few mosques in the world with 6 minarets, and it has a 22.5m (74ft) diameter dome that nearly equals that of Aya Sofia in size. The dome, which is 43m (141ft) high, is supported by four large fluted columns each measuring 5m (16ft) across.

The main entrance is reached through a spacious courtyard surrounded by granite columns with a hexagonal wrought-iron ablutions fountain at the centre. Visitors, however, should use the side entrance and keep within the partitioned area so as not to disturb worshippers. Head-scarfs and coverings are issued at the door.

Inside, the hall measures 72m (236ft) by 64m (210ft) and is well lit by 260 small windows set into the walls. The walls are clad with over 21,000 blue-coloured tiles which were made in Iznik and give the mosque its name. The best tiles are set in panels along the galleries on the first floor. The *mimber* is carved from white Marmara marble and the prayer niche contains a piece of the black kaaba stone from Mecca. The sultan's royal box, originally entered by horseback, is to the left. Ahmet I, who commissioned the mosque, died just 6 months after the building was completed at the age of 28 and his tomb is attached to one side. The mausoleum also contains his brothers and two other sultans, Osman II (1622) and Murat IV (1640).

 The **Kilim and Carpet Museum** is housed in the imperial suite of rooms joined to the north corner of the mosque, known as the Hunkâr Kasri, where the sultan formerly rested before and after praying.
A Son et Lumière outlining the history of the mosque is held free of charge, in four languages, on alternate evenings, in front of the mosque during the summer season.

 The solid brick-red walls of **Aya Sofia** look somewhat clumsy next to the elegant contours of Sultanahmet Cami, but the broad buttresses and outer walls were never part of the original design. They were added later to support the dome, the fifth largest in the world, with a diameter measuring 31-3m (101-8ft), which has collapsed on more than one occasion.

The earliest basilica on the site was made of wood and was built in AD360. It burnt down but was rebuilt by Theodosius II in 415, and destroyed again in 532 during the Nika revolts. The basilica seen today was founded by Justinian, just 9 days after the revolts; construction work started in 532 and the basilica was officially opened in 537. It was designed by the well known architects Isidoros of *Miletos* and Anthemios of *Tralles*, and the very finest materials were used in its construction: yellow marble from North Africa, red porphyry and granite from Egypt, green columns from the Artemis Temple at *Epheseus*, local marble from the island of Marmara, as well as light bricks made in Rhodes for the dome. The inner surfaces were coated with mosaics and gilded with gold, but were badly destroyed in the iconoclastic movements of 726-842.

In 1453 Mehmet II officially converted the basilica to a mosque and added a *medrese* (a religious school) and a minaret. His son Beyazit added another minaret and Murat III built the last two. In the eighteenth century the mosaics were plastered over and four large piers were built onto the exterior to support the dome. Mahmut I added a library, another school and an ablutions fountain, and converted the baptistry to a mausoleum for Mustafa I and his son Ibrahim. At the end of the Ottoman empire there was great dispute as to whether the republic would recognise Aya Sofia as a church or a mosque. The matter was settled in 1935 when it was opened as a museum.

A ninth-century bronze door on the west side leads into the narthex, a large hallway with nine doors gaining entrance to the basilica. The largest door, used for royal ceremonial processions, has a ninth century mosaic in the lunette above showing the Emperor Leo VI kneeling before Christ. The main hall measures 77m (252ft) by 72m (236ft) and the highest point of the dome, which gives the impression of floating above the forty windows that surround its base, is 55m (180ft) above the floor. Of the four great columns supporting the dome the one to the left nearest the door is known as the sweating column of St Gregory. An indentation has been worn in the marble by generations of people placing their fingers into the cavity for good luck; if a damp, 'sweaty' sensation is felt, wishes are meant to come true.

A circular mosaic in the floor of the hall marks the place where Byzantine emperors were crowned in the eighth and ninth centuries, and some of the column capitals bear the monograms of Justinian and Theodora, but the best remaining Byzantine decorations are the mosaics in the upper galleries. The four Islamic cartouches hanging in the main hall were added in the seventeenth century and the alabaster vessels, from ancient *Pergamum*, were also brought to the mosque during the Ottoman period.

A winding ramp leads from the north end of the narthex to the galleries. The south gallery was used by the emperor and his family and contains impressive mosaics dating from the eleventh and twelfth centuries. Only the upper section remains of the Deisis, a magnificent mosaic depicting Christ with the Virgin Mary and John the Baptist, but there are two well preserved smaller mosaics at the east end of the south gallery.

Topkapi Palace was first built in 1459-78 by Mehmet II on the site of the Byzantine and Roman acropolis, overlooking the Sea of Marmara, the Golden Horn, and the Bosphorus. It served as the centre of the Ottoman administration and the imperial residency for 400 years and was opened as a museum in 1924.

The palace is a 10 minute walk from Aya Sofia and can be reached by following the road along its east wall. Before entering the palace compound to the left of the Imperial Gate, Soguk Çesmesi Sokak runs along the outer wall and is a fully restored street with many of the Ottoman houses opened as cafés and hotels; there is also a restaurant in a vaulted cistern at the far end. To the right of the Imperial Gate there is a monumental fountain, known as **Ahmet III Çesmesi**, which was built in 1728.

The **Imperial Gate**, formerly known as Bab-i Humayin, is one of the few structures remaining from the original palace built by Mehmet II. The large car park inside, the first courtyard of the palace, was originally a military training ground. **St Irene's Church** is to the left. It is seldom open except for occasional classical concerts, details of which can be obtained from the tourist information office at Sultanahmet. It stands on an ancient religious sanctuary dedicated to Aphrodite and is one of the oldest churches in the city. Like Aya Sofia it was rebuilt many times; the present structure was first constructed by Justinian in 537 and later repaired by Constantine V in 750-75.

The ticket office is at the **middle gate** previously known as Bab-us Selam. Visitors should check the opening times of the harem and other exhibitions before purchasing a ticket. The middle gate leads under the courts of justice and the executioner's quarters into the second courtyard which was used for ceremonial purposes and council meetings. The stables and harness rooms are on the left side of the courtyard, and a 42m (137ft) high tower known as Kübbealti marks the entrance to the harem.

The right-hand side of the courtyard is lined by the **palace**

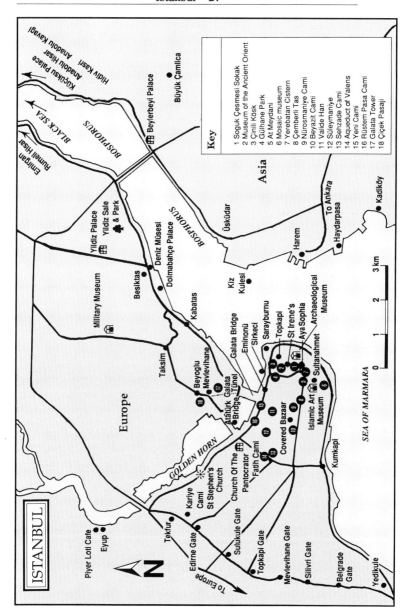

kitchens with their distinctive row of chimneys. The ten kitchens were designed by the great architect Sinan and now house the imperial ceramic collection. Chinese porcelains from the Song, Ming and Yung dynasties and rare celadons are amongst the oldest pieces and date from 960 to 1368, while Japanese and European porcelains and crystals make up the rest of the collection, one of the best in the world. The last kitchen contains an impressive assortment of cooking utensils, including caldrons large enough to cook for 6,000 people at a time. The kitchens were the largest in the Ottoman empire and employed up to 1,200 kitchen staff.

The **harem** consists of over 400 rooms which cover an area of 6,720sq m (72,334sq ft), less than a tenth of which is open to the public. Most of the building was constructed by Murat III (1574-95), but large sections were rebuilt by Mehmet IV (1648-87) after the great fire of 1665, and still later additions were made by Osman III in the eighteenth century. The rich tilework which covers many of the rooms dates from all these periods.

The ticket office for the harem is near the entrance, the carriage gate, which leads into the **court of the black eunuchs**. The eunuchs were black Sudanese slaves who worked in the harem which at times contained as many as 3-4,000 women. The first suite of rooms on the tour belonged to the sultan's mother and are known as the **valide apartments**. Victorian clocks, Chinese porcelain vases and nineteenth-century classical scenes painted on the wood-panelled walls reflect the western interests of the late Ottoman era. The **sultan's bathroom** complete with Delft tiles is next door.

The tour continues through the **imperial hall**, where the sultan was entertained, to the **cage**, known as the *kafes*. This is a pair of rooms thought to have been used by the sultan's eldest son. The sultan's quarters are perhaps the most magnificent rooms in the harem. **Murat III's salon** with its Iznik tiles and elaborate fireplace looks out over the palace gardens. Next door is **Ahmet I's library** and a beautifully painted reading room. The wood panelling is decorated with painted fruit, animals and flowers, and was added by Ahmet III in 1705. The tour passes out of the harem through a long passageway called the **golden way**, where women once lined up to catch pieces of gold the sultan distributed as he left.

Bab-us Saade, the **Gate of Felicity**, leads into the third courtyard. Inside is the **audience hall**, a grand building surrounded by porticoes, used as the reception room for foreign ambassadors. Sultan Süleyman's throne dating from 1596 is in a display case inside and the walls are decorated with nineteenth-century Viennese woodwork. The **palace library** behind it was built in 1719 by Ahmet III.

The buildings on the right of the courtyard were originally used as a suite of reception rooms, and now contain the **treasury** and a **costume collection**. The costumes range from the caftans of Mehmet I (1432-81) to the military uniforms of Mehmet Resat (1844-1918). The treasury contains a dazzling collection of Ottoman jewels, including an 86 carat diamond, one of the largest cut diamonds in the world. It is said to have been found by a spoonmaker in the ruins of the Byzantine palace and sold to the sultan, and hence its name. A dagger with a handle carved from a single emerald is also on display as is the golden ceremonial throne of Ahmet I (1604-17).

The **holy relics** are housed on the opposite side of the courtyard and were traditionally brought out on ceremonial display for the sultan every year during the holy fast of Ramazan. The most important relics, the holy mantle and the bow and sabre of Mohammed are protected behind a glass screen. Other exhibits include the doors of Kaaba, a hair from Mohammed's beard and soil from his grave. The collection is of great religious significance to Moslems and visitors should take care not to offend. Photography is forbidden.

The fourth courtyard, set on a high terrace at the tip of the peninsula, was the sultan's private residence. It consists of a number of secluded pavilions surrounded by gardens. The **Revan pavilion**, with its beautiful Iznik tiles, is to the left near a square pool. It was built in 1635 after the capture of Erivan. The terrace below has a small bower in the centre covered by a gilded baldachin, the iftariye. It was built by Ibrahim in 1640 and offers good views across the Golden Horn to the Galata tower. The **Baghdad pavilion**, built to commemorate Murat IV's conquest of Baghdad in 1638, is at the far end of the terrace. It is decorated with sixteenth-century Iznik tiles and finely inlaid woodwork.

Before the railway was built along the Marmara coast in 1840 the palace extended to the water's edge. Now the railway track passes below the **Mecidiye pavilion**, one of the latest additions to the palace. Built in the nineteenth century by Abdül Mecid it has now been converted to a restaurant and is the perfect spot to finish a tour of the palace and enjoy the views across the water.

From the car-park in the first courtyard of Topkapi Palace there are signposts down the hill to the museums. The ticket office is at the gate on the right which leads into the museum compound. The **Museum of the Ancient Orient** is the first building on the left and contains an extensive collection from ancient Nineveh and Babylon. A ceramic tile relief of lions and mythological beasts taken from the sixth century BC monumental way to the Ishtar Gate of Babylon is one of the most important exhibits. The collection of Hittite artefacts is also notable and includes a large number of cuneiform tablets dating from 1790BC. They record the earliest written laws, and the

The church of Aya Sofia, now a museum

oldest known peace treaty, the Treaty of Kadesh, which was made between the Hittite empire and Egypt in the second millennium BC.

The **Archaeological Museum** is under long-term restoration and the upper floors are permanently shut. The ground floor has a collection of funerary monuments, sarcophagi and statues from the Greek and Roman periods. Many of the tombs come from the royal necropolis at Sidon in Lebanon. The most important of these is the **Sarcophagus of Alexander**, the tomb of an unknown fourth-century BC Seleucid ruler, and not of Alexander the Great as was once believed. The finely carved scenes on the sides of the sarcophagus depict battles between the Greeks and Persians. The **Mourner Sarcophagus**, dated 350BC, comes from the same burial site and takes its name from the grieving women carved on its sides.

The **Çinili Kösk** is opposite the Archaeological Museum. It has a distinctive Eastern style with pointed-arched porticoes supported on slender polygonal columns. Built in 1472, it was one of one of the first pavilions in the palace grounds and Mehmet II is said to have watched *cirit* javelin matches in the park below from here. It contains a fine collection of early Islamic ceramics.

At Meydani is along the north-west side of Sultanahmet Cami, and the present day public gardens mark the site of the ancient

The Deisis mosaic in Aya Sofia

hippodrome built by the Roman emperor Septimus Severus in AD203. During the Byzantine era it was extended to hold 150,000 spectators and measured some 440m (1,443ft) long and 120m (394ft) wide. As Byzantine politics and sports became entangled, the hippodrome was the scene of numerous disturbances between the opposing factions, the greens and the blues. Thirty thousand people were executed here during the Nika revolt.

When the crusaders invaded in 1204 the fine statues and monuments adorning the arena were plundered and the hippodrome fell into disuse. One of the most notable monuments, an ancient Greek statue of four golden horses and a chariot, was carried off by the Venetians and can still be seen at St Mark's in Venice today. During the fifteenth century the Ottomans used the hippodrome as a marble quarry and later in the seventeenth century as an archery field.

The **German fountain** presented by Kaiser Wilhelm II to Sultan Abdül Hamit II in 1895 stands at the northern end of the hippodrome. The fountain has a copper dome, decorated with the imperial monograms of the sultan and the kaiser, supported on black porphyry columns.

Dikili Tas, the Egyptian obelisk, is the first of the three surviving monuments of the Byzantine hippodrome. It was taken from an ancient Egyptian temple built by the Pharaoh Tuthmosis III in 1504-1450BC and is carved with Egyptian hieroglyphics. It weighs 800 tons and is 20m (66ft) tall, just a third of its original height. Theodosius raised the obelisk in the fourth century above stone-carved reliefs which depict: the imperial family in their royal box at the hippodrome; scenes of chariot racing; and the ceremonial raising of the obelisk.

The second monument is **Yilanli Sütun**, serpent column, which dates from 479BC and originally stood at the Temple of Apollo in *Delphi*. Constantine brought it to the hippodrome in AD300. Only a small section has survived and the heads of the three entwined snakes are sadly missing.

Örme Sütun, mortar column, is the tallest of the three monuments and is 32m (105ft) high. It was raised by Constantinos VII in the tenth century and was originally clad in gilded bronze. The plates were removed by the crusaders and only the nail holes in the stone, which were used as footholds for column climbing contests by the Ottomans, are left.

Yellow signs at the south end of the hippodrome point to the **Mosaic Museum** which is located in the *arasta*, an Ottoman market building behind Sultanahmet Cami. The *arasta* was built on top of the Byzantine palace and the mosaics that have been unearthed here were once part of the palace portico and date from the fifth and sixth centuries.

The **Museum of Turkish and Islamic Art** is housed in the palace of Ibrahim Pasa, the Grand Vizier to Süleyman the Magnificent who was executed in 1536 for plotting against the sultan. The museum collection is well displayed and includes very early Anatolian ceramics as well as Seljuk and Ottoman tiles. There is also a fine collection of metal crafts and imperial Ottoman carpets. The museum shop is good for souvenirs and there is a traditional coffee house.

The **Haseki Hürrem Hamam** is a beautiful Ottoman baths located between Aya Sofia and Sultanahmet Cami. It has recently been restored and opened as a carpet museum. The building was designed as a double bath by Sinan in 1556 for the Sultana Haseki Hürrem, also known as Roxelana, wife of Süleyman the Magnificent. It provides an attractive setting for the carpet exhibition which is part of a government funded project to promote Anatolian carpets and prevent traditional designs from dying out. The carpets seen in the exhibition are all hand-made reproductions and are for sale at fixed rates.

On the opposite side of Divan Yolu from the At Meydani is a small building that marks the entrance to the underground cistern known as **Yerebatan Saray**. It is thought to have been built by Constantine and later enlarged by Justinian. The water was supplied by aqueducts leading from the Belgrade Forest 19km (12 miles) away. It is one of the largest and most impressive cisterns in the city, measuring 140m (459ft) by 70m (230ft). The ceiling has fine brick vaults supported by 336 columns with Corinthian capitals. Footpaths lead visitors around the floodlit chamber to the strains of classical music. During the summer season there is a restaurant at the water's edge.

Divan Yolu is the main road from Sultanahmet to Aksaray. It follows the route of the original Byzantine road through Constantine's forum. **Çemberlitas**, the large stone column on the right of the road, is all that remains of the Byzantine commercial centre. A bronze statue of Constantine once stood on the top, but the upper section is now completely missing and the segments that remain are bound with unsightly metal hoops.

Nürosmaniye Cami is on the right behind the column. Construc- tion was started by Sultan Mahmut I in 1748 and completed by Osman III in 1755. Divan Yolu continues up to **Beyazit Meydani**, a large square on the right, named after Sultan Beyazit II, who built the mosque complex in 1501-5. It is the earliest surviving imperial mosque in Istanbul and was the greatest monument built during Beyazit's reign; it also marks an important architectural development from the earlier Bursa-style towards the classical style. The adjacent courtyard, which measures exactly the same size as the mosque, has three tall portals decorated with stone-carved arabesque designs. The courtyard is surrounded by twenty-four small domes with an ablutions fountain at the centre. The two terracotta patterned minarets are 87m (285ft) apart, an unusually large distance. The main door into the mosque is inlaid with ivory and inside two open aisles flank the central hall which is covered by a dome 17.5m (57ft) wide. The *mihrab* and *mimber* are both carved from marble, the latter has a very high tapering roof. The sultan's loge is also carved from marble and is supported on ten fine marble columns.

The Beyazit *medrese* on the left side of the square served as an influential school of law during the Ottoman era; it now houses the **Museum of Calligraphy**. The monumental triple arch on the north side of the courtyard has nothing to do with the mosque but leads into the university grounds. The tall tower inside the grounds, visible from all over Istanbul, is 85m (279ft) high and was built as a fire watch tower. Unfortunately it is not open to the public.

The **Spoon-Maker's Gate** in the north-east corner of the square, between the mosque and the Beyazit library, leads into the **Sahaflar**

The Church of St Irene, Topkapi Palace

Carsisi, a second-hand book market. It has been a book market since the eighteenth century and continues to trade in both new and old books as well as miniatures.

The **covered bazaar**, or *kapali çarsi*, can be reached by walking through the book market and crossing Cadircilar Sokak, which is a street of copper-makers, to the **Beyazit Gate**. Inside the gate is one of the busiest thoroughfares in the bazaar, Kalpakcilar Caddesi. It leads right across the south side of the bazaar to the **Nürosmaniye Gate**.

There are sixty-five streets altogether and at least 4,000 shops beneath the multitude of domes and vaulted roofs. Although the bazaar is rather like a maze, shops selling similar goods are all found in the same area. Jewellers gather in one section, carpet sellers in another, and so on, which is practical for shopping purposes. This system derives from Ottoman times when traders and craftsmen worked together under the protection of a guild. The streets are still named after some of the trades that existed in Ottoman times, but the guild system was dissolved in the nineteenth century and there are now fewer craftsmen working in the bazaar.

The covered bazaar was first built in the fifteenth century by Mehmet II, probably on the site of a Byzantine market. It has been in use ever since although it has been rebuilt many times. The most extensive reconstruction took place after the earthquake in 1894 when more than half the bazaar was flattened. It took 4 years to repair the damage and traders had to move to Galata on the other side of the Golden Horn. The bazaar has only regained its popularity in the last 20 years, and now it is a thriving centre for tourism as well as local business. Carpets, leather, jewellery, copper and souvenirs are amongst the top merchandise on offer. The bazaar also has its own banks, post offices, snack bars and restaurants; the Sark Kahvehanesi is one of the few surviving traditional coffee houses.

The **Cevahir Bedesten** is the stronghold building at the centre of the bazaar which was originally built by Mehmet II in 1461. It has a domed roof supported on eight columns and four heavy iron gates set into the 1.5m- (5ft-) thick walls. In Ottoman times it served as a bank and there were 128 safes built into the walls and in the ground. Today the 106 small shops inside the *bedesten* sell antiques, silver jewellery and copperware. There is a second *bedesten*, also built by Mehmet II, near Nürosmaniye Gate. It is known as the **Sandal Bedesten** after a type of woven silk cloth that used to be traded here. The building has recently been well renovated and has twenty brick domes supported on twelve large pillars. It serves as an auction room twice a week and also contains a number of small shops.

Commercial market buildings are known as *han*. Many were built around the outside of the bazaar and served as inns for travelling merchants and stores for their merchandise. Of the twenty-four *han* that were built, each with its own trade, only a small number have survived today. These date from the fifteenth and sixteenth centuries and are in varying states of dilapidation.

Zincirli Han is one of the best preserved *han* buildings. It stands just inside the north-east corner of the bazaar and serves as a jeweller's market. **Büyük Yeni Han** and **Valide Han** are outside the bazaar located on Çakmakcilar Sokak, the steep road that leads downhill from the bazaar towards Eminönü. Büyük Yeni Han is the largest of the two and was built in 1764, while Valide Han is older and dates from 1651.

The third hill of ancient *Constantinople* is crowned by the most important of the city's imperial mosque complexes, the **Süleymaniye**. It is built on the foundations of a former Byzantine palace, on a high terrace overlooking the Golden Horn. The complex was commissioned by Süleyman I in 1550 and took 7 years to complete. It was designed by the architect Sinan who based the proportions and measurements of the building on mystical numbers, multiples of three being of particular significance.

The complex includes four religious colleges, of which two now house an important library containing over 32,000 Ottoman manuscripts. There is also a soup kitchen, a hospital, a public bath and a caravanserai. The entire complex is built of locally quarried limestone and materials taken from the former palace, while the twenty-four columns surrounding the mosque courtyard are from the Byzantine hippodrome and are made of porphyry, white marble and pink granite. The courtyard has a minaret at each corner, the two largest are next to the mosque, and in the centre there is a low rectangular *sadirvan* (fountain).

Inside, the mosque is lit by a myriad of small windows surrounding the domes and covering the east and west walls. The windows above the *mihrab* have decorative stained glass thought to have been added by Sultan Ibrahim (1640-48). The dome measures 26m (85ft) across and is exactly twice this measurement in height. It is supported on vast granite piers each 47m (154ft) high. The inscriptions, carved in stone and painted on plaques, were originally the work of Çerkes Hasan Celebi, who was the pupil of one of the most famous calligraphers in Ottoman times, Ahmet Karahisari. The narrow galleries, which are supported on consoles around the top of the mosque, were formerly used for lighting the oil lamps which have now been replaced by electric lighting. The ebony *Koran*-reading chair is beautifully inlaid with ivory and mother-of-pearl and is one of the few pieces of original furniture that remain. The *mihrab* is decorated with Iznik tiles, and the *mimber* on the right is carved from Marmara marble.

Süleyman's wife, Roxelana, (Haseki Hürrem) died a year after the mosque was completed. Her tomb is in the graveyard behind the mosque and is decorated with fine panels of Iznik tiles. Süleyman's tomb is nearby, and is the largest mausoleum ever built by Sinan. Sinan's own tomb can be seen below the east wall of the complex and is by comparison very modest.

 Sehzade Cami was Sinan's first royal commission. Süleyman had it built in memory of his eldest son Saruhan Sehzade Mehmet, who died at the early age of 22. The mosque is often considered Sinan's 'apprentice work' and was only the fourth imperial complex ever to be built in the city. It is built of an attractive grey stone and has an impressive cascade of domes with two decorated minarets either side of a courtyard. The interior is very plain, the carved marble *mimber* is the most decorative feature. The young prince is buried in the graveyard behind the mosque in an octagonal tomb faced with marble, green breccia and terracotta.

The **Aqueduct of Valens** straddles the third and fourth hills and can be seen next to the mosque. It was built in 370 by the Emperor Valens to supply the city with water; 920m (3,017ft) of it is still standing and at its highest point it is 26.5m (87ft) tall.

Mehmet Fatih Cami stands on the fourth hill and is raised on a vaulted terrace making it visible from Sehzade Cami. It was first built in 1460 but was completely destroyed by earthquakes in 1509 and 1766. The building seen today was built in 1771. It is one of the most active mosques in the city and the eight *medrese* built in the spacious courtyards surrounding the mosque still function as *Koran* schools.

Mehmet's tomb, which was also rebuilt in the eighteenth century, is well attended as a shrine and stands in the graveyard behind the mosque. The mausoleum of his wife Gülbahar, and Sultan Abdül Hamit I stand alongside. The complex is particularly lively on Wednesdays when there is a large market and the courtyards are used as busy thoroughfares.

Itinerary 1b — City Walls and Golden Horn

Itinerary 1b follows the old city walls from the Sea of Marmara to the Golden Horn, finishing at the Galata Bridge.

Yedikule is roughly 5km (3 miles) along the Marmara shore from Sultanahmet. The fortress was originally built in 380 by Theodosius I to protect the triumphal arch known as the **Golden Gate**. It was greatly enlarged by the Ottomans who added five new towers, giving the fortress seven towers in all, and was used as a jail for foreign ambassadors and other notables including the Grand Vizier Mahmut Pasa who was executed here in 1474, as was the Sultan Osman II in 1622.

The Golden Gate is no longer gilded but all seven towers are well restored and it is possible to walk along the crenellated parapets. The east tower is known as the **Tower of Inscriptions** as the walls are covered with messages engraved by prisoners. The south tower, which is 20m (65ft) high, flanks the Golden Gate and contains the remains of the executioner's scaffold and the pit where dismembered heads were thrown. The cell where Osman II was hanged is on the fourth floor.

In 413 Theodosius II built a wall across the land stretching from the Sea of Marmara to the Black Sea. The Ottomans strengthened it with an inner defence wall and a moat 18m (59ft) wide and 6-7m (20-23ft) deep. The wall from Yedikule to the Topkapi Gate has recently been restored and a total length of 6.5km (4 miles) remains standing complete with ninety-six 18m-high (59ft-) towers.

A busy highway skirts the foot of the walls from the Belgrade Gate past Yedikule to the Silivri, Mevlevihane, Topkapi, Sulukule and Edirne gates. Close to the Edirne Gate is the site of the former palace of Blachernae, **Tekfür Saray**. It served as the Byzantine imperial residence from the twelfth century onwards. Only a section remains

Fourth-century Byzantine obelisk base
showing the Emperor Theodosius, At Meydani

of the attractively patterned marble and brick façade which dates from the tenth century. It was outside these walls that the last Byzantine emperor, Constantine XI, fell defending the city walls against the Ottomans in 1453.

St Saviour in Chora now called **Kariye Cami** is just inside the city walls to the north of the Edirne Gate and is signposted off Fevzi Pasa Caddesi. The church dates from the fifth century and was part of a monastery until the eighth century after which it fell into disuse. In 1057 Mary Ducas, a niece of the Comnene emperor Isaac, rebuilt the church, but the beautiful mosaics that cover the walls today were added in the early fourteenth century by Theodore Metochites, the Lord High Treasurer to Emperor Andronicus II. The church lay abandoned after the Ottoman conquest until the end of the fifteenth century when the Grand Vizier Atik Ali Pasa converted the bell tower to a minaret and the church to a mosque.

Kariye Cami is now open as a museum. The surrounding wooden Ottoman houses have been restored and there is an outdoor café in the courtyard in front of the church. The church is constructed of brick and stone and has a finely carved marble porch. Inside, the lower walls are faced with matching panels of grey, red and green veined

Antique shop near the covered bazaar

marble, while the upper walls and ceilings are covered with gilded mosaics and painted frescoes dating from 1315-21. There are seventy mosaics and twenty frescoes in total, all of which were carefully restored to their former beauty by an American team in 1948-9. The mosaics show scenes from the life of Christ and are arranged in a chronological sequence around the inner and outer narthex of the church.

Eyup is a suburb of Istanbul located at the upper end of the Golden Horn. It has been of religious importance since 1458 when Mehmet I identified the site as the burial place of Eyup Ensari, a disciple of Mohammed the Prophet who was killed during the Arab invasions of *Constantinople* in 674-678. A mausoleum and mosque were built in his memory and in the eighteenth century Sultan Ahmet III enlarged the mosque adding two minarets. Most of the structures seen today date from 1800 when Selim III completely rebuilt the complex.

The two courtyards flanking the mosque are entered through

baroque-style gateways. The *sadirvan* is in the outer courtyard and the mausoleum, decorated with attractive sixteenth- to nineteenth-century tiles, is directly opposite the mosque entrance. People offer their prayers through the gilded copper grille which looks onto the tomb.

Inside, the main dome is supported on eight columns and the marble *mihrab* and *mimber* are painted with gold. The *Koran* school attached to the mosque is still in use, and the public kitchen still provides food for the needy.

Eyup's religious significance makes it a popular place for Moslems to be buried. A number of monumental tombs surround the mosque, and the hillside above is covered with graves. Kirkmerdiven Caddesi leads up through the graveyards to the hill summit where the **Piyer Loti Café** commands good views over the Golden Horn. The café is named after the French writer Pierre Loti who is said to have been a regular customer in the nineteenth century.

The **Golden Horn** is 11km (6.8 miles) long and is up to 40m (131ft) deep in places. As one of the world's best protected natural harbours and a natural defence, it has contributed much to the life of the city. During the Ottoman era the shores were lined with luxury palaces but the Golden Horn has since become industrial dockland and the water polluted with toxic waste. A major project is underway to clear the shores and replace the tumbled down buildings with parkland. None of the Ottoman palaces have survived, though the Golden Horn, so popular in its heyday, is once again attracting visitors.

Ferry boats operate from the small pier at Eyup to the Galata Bridge calling at the suburbs on the way. The **Church of St Stephan of Bulgars** in Fener is passed on the right and is remarkable for being built entirely of iron. It was prefabricated in Vienna, floated down the Danube and assembled in Istanbul in 1871. Higher up on the hilltop on the right is another church, originally known as the **Church of the Pantocrator** which dates from the twelfth century.

The **Galata Bridge** was built in 1909-12. It stretches for 468m (1,535ft) across the mouth of the Golden Horn and is 26m (85ft) wide. The bridge actually floats as it is constructed on twenty-two pontoons, and moves up and down with the swell. The middle section swings open to allow ships to pass through early in the morning. The lower pedestrian level of the bridge is lined with fish restaurants and tea houses.

Yeni Cami is at the south end of the Galata Bridge overlooking the Golden Horn. It is often likened to Sehzade Cami and it has a similar cascade of domes. The mosque was founded in 1595 by the mother of Mehmet II, and finished after a series of delays in 1663 by Türhan

Hatice, mother of Mahmut IV.

It is one of the most active charitable mosques in Istanbul with one of the largest public kitchens. The north and south sides of the mosque have porticoed galleries, and a covered bridge connects the mosque to the royal apartments. On the west side there is a large arcaded courtyard. The main entrance is decorated with faience tiles and fine marble columns. Inside, the *mihrab* and *mimber* are also decorated with tiles and the main dome, which is 36m (119ft) high, is painted with arabesques.

The Egyptian bazaar known as the **Misir Çarsisi**, is built in an L-shape and stands next to Yeni Cami. It was constructed just before the mosque was completed in 1660 on the site of a former Byzantine market. Its name derives from the quantity of Egyptian spices traded here during the Ottoman era. There are two main gates and four entrances, and eighty-six shops inside. The guard house above the main entrance is restored as a restaurant and serves traditional Turkish food.

The building was renovated in 1943 and continues to be active in the trading of food and spices. Turkish specialities such as *sucuk,* spicy salami, *pastirma*, smoked beef, white cheeses and Turkish Delight are readily available; there is also a wide range of herbs, spices, nuts and seeds.

Ragip Gumuspala Caddesi leads beyond the Egyptian bazaar to one of the most ornate mosques ever built by Sinan, **Rüstem Pasa Cami**. It is built above a block of warehouses on a secluded terrace reached by staircases at either end. The mosque was built in 1561 by Rüstem Pasa, Grand Vizier to Süleyman and his later son-in-law, and is decorated with a wealth of Iznik tiles. The patterns are very varied with the popular motifs of the era — tulips, pomegranates and other flowers — in great profusion. The galleries are lined with faience panels, even the piers supporting the dome are tile-clad, and every tile is different. The stunning effect is enhanced by the daylight which floods in through the unusually large windows. The *mimber* has a high hood and is carved from marble, and the finely inlaid *Koran*-reading chair is the sixteenth-century original.

Itinerary 1c — The Bosphorus

The Bosphorus is dotted with Ottoman palaces, timber houses and picturesque fishing villages. The strait measures 32km (20 miles) from end to end, is 3.3km (2 miles) at its widest point and varies in depth from 30-120m (98-394ft). It separates Europe from Asia, but connects the Sea of Marmara with the Black Sea and there is a constant flow of ships. Two suspension bridges spanning the straits allow road traffic to cross between the two continents.

Sultan Ibrahim's Baldachin, overlooking the Golden Horn and the Galata Tower

The best way to see the Bosphorus is by boat, although buses run regularly along both the Asian and European shores. In the summer a daily Bosphorus tour ferry departs from Sirkeci pier. The boat calls at various points along the Asian and European shores and stops for lunch at Anadolu Kavagi. The round trip takes about 6 hours. Timetables for other ferries along the Bosphorus are posted near the ticket office at Sirkeci.

THE EUROPEAN SHORE

The first landmark along the European shore is **Dolmabahçe Palace**, a grand, white marble building on the waterfront midway between Kabatas and Besiktas. It was built for Sultan Abdül Mecit in 1843-56 by the Balians, the imperial architects of the nineteenth century. The palace served as the sultan's residence until the dissolution of the empire in 1918, and continued to be used by the Turkish republic until it was opened as a museum. Atatürk died here on 10 November 1938 at 9.05am, and all the clocks in the palace are

Mosaic of a leper,
Kariye Cami

fixed at the hour of his decease.

The palace is set amongst formal gardens surrounded by a high wall with an ornate screen along the water's edge. A clock tower marks the entrance way and guided tours depart regularly from the main doors. There are some 285 rooms and the vast scale of the palace makes for an impersonal atmosphere. The throne room is in the centre of the palace and is covered by a large dome 35m (115ft) high. The chandelier in the throne room weighs 4.5 tons, has 750 candles and was a gift from Queen Victoria. The architecture and the décor are European although the living quarters are still segregated, men being restricted to the *selamlik* and women to the harem, in the Islamic tradition. Two-thirds of the palace is contained within the harem while only one-third is made up of state rooms and the *selamlik*. The north wing which was formerly used by the sultan's heir now houses the Besiktas art gallery.

The **Deniz Muzesi** or Maritime Museum is located near the landing stage at Besiktas and has an interesting collection of

Ottoman *kayak*, or barges. These range from the huge imperial vessels used to transport the Sultan around, to the smaller everyday craft that used to ferry across the Bosphorus.

Yildiz Sale is a part of the Yildiz Palace, the former residence of Abdül Hamit II. It is set in an attractive park with three late nineteenth-century pavilions which have been renovated as cafés. The main gate is at the roadside, midway between Besiktas and Ortaköy.

The palace is made up of a number of independent buildings, the guest wing located at the top of the park is open as a museum. There is a vast Hereke carpet in the ballroom which is 406sq m (4,368sq ft) and attractive porcelain stoves and crystal chandeliers and candelabra are seen throughout the palace.

Bogaziçi Köprüsü (The Bosphorus Bridge) is the fifth largest suspension bridge in the world and is 1,560m (5,117ft) in length. It was built by a British and German consortium and opened in 1973. There is a toll for crossing the bridge and traffic is always very heavy.

Rumeli Hisar and Anadolu Hisar guard the Bosphorus at its narrowest point which is only 650m (2,132ft) wide. Built by Mehmet II in 1452, the fortress played a vital role in the Ottoman capture of *Constantinople* as the sultan was able to control all seafaring traffic. It is the best-preserved of the Bosphorus castles with its 7m (23ft) thick walls and tall towers. The castle is entered through the original gateway on the east side, and there are splendid views over the Bosphorus from the crenellated parapets and towers. An open-air theatre has been built at one end and is a popular venue for concerts during the Istanbul Summer Festival. Istanbul's second suspension bridge, **Fatih Sultan Mehmet Köprüsü**, opened in 1988, crosses the Bosphorus just north of the castle.

The first tulips were exported to Holland in the seventeenth century from Turkey, and the park at **Emirgan** is well known for its tulip gardens covering the hill slopes above the village. There are good views of the Bosphorus and an Ottoman pavilion has been restored as a café.

The road ends at the sleepy fishing village of **Rumeli Kavagi** which has a number of modest fish restaurants, and deep-fried mussels known as *midiye* are a local speciality. The remaining coastline as far as the Black Sea is a military zone.

THE ASIAN SHORE

Üsküdar, formerly known as *Scutari* is the lively Asian suburb along the shore where the Bosphorus meets the Sea of Marmara. There are a number of notable Ottoman mosques in Üsküdar, including Iskele Cami, Yeni Valide Cami, and Çinili Cami, it is also the site of one of the largest Moslem cemeteries in Asia Minor. Just offshore from

Üsküdar there is a small island with a 30m- (98ft-) high tower known as Kiz Kulesi, or Maiden's Tower. It was built in 1763 and is now used as a coastguard's station.

The Harem railway station to the east, was originally built in the early twentieth century as the Istanbul terminal for the Baghdad line. Just behind the station are the **Selimiye Barracks**, built in 1826 by Mahmut II and where Florence Nightingale tended the wounded during the Crimean War in 1854.

Beylerbeyi Palace lies on the waterfront in the shadow of the Bosphorus bridge. It was built for Sultan Abdül Aziz in 1861-65 and has a similar architectural style to Dolmabahçe Palace only on a smaller and more intimate scale. There are twenty-four rooms and six large halls, and several attractive fountains and pools. Some of the palace furniture was made by the sultan himself. Abdül Aziz took up woodwork, as it was customary for sultans to learn a craft, and the inlaid chairs in the dining hall are a testimony to his skill. Egyptian rush mats are fitted throughout the palace as insulation and many of the rooms have fine mahogany panelling. The imperial bath tub gives some idea of the size of the sultan who was 2m (6.5ft) tall and weighed 160kg (352lb).

There is a hunting lodge inside the well-kept gardens that sur- round the palace which offer pleasant views onto the Bosphorus. Outside the palace grounds the shore is lined with restaurants and souvenir shops, and a mosque built by Abdül Hamit I in 1778.

Büyük Çamlica, a hill 267m (876ft) high, has been a popular leisure park since the early eighteenth century. The hilltop has recently been restored, new paths have been laid and trees planted, and the original kiosks and coffee-houses renovated. There are excellent views across the Sea of Marmara, the Golden Horn and the Bosphorus.

Küçüksu Palace is one of the smallest of the Ottoman palaces along the Bosphorus and was built for Sultan Abdül Mecit I in 1856-7 as a shooting lodge. It has attractive wooden floors and ornate fireplaces, and the ceilings are decorated with stucco and gilt work. It is similar in style to the palaces of Dolmabahçe and Beylerbeyi, being designed by the same family of architects, the Balians.

Anadolu Hisar stands opposite Rumeli Hisar, on the Sweet Waters of Asia, now known as the Göksu river. The fortress was originally built by Yildirim Beyazit at the end of the fourteenth century, but was considerably enlarged by Mehmet II in 1452. The ruins are not as impressive as Rumeli Hisar as only the outer wall of the central keep is left standing.

Up until the 1930s the last Khedive of Egypt, Abbas Hilmi Pasa, lived in **Hidiv Kasri**, an art nouveau-style palace located in the

Mussel cleaners at Kumkapi, with the Black Sea fishing fleet

wooded parkland above the village of Çubuklu. With the formation of the republic, the Khedive fled the country and the palace stood deserted until 1982 when it was restored by the Touring Club. It is now the setting for a stylish restaurant and tea rooms as well as a small, exclusive hotel.

Anadolu Kavagi is clustered around a picturesque harbour lined with fish restaurants, and in the summer ice-cream of every flavour is sold from small kiosks. Up above the village the castle of Anadolu Kavagi stands guarding the mouth of the Black Sea. It has recently been opened to the public and although the remains are not very impressive there are panoramic views out to sea. The coastline further north is all within military territory.

Itinerary 1d — Beyoglu and Taksim

The area of Beyoglu, formerly known as *Pera*, covers the hilltop north of the Golden Horn and was an influential centre of western culture during the late Ottoman empire. Foreigners first settled here in the

Selling fish on the Golden Horn

fourteenth century under the protection of the Genoese trading colony at Galata. In the nineteenth century it became popular for Europeans to travel on the Orient Express from Paris to *Constantinople*, and the **Pera Palas Hotel** was built to provide suitable accommodation for the travellers. Today, Beyoglu is still an important centre of business and commerce and the Pera Palas Hotel continues to attract customers even though the grand days of the Orient Express are over.

The **Tünel** is one of the world's shortest underground funiculars. It was built by French engineers in 1875 and the track, a mere 614m (2,014ft) long, climbs up the steep hill from the Golden Horn to Beyoglu. The service runs every few minutes until 9pm.

The **Mevlevihane** is a former dervish convent located on Galipdede Caddesi, the first turning on the right after the Beyoglu Tünel. The convent was founded in 1491 by Iskender Pasa and rebuilt after a fire in 1756. The sect was officially banned in 1928 and the convent, set in a secluded cemetery where many prominent members of the Mevlana dervish sect are buried, is now open as a museum. The exhibits are displayed in a series of small rooms surrounding the main hall where the dervishes performed their whirling rituals, and include dervish costumes, musical instruments and illuminated manuscripts.

Yeni Cami, one of the most active charitable mosques in Istanbul

❊   The **Galata Tower** is built on a hill summit 140m (459ft) above sea level and its high conical roof is a prominent landmark on the skyline. It was first built in 1338 as part of the Genoese fortifications and during the Ottoman era it served as a fire-watching tower. The tower seen today was built in 1875 and is 68m (223ft) high. It contains a nightclub and restaurant on the top floor, and a circular viewing platform which affords panoramic vistas across the entire city. It is reached by walking downhill from the Mevlevihane.

    Istiklal Caddesi the former Grand Rue de Pera, is the main thoroughfare linking Beyoglu to Taksim, and is the central location for the consulates, foreign cultural centres, churches and cinemas. Most of the buildings date from the late nineteenth century, although their former elegance is often obscured by the throng of people, traffic and the modern shop fronts.

    The ornate gates of the Galatasaray high school, built in 1868, marks the intersection midway along Istiklal Caddesi that leads to Tepebasi, the site of the Pera Palas Hotel. **Çiçek Pasaji**, a lively

Dolmabahçe Palace gardens

market street, is next on the left, and **Cité de Pera**, an arcade adjoining the market has recently been restored with restaurants, tavernas and beer houses.

Taksim Meydani is a busy square with wide streets radiating out on all sides. An independence monument, built in 1928, marks the western end and the Atatürk Kültür Merkezi, a cultural centre opened in 1976, runs along the east side. Cumhuriyet Caddesi, which heads north, leads to the main shopping and business centres of Osmanbey and Sisli.

The **Military Museum** is in the district of Harbiye, 1km (0.6 mile) north of Taksim Meydani along Cumhuriyet Caddesi. It contains a large collection of weapons and armoury dating from the twelfth century to the present day. In the afternoons the military band hold outdoor performances of *mehter,* Ottoman janissary music. Performance times should be checked at the tourist information office.

Excursions from Istanbul

Each of the following are day excursions from Istanbul. All can be reached by public transport except for the Belgrade Forest.

Rumeli Hisar Castle guarding the Bosphorus at its narrowest point

Sariyer, on the European side of the Bosphorus

Market day in Sariyer

PRINCES' ISLANDS

The Princes' Islands, known as the *adalar,* are a cluster of nine islands in the Sea of Marmara about 20km (12.4 miles) south-east of the city. During the Byzantine and Ottoman eras the islands were places of exile, and they only became popular as holiday resorts in the nineteenth century. Today many Istanbul families have summer houses on the four largest islands, and at the weekends the beaches and restaurants are very busy. There is a frequent commuter ferry service from Bostanci on the Asian shore, and a service three or four times daily from the *adalar iskelesi* port at Sirkeci.

 Büyükada is the largest and most southerly of the islands. The town is well kept and clean, and old-fashioned, horse-drawn phaetons are the main form of transport as motorised vehicles are not allowed. A clock tower marks the centre of the harbour, and there is a selection of restaurants on one side with grand timber mansions and Victorian-style guest houses on the other. A working Greek Orthodox monastery, the **Monastery of St George**, lies between the two pine-covered hills Isa Tepe 163m (535ft) and Yuce Tepe 201m (659ft), and is a 45 minute hike from the town. Phaetons are hired from the square near the harbour and fixed fares are charged for various destinations including the sandy beach at Yörükali. Phaetons also make circular tours of the island.

Heybeliada is the second largest island and is dominated by a Turkish Naval Academy. Until 1973 the Greek Orthodox Patriarchate had a theological seminary on the northernmost of the three hills of the island and there is an Orthodox orphanage as well as a Byzantine monastery which was built in 1431. These monuments can now only be visited with permission from the Naval Academy. The small beach on the far side of the island can be reached by hiring a phaeton, as on the other islands motorised vehicles are not allowed.

 Burgaz Ada has elegant wooden houses built around the harbour with a domed Greek church at the centre. The house of a well known Turkish poet, Sait Fail (1907-54), is open as a museum and phaetons are for hire although it is quite easy to cover most of the island on foot. There is a footpath marked alongside the church leading to the plateau at the highest point of the island and there are grand views of the Gulf of Izmit and the Sea of Marmara on one side, and Istanbul on the other.

Kinali Ada is a rocky, treeless island, popular at the weekends as it is the closest to the city.

KILYOS

Kilyos is a popular beach resort on the Thracian side of the Black Sea coast, and is well marked by yellow road signs from the city. Buses also run to Sariyer, a small town on the European side of the Bosphorus, from where *dolmus* continue on to Kilyos. There are both hotels and restaurants in Kilyos, and the fee-paying section of the beach is supervised by lifeguards. The undertow is very strong along this stretch of the Black Sea coast and although the empty sand beaches may seem appealing, visitors are recommended to swim in protected areas only.

BELGRADE FOREST

The Belgrade Forest is the largest area of woodland close to the city, and contains the reservoirs that supply the city with water. It has been the main source of water supply to Istanbul since Byzantine times, but received its present name from serfs who were brought from Belgrade to work on the water system after the Ottoman capture of Belgrade in 1522.

The forest begins about 20km (12.4 miles) north of the city on the road to Kilyos. The highway passes by a fine aqueduct that was built in 1732 by Mahmut I, at Bahçeköy, before reaching the main gate of the park. It is one of the many aqueducts and small dams that are scattered throughout the park.

The forest is well laid out, the road leads to a central car-park from where footpaths and smaller tracks spread out in all directions. Maps are on display at a number of points, and signposts indicate the direction of the reservoirs and picnic areas. The most popular part of the forest is around **Büyük Bent** (Big Reservoir), where there is a jogging track and physical fitness equipment. Other facilities include a tea-house, fresh spring-water fountains and numerous picnic areas.

2
THRACE AND MARMARA

The Sea of Marmara is an inland sea, about 300km (186 miles) long and 100km (62 miles) wide, enclosed by Europe on one side and Asia on the other. The Bosphorus joins the eastern end to the Black Sea, and the Dardanelles, the western end, to the Aegean. The Asian shore, known as the Marmara, is generally lush and hilly, while Thrace, on the European side, is flatter and drier. Both coastlands attract holidaymakers from Istanbul and although there is growing alarm at the pollutants dumped in the sea by local industries, holiday developments continue to expand.

Both Thrace and Marmara are important agricultural regions, with fertile soils and favourable climates which provide most of the food for Istanbul. In winter it is wet and cold with an average temperature in January of 7°C (44°F). Temperatures are slightly lower in Thrace and severe frosts and snow are quite common. In summer it is hot and dry with a July average of 28°C (82°F), soaring up to 40°C (104°F) during heat-waves.

The area has a long history that dates back to the ancient Greeks and Romans, but the chief historical remains seen today are Ottoman. Bursa became the capital of the new Ottoman empire in 1326 and the capital was later transferred to Edirne. These two cities contain some of the finest early Ottoman architecture in Turkey.

There are regular ferries (most carry cars) from Istanbul across the Sea of Marmara to Yalova, Mudanya, and Bandirma on the Asian coast. The route is circular and is divided into five stages, each of which can be covered in a day. It is possible to join Route 3 at Çanakkale.

Route 2a — Istanbul to Edirne

There is little of interest to see on the journey from Istanbul to Edirne,

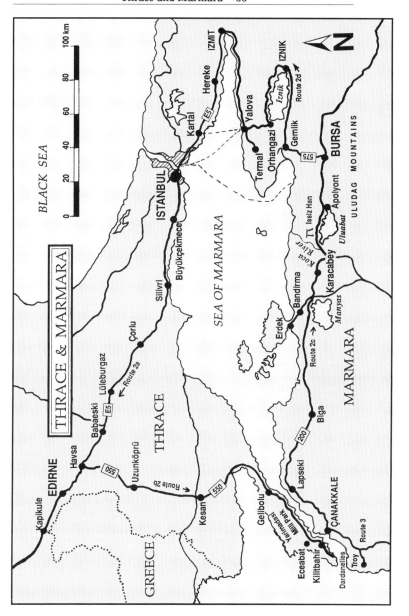

but there are long sections of dual carriageway and the drive can be made in under 4 hours. Follow the E5 signposted to Edirne, past the airport, over some large hills to Büyükçekmece, an industrial town next to a large lagoon. The old road crosses the lagoon on an **Ottoman bridge** built in 1538 by Mimar Sinan. At Silivri there is another Ottoman bridge, the **Silivri Köprüsü**, which has over thirty arches. Ancient burial mounds dot the landscape and tumuli can be seen close to the road at the villages of Seymen and Yenibedir. Lüleburgaz is one of the largest towns on the route and a yellow signpost points to **Sokullu Külliyesi**, an Ottoman mosque complex built in the sixteenth century by Mimar Sinan. Six kilometres (3.7 miles) before Edirne the road passes the turning to Sofya and Kapikule, the Bulgarian border point.

The E5 leads straight to **Edirne** town centre, Cumhuriyet Meydani, marked by the city's finest monument, Selimiye Cami. The road veers left at the mosque, along Saraçilar Caddesi, to the bazaar area. Most of the city's monuments are within easy walking distance of the town centre. The city has declined dramatically in size since its days as the capital of the Ottoman empire and some mosques that once stood on the edge of the city now lie isolated and abandoned in the outlying fields. Edirne is best known nowadays as the venue of the national oiled-wrestling tournament which is held every year at Kirkpinar on the town outskirts.

Selimiye Cami is a good starting point for a tour of the town. Steps lead up from Cumhuriyet Meydani to the *arasta*, or market building, which was built along the bottom of the mosque during the reign of Murad III (1574-95). The *arasta* is well restored and still functions as a bazaar dealing in cheap clothing and souvenirs. The steps in the centre lead up to the mosque terrace. Selimiye Cami was built for Sultan Selim II in 1569-75 by Mimar Sinan. It is one of Sinan's latest works, built when he was in his eighties, and succeeds in his life-long ambition to combine splendour, elegance, light and space as a harmonious whole.

Four slender tapering minarets, each with three balconies, stand at the corners of the precinct. The main entrance is approached through an enclosed courtyard with a marble-carved *sadirvan* at its centre. Inside the mosque the sense of light and space is partly achieved by the spacious dome, 43.28m (142ft) high and 31.5m (103ft) in diameter, and partly by the myriad of arched windows high in the upper walls. In the centre a fountain trickles beneath a balcony supported on eight columns. The *mihrab* is decorated with ceramic calligraphy and the *mimber* is skilfully carved from one solid piece of marble.

The *medrese*, in the north-west corner of the precinct, has been converted to a small **Ethnographical Museum** and the former students' cells surrounding the courtyard now contain a variety of Ottoman artefacts, ranging from embroidery and knitted socks, to carved wood, furniture and weapons. There is also a room containing photographs documenting the tradition of oiled-wrestling at Kirkpinar.

The **Archaeological Museum** is just outside the mosque pre- cinct and contains Ottoman costumes and crafts, as well as jewellery and artefacts found in local burial sites from the second millennium BC. **Muradiye Cami** is on the hilltop to the right beyond the museum. It was built in 1435-6 as a dervish convent and was still in use up until 1926. The interior is decorated with attractive Iznik tiles, but the mosque is kept locked except at prayer times.

Ulu Cami is directly opposite Selimiye Cami. It is also known as Eski Cami as it is the oldest Ottoman building in Edirne and dates from 1403-14. The entrance is on the east side. Inside, nine domes each measuring 13m (43ft) in diameter, are supported on four large piers and the walls are painted with black calligraphic figures. Behind Ulu Cami there is an Ottoman market building, the *bedesten*, built in 1418 and covered by fourteen domes. **Rüstem Pasa Kervansaray** is opposite the *bedesten* and is thought to have been built by Mimar Sinan. It is still in use today and a section has been tastefully converted to a hotel.

The 1443 Ottoman baths, known as **Tahtakale Hamami**, are still in working use and lie at the far end of Saraçilar Caddesi. Visitors are welcome to look inside. **Ali Pasa Çarsisi**, the main bazaar street is built parallel to Saraçilar Caddesi. It is said to have been designed by Mimar Sinan for the Grand Vizier Semiz Ali Pasa during the reign of Süleyman I (1520-66). At the far end of the bazaar, on Kapikule Caddesi, stands part of the Roman city wall which was restored by John Comnenus in 1123, and converted to a clock tower in 1886. Just past the tower is the **Sokullu Mehmet Pasa Hamam**, another Turkish bath designed by Mimar Sinan.

Üç Serefeli Cami, opposite the baths, takes its name from its minaret which has three balconies each with a separate stairway. The mosque was built in 1438-47 by Murad II. The proportions are unusual, the main dome sits over a narrow rectangular room with two smaller domes joined awkwardly at either side.

Beyazid Külliyesi, the largest charitable foundation in Islam and one of Edirne's most impressive monuments, now stands a good kilometre outside the town. The road crosses the Tunca river and passes through the fields to the complex. A path leads from the entrance of the enclosure to the mosque at its centre. On the left is a soup kitchen, and on the right a medical school, a pharmacy and

Selimiye Cami, Edirne

Beyazid Külliyesi, one of Edirne's most impressive monuments

a hospital. The complex was built between 1484 and 1485 by Sultan Beyazit II, but only the mosque is now in use. The other buildings are under restoration and are usually locked. The hospital, in the corner of the compound nearest the bridge, has an octagonal treatment room with a fountain on a raised platform in the centre.

There are good footpaths along the dykes either side of Beyazid Külliyesi. To the east is Sarayiçi, the ruined site of an Ottoman palace and Kirkpinar, and to the west are the ruins of Yildirim and Gazi Mihal Cami.

Route 2b — Edirne to Çanakkale

From Edirne follow signposts on the E5 to Istanbul as far as Havsa, then take the right turn to Çanakkale on highway 550. At Uzunköprü the road passes within 8km (5 miles) of the Greek border and then crosses the E25 just before the busy market town of Kesan. The highway climbs over the Karadag mountain range to the Aegean coast and then along the Gelibolu peninsula. The peninsula is a

national park area, the **Yarimadasi Milli Park**, which covers 33,000 hectares (81,510 acres) of land. The park contains the war monuments and many cemeteries that commemorate the thousands of lives lost during the 9-month Gallipoli Campaign. Tours of the war monuments can be arranged in Çanakkale and Gelibolu.

Gelibolu, known by the Allied Fleet in 1915 as Gallipoli, is now an insignificant fishing town with little of interest apart from the remains of a fortress built to defend the Byzantine city *Callipolis*. The tourism office on the main square and the travel company Yilmaz Tur, organise excursions to the battlefields. Taxi drivers offer private tours, but the price and itinerary should be checked beforehand.

Car ferries make the half-hour crossing to Lapseki from the harbour every 30 minutes. A second car ferry operates an hourly service across the straits between Eceabat and Çanakkale. At Eceabat yellow signs point the way to the Helles and Anzac War Cemeteries.

Kilitbahir is a small village slightly further down the straits directly opposite Çanakkale. The name Kilitbahir, lock of the sea, is derived from the defensive gateway formed by the two fortresses either side of the straits. The castle at Kilitbahir was built in the fifteenth century by Mehmet II on the foundations of a Byzantine fortress. The crenellated walls are patterned with brickwork and visitors are free to wander about the barracks but not in the central keep which is a restricted military zone.

A small ferry carrying a few cars leaves for Çanakkale every 15 minutes. The straits here are only 1,460m (1,600 yd) wide and the crossing takes a mere 10 minutes. From the ferry there is a good view of the war poem carved in chalk on the hillside north of Kilitbahir. It is written by Necmettin Halil Onan, and the first few lines read:

> Stop O passer-by,
> This earth you thus tread unawares
> Is where an age sank,
> Bow and listen.
> This quiet mound
> Is where the heart of a nation throbs.

Çanakkale is a suitable base from which to visit the ruins of *Troy* and the war memorials on the Gelibolu peninsula. It is the largest town in the region as well as the provincial capital. *Çanak*, is the Turkish for earthenware, and appropriately enough the town has been a centre for ceramics since the mid-eighteenth century. The local pottery is made of a coarse clay, decorated with stylised motifs of ships, mosques and plants.

There is a large plaza at the centre of the town with a clock tower on one side and a busy fishing harbour along the waterfront. Battlefield tours can be organised with the help of the tourism office on the quayside or directly from the agent Troy Anzac Travel near the clock tower.

One of Çanakkale's main attractions is the castle, **Çimenlik** **Kalesi**, at the southern end of the harbour on the Kocaçay river. It was first built in 1452 by Sultan Mehmet II, and ammunition shelters, a mosque and an inner keep were added in 1875 by Sultan Abdül Aziz. The **Military Museum** to the right of the outer gate contains a collection of weapons, uniforms and war-time photographs, as well as objects washed ashore from the Allied warships. Beyond the museum is a reconstruction of the **Nusrat mining boat** which mined the straits during the night of 17 March 1915. The next day the Allied ships, believing the straits to be clear, sailed to their destruction and hastened the Turkish victory. There is further war memorabilia from the Gallipoli Campaign exhibited in the inner keep. Nearby is the **Piri Reis Tower**, named after the Ottoman admiral, which has a collection of books and maps dating from the sixteenth century.

The **Archaeological Museum** is on the road to *Troy* about 25 minutes walk from the town centre. It houses a modest but interesting collection of archaeological finds dating back to the prehistoric era.

There is a regular *dolmus* service from the bus station at Çanakkale to the ancient site of *Troy*. The ruins are just off the E24/550, 33km (20 miles) south of Çanakkale.

Troy was no more than a Homeric legend until 1870, when a German named Schliemann identified a mound 5km (3 miles) from the sea which matched the description in the Iliad. With the permission of the Ottoman government and the help of some 150 Turkish workers he started to dig deep trenches across the site. After 20 years Schliemann found what he was looking for, the treasure of King Priam, and fled the country leaving the site in considerable chaos. From 1932-38 Cincinnati University excavated and discovered nine city layers built one on top of another, the earliest dating from 3000BC and the latest from 300BC. The positive identification of Priam's *Troy* is still unresolved. Some scholars believe it to be *Troy* 6 (1800-1275BC), while Cincinnati University say it is *Troy* 7 (1275-1190BC). Indeed, uncertainty shrouds much of *Troy's* history; careless excavations have destroyed a lot of the evidence and the remains seen today are scanty, but the romantic setting in the heart of the Troad countryside and the Homeric legend lend the site a special attraction.

It takes less than 2 hours to visit the ruins of *Troy* as the city was never more than a small citadel. A footpath makes a circular tour of the clearly-marked ruins. The path starts at a section of defensive wall from *Troy* 6 (1800-1275) built of angled limestone blocks with a large defensive tower. The city is entered by an overlapping gate and the path leads to the site of the Temple of Athena now a large pit next to a rampart from *Troy* 2 (2500-2200BC). In 480BC the Persian King Xerxes sacrificed 1,000 oxen here before setting off to attack Greece. In 334BC Alexander the Great took a similar precaution before embarking on his campaign to liberate Asia. The watch tower nearby dates from *Troy* 6 and has a deep cistern.

Schliemann found his treasure on the acropolis in the centre of the citadel. The best remaining structure here is the sturdy limestone ramp that dates from *Troy* 2 (2500-2200BC). The footpath leads from the acropolis to a Hellenistic sanctuary from *Troy* 8 (700-300BC), built against the outer city wall of *Troy* 6. Before completing the circuit the remains of a Roman bouleuterion and theatre dating from *Troy* 9 are passed on the left. Their small scale gives some indication of the dwindling importance of the city in its final phase.

Route 2c — Çanakkale to Bursa

Bursa is signposted from Çanakkale on highway 200 which winds up and down hills that offer occasional glimpses of the Dardanelles. **Lapseki** stands on the ancient site of *Lampsacus*, the alleged birthplace of the phallic god Priapus. There are a number of modest restaurants around the dock. At Sevketiye the road heads inland, passing the busy agricultural town of Biga to the plain behind Bandirma. Manyas Lake and Balya are signposted off right, on highway 565.

A diversion to the ornithological reserve, **Kuscenneti Park**, on Manyas lake is to be recommended for bird-spotters and nature-lovers. A wide range of migratory birds can be seen from the hide built on the edge of the reedy lake. Herons, spoonbills, glossy ibises and pelicans are but a few of the 239 bird-types that have been recorded here. It is estimated that some 2 to 3 million birds visit the lake every year, mostly between March and July, and in September and October.

At Edincik take the left turn signposted to Erdek and follow the road across the narrow marshy isthmus joining the **Kapidag penin-sula**, known in ancient times as *Arkonnesos*, to the mainland. About 6km (3.7 miles) before Erdek a small black and white sign points right to **Hadrianus Mabedine**, the ruined foundations of a temple to Hadrian. The temple was built in the second century AD in the city of **Cyzicus**. Further remains of the city are reached by following the narrow unsurfaced road on the right that heads towards Hamamli, for about 3km (1.8 miles), bearing right where the choice presents itself.

Cyzicus originally stood on the hill and stretched all the way down to the sea. It was founded by colonists from *Miletos* in 750BC but what remains of the city today is obscured by a dense mass of undergrowth and has never been excavated. However, the abundant vegetation and the charming setting in the gentle valley of the ancient *Kleite* river make wandering round the ruins a real pleasure. The most interest-ing building is the circular amphitheatre. The sections that survive give some idea of the huge scale of the city.

Erdek, ancient *Artake*, is a small seaside town, popular with local holidaymakers, on the south-west shore of the Kapidag peninsula. There is a good selection of fish restaurants and tea-houses along the sea front, but little in the way of accommodation; most people stay in the camp-sites or hotels on the sandy beaches to the north of the town. Carved stones and capitals from *Cyzicus* are displayed along the promenade.

Highway 200 passes the town of Bandirma and crosses the agricultural plain to Karacabey. **Uluabat Lake** first comes into sight at the village of Uluabat which sits along the bank of the Koca river, the ancient *Rhyndacus*. A couple of kilometres after the village a yellow signpost points right to **Issiz Han**, a caravanserai 2km (1.2 miles) from the main road. At the east end of the lake a right turn is marked to Gölyazi and Apolyont. A narrow road winds for about 6km (3.7 miles) down to the village of Gölyazi, which is built on top of the ancient ruins of **Apollonia**. Most of the ruins are on the islet in the lake which has been joined to the mainland by a bridge. Vehicles should be left at the bridge as there are no roads in the village.

Apollonia is said to have been founded by a Milesian trading colony in the seventh century BC and was originally connected to the sea by a wide canal. The site has never been excavated but the earliest remains appear to date from ancient Greek times. A derelict Greek church can be seen on the left before reaching the bridge.

Today, Gölyazi is a simple fishing village dependent largely on bartering its fish for other products such as cheese from Bandirma. There are no substantial structures remaining from *Apollonia*, but ancient stones are scattered throughout the village and have been incorporated into many of the village houses.

 The city wall, built with ancient stones, encircles the islet and is one of the most impressive structures. During the summer when the level of the lake gets quite low it is possible to walk around the outside of the walls. In the winter it is worth hiring a fishing boat to tour the island. One of the best remaining sections of the wall on the land is behind the new mosque. It has a fine Roman inscription set beneath a decorative frieze of garlands and bulls' heads.

Kisadasi is a tiny island just offshore, thought to have served as some kind of harbour monument and once connected to the mainland by a bridge. The edges of the island are finely paved and there are stone carved bollards and rings for mooring boats. The island takes its name, Girl Island, from more recent history, when a woman carrying the plague lived here in confinement.

It is 40km (25 miles) from Uluabat Lake to Bursa. The road is straight and well surfaced and dips up and down long hills into the fertile plain surrounding Bursa.

The provincial capital of **Bursa** is built on the foothills of Mount Uludag. The province is rich in agriculture and is well known for top quality peaches and sweet chestnuts. The city has one of the fastest expanding industrial zones in Turkey and is a leading manufacturer of cars and textiles.

Highway 200 passes the extensive factory developments west of the city, and the centre, Heykel, is marked by signs to *centrum*. Heykel is the crossroads in the centre of the city, marked by an equestrian statue of Atatürk. Accommodation in the city centre is mediocre and most visitors stay in the hotels in Çekirge, a suburb built on hot natural springs 2km (1.2 miles) west of Heykel.

Bursa first rose to importance as the capital of the Ottoman empire and the city has some fine examples of early Ottoman architecture. It grew up around a series of mosque complexes which acted as charitable foundations, providing the community with hospitals, libraries, schools, and soup kitchens. These complexes, along with their mosques, are now amongst the city's main monuments, and at least a day is required to see them all.

Ulu Cami, identified by its thick minarets and high walls, is a prominent landmark and a good point from which to start a tour of the city. It is directly above the bazaar on the corner of Atatürk Caddesi next to the plaza. The mosque was started in 1379 for Sultan Murat I and finished in 1421 during the reign of Mehmet I. It is built on a simple rectangular plan and is covered by a series of twenty small domes. Inside, there is a marble pool in the centre, and the original *mimber* is intricately carved from cedar wood. The walls and vast structural piers are painted with quotations from the *Koran* in elegant calligraphic figures.

The **bazaar**, which extends downhill and east of Ulu Cami, was constructed by Yildirim Beyazit in the fifteenth century and although many changes have taken place the basic layout has remained the same and the area is still the main shopping and trading centre of the city. The original *bedesten*, now a gold market, is at the centre and has four gateways, each leading to the surrounding commercial buildings, called *han*. One of the best preserved examples is **Koza Han**, a silk trading centre, situated behind the fountain in the plaza next to Ulu Cami. It was built around a courtyard with a stone *mescit* (prayer kiosk), in the middle, in 1491. **Emir Han** is directly behind Ulu Cami and has a small tea-house in its courtyard, while **Eski Ipek Han** and **Pirinç Han** are slightly downhill from the bazaar. Pirinç Han was built as a fur-trading centre in the sixteenth century. It is currently being restored and is one of the largest *han* in Bursa.

Yesil Külliyesi is one of Bursa's finest mosque complexes and can be reached by following Namazgah Caddesi from Heykel, and then taking the left fork marked by a signpost to Yesil Türbe. The complex includes a tomb, a mosque and a school, and was built in the fifteenth century by Mehmet I.

Yesil Cami is made of honey-coloured stone, except for the façade which is entirely clad in marble, and has an exceptionally fine portal. It was built in 1421 in the traditional Bursa-style with two large domes and takes its name, green mosque, from the turquoise-coloured Iznik tiles which clad the interior. The **sultan's apartment** above the main door is particularly notable for the richly patterned faience tiles but can only be visited with the permission of the mosque attendant.

Yesil Türbe, an octagonal mausoleum covered in turquoise tiles, stands on a mound opposite the mosque and contains the remains of Sultan Mehmet and his family. The Sultan's coffin is on a raised platform decorated with tiled inscriptions. The tiles on the exterior walls were replaced in the nineteenth century, but most of the faience work inside is original. The tiles in the prayer niche are especially fine.

The theological school next to the mosque now houses the **Turkish Islamic Arts Museum**. The students' cells and the main lecture hall now contain a collection of Ottoman objects, including local embroidery, Bursa velvet, jewellery and armoury.

The stone mescit *in Koza Han, a silk trading centre in Bursa*

The tea-house and restaurant opposite the mosque offer panoramic views across the city. The two domes of **Yildirim Beyazit Cami**, built in 1402 by Beyazit I, stand on the edge of the city in the plain below. The mosque was the prototype for what became known as the Bursa style and is part of a complex including a hospital and tomb. **Emir Sultan Cami** is to the right, surrounded by tall cypress trees and a vast cemetery. The mosque was built in 1804-5 on the site of a previous mosque which was destroyed by an earthquake.

The tombs of Orhan and Osman, the founders of the Ottoman empire, stand on the ancient citadel walls above Atatürk Caddesi. The original mausolea were destroyed in an earthquake in 1855 and were rebuilt in 1863 by Sultan Abdül Aziz. The tomb of Orhan is built on the site of a Byzantine monastery, St Elija, and patches of mosaic can be seen on the floor. A clock tower stands in the gardens behind the tombs, and a tea-house offers fine views across the city to Uludag. There are numerous cafés built on the slope below the citadel walls and a network of footpaths lead down to Altiparmak Caddesi.

A taxi or *dolmus* can be taken from Altiparmak Caddesi past the stadium along Çekirge Caddesi to the **Archaeological Museum**, located inside the main gates of Kültür Park. The museum contains

Yesil Türbe, Bursa, a mausoleum decorated with turquoise tiles

local archaeological finds and an interesting collection of funerary stellae which are displayed in the garden.

Muradiye, located directly above Kültür Park, is an imperial cemetery founded by Murat II in 1425-27 along with a **mosque** and a **theological school**. Eleven monumental tombs now stand in well-tended rose gardens, the largest of which belongs to the founder and dates from 1451. The coffin is positioned beneath a glass cupola supported on columns which originate from ancient *Prousias*. The adjoining chamber contains the coffins of Murat II's four sons. Some of the tombs have fine Iznik tiles, and those belonging to Prince Mustafa (1522), Prince Cem (1495) and Sehzade Mahmut are particularly good. Across the square from Muradiye is **Osmanli evi**, a seventeenth-century Ottoman house which is open as a museum.

From Kültür Park, Çekirge Caddesi heads west to **Çekirge**. The right turn, opposite the city's best known hotel, the Çelik Palas, leads downhill to **Yeni Kaplica**, one of Bursa's finest bath complexes. It is said to have been designed by Mimar Sinan in 1522 and visitors are welcome to look inside.

The main road passes by the Karagöz monument on the right, built to commemorate the creator of the shadow puppet theatre which originated in Bursa during the fourteenth century. The puppets were made of camel skin and coloured with translucent dyes and reproductions can be seen in most souvenir shops.

The **Eski Kaplica** baths are in the centre of Çekirge, on the right overlooking the plain. They are the oldest baths in Bursa, founded by Justinian in the sixth century, and have recently been connected to a modern five-star hotel.

The peak of **Uludag**, 2,543m (8,341ft) above sea level, is surrounded by a national park area covering 11,338 hectares (28,000 acres). It is accessible either by a tortuous road 36km (22 miles) up the mountain above Çekirge, or by the *teleferik* which leaves from the east end of the city above Emir Sultan Cami. The cablecar runs every hour, weather permitting, to the lower slopes of the resort. The mountain is an area of great natural beauty and on clear days there are outstanding views to the Sea of Marmara and across the city. In spring and summer it is excellent for hiking, while in winter it is a busy ski resort. Uludag is also popular for its Et Mangal restaurants which specialise in meat grills. The *kendin pisir kendin ye* signboards, mean 'cook it yourself and eat it yourself'.

Route 2d — Bursa to Istanbul

There are two routes from Bursa to Istanbul, one goes by ferry across the Sea of Marmara, the other by road around the Gulf of Izmit. There are passenger ferries to Sirkeci from the attractive fishing towns of Mudanya and Yalova which depart two or three times a day. There is also a 2-hourly car ferry service to the Istanbul suburb of Kartal from Yalova. The quickest crossing by the hydrofoil service from Yalova to Kartal takes 26 minutes, but does not hold cars.

From Bursa, highway 575 climbs over picturesque hills to the port and olive growing centre of Gemlik. It then winds up a river valley, at the head of which a yellow signpost points right to *Nicaea*, which is 45km (28 miles) along the shore of Lake Iznik.

Modern day **Iznik** stands on the site of ancient *Nicaea* at the foot of the Katirli mountains. The town is surrounded by an impressive city wall and the road enters through the **Yenisehir Gate** which is attributed to Claudius II (AD268-270). Just inside the wall, a sign points left to a third-century Roman theatre which has been recently excavated, but much of the stone was removed to construct and strengthen the city walls.

The town is built along two main roads, Atatürk Caddesi which runs north from the Yenisehir Gate to the Istanbul Gate, and Kili-

Window of the Turkish Islamic Arts Museum, Bursa

çaslan Caddesi which runs west from the lake edge to Lefke Gate. During the summer hotels and restaurants open along the lake edge, but in winter facilities for tourists are limited.

The town was founded in 310BC by Lysimachus and named *Nicaea* after his wife, but was renamed Iznik in 1078 when the Seljuk leader, Melik Shah, captured the city. In 1514 the Ottomans brought 500 potters from Tabriz and established the Iznik pottery. By 1575 there were up to 375 kilns in operation and for the next 200 years Iznik was to be the centre of Ottoman ceramics. When the potteries were moved in the eighteenth century to Tekfür Saray in Istanbul the city fell into a decline.

Lefke Gate in the east wall is a suitable point from which to start a tour of the town. It was built in AD123 in honour of a visit by Hadrian. Just outside the walls is a Byzantine aqueduct which was built during the reign of Justinian and is still in use. **Yesil Cami** is along Kiliçaslan Caddesi close to the museum. The mosque was built in 1378-1391 and the chunky minaret which has been renovated with modern

The tiled minaret, Yesil Cami, in Iznik

The döner *kebab is popular throughout Turkey*

turquoise tiles is typical of the Seljuk style. The porch is carved from white marble and the high central dome is supported on red and green granite columns. The mosque is normally locked except around prayer time.

The museum is housed in the **Nilufer Hatun Imaret**, one of the earliest known charitable foundations, built in 1388 by Murat I for his mother, Nilufer Hatun. The building is well preserved and contains an interesting collection of locally excavated objects, ranging from Roman oil lamps to Ottoman ceramics and tiles. The museum janitor has the key to St Sofia, and visitors should check whether it is open before leaving the museum.

The ruins of **St Sofia** are situated at the main crossroads of the ∏ town. They date from the fourth century and are built on the site of the Roman gymnasium. Only the main structural walls and the curved apse are standing, although there are visible traces of frescoes and mosaic flooring. The seventh Ecumenical Council, which abolished iconoclasm, was held here in 787. Atatürk Caddesi leads from St

Sofia to the **Istanbul Gate** which was built by the Emperor Vespasian (AD69-79). There are three gates in total, the upper walls of the innermost gate have stone-carved masks taken from the theatre built into them.

The city walls offer plenty of scope for walking, it is possible to follow the sentry walk between the double fortifications in many parts. The oldest walls date from the third century, but most of them were constructed by the Byzantine emperor Justinian and later in the thirteenth century by Theodor I Lascaris.

Yeralti Mezari is 3km (1.8 miles) north of the town. It is an underground Byzantine tomb beautifully decorated with frescoes of peacocks and flowers. Visitors must be accompanied either by a guide from the museum or the tourism office to see inside.

After Orhangazi highway 575 becomes single lane and slow lorries block the road over the last range of hills before Yalova. There is little of interest to see in Yalova itself, however there is an attractive spa resort 11km (7 miles) west of the town at Termal.

There is a regular *dolmus* service from Yalova to Termal. The road out of Yalova is signposted to Armutlu, the turning to Termal is on the left. The resort is set in a wooded valley on the site of a Roman spa which was known as *Pythia*. The only Roman remains today are the funerary stellae built into the outer walls of the **Kursunlu Kaplica**, the oldest baths in the resort. On the slope opposite the open-air swimming pool are the remains of a Byzantine church dedicated to St Michael which is thought to have been built on the site of the Roman temple to Apollo. The spa was re-opened by Atatürk and the house where he stayed is now open as a museum. The Turban hotel chain run the resort and have two main hotels, the Çinar and the Çamlik. *Pansiyon*-type accommodation is available at the village of Gökçedere.

There is little of interest to see along the shores of the **Gulf of Izmit** although **Izmit** itself has an impressive history. It was founded in 712BC, destroyed by Lysimachus and rebuilt by Nicodemus in 262BC as *Nicomedia* the capital of Bithynia. The city was destroyed a second time by the Goths, but rebuilt by the Roman emperor Diocletian. Today it is an industrial town and the waterfront is lined with factories.

From Izmit the E5 motorway follows the shore to Istanbul. The road passes by **Hereke** which is famous for its silk carpets. The E5 continues into Istanbul through the extensive city suburbs.

3
NORTH AEGEAN

T he north Aegean coast is dotted with Greek islands, and ferries operate during the summer from Ayvalik and Çesme to the two largest islands, Lesvos and Chios. The coast is built up with holiday homes and resorts around Kusadasi and Çesme, but less popular parts of the coastline remain largely unspoilt. The coast also boasts two of the best known classical sites in Asia Minor, *Pergamum* and *Epheseus*, while the modern regional capital, Izmir, is the third largest city in Turkey.

The highest mountains in the region, the Kaz Daglar, are in the north between Ayvacik and Edremit. Mount Kaz, ancient Mount Ida, is 1,767m (5,795ft) in height. The land becomes less mountainous towards the south, and olive groves give way to tobacco and corn fields, while cotton grows in the fertile river plains of the Bakir, Gediz and the Menderes.

The Aegean climate is a little cooler than that of the Mediterranean, but summers are hot and dry with average midday temperatures in August reaching 28˚C (82˚F) and the sea temperature is a comfortable 26˚C (79˚F). Winters are mild and frosts are rare with an average midday temperature in January of 9˚C (48˚F).

At least one day should be allowed for each stage of the route unless otherwise stated. Visitors who do not have time to continue beyond Kusadasi can travel directly from Izmir to Istanbul by plane (1^1/$_2$ hours), by road (8 hours), or by ferry (18 hours). Car-ferry facilities are available, but summer reservations should be made at least 6 weeks in advance. Visitors who wish to continue travelling down the coast can join Route 4 at Selçuk.

Route 3a — Troy to Ayvalik

The E24/550 south of *Troy* is a narrow, poorly-surfaced road, but the

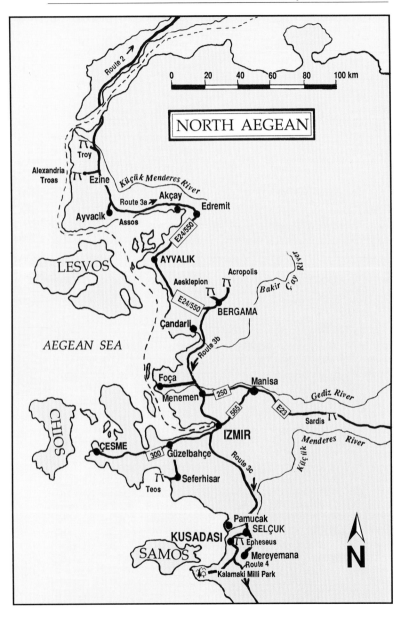

Peasant women selling fruit at Edremit

Hamidiye Cami, Ayvalik

countryside is pleasant. From Ezine there are road signs to **Alexandria Troas**, a classical city founded in the fourth century BC by Antigonus, King of Thrace. It is on the coast approximately 40km (25 miles) from the main highway. Due to its proximity to Istanbul the city was plundered for stone to build the Ottoman mosques and the remains are poor. An unsurfaced road follows the coast in a southerly direction from *Alexandria Troas* to Behramkale, which can also be reached by the E24/550.

The remains of the classical city of **Assos** lie on the coast 20km (12 miles) from the E24/550. Yellow signs indicate the route from the market town of Ayvacik, and the road climbs up and down hills until the ruins of *Assos* come into sight on the hilltop ahead. Just before the ruins the road passes a fourteenth-century Ottoman bridge that spans the Delicedere river and a yellow sign points right to **Apollo Smintheion**, a temple located 25km (15 miles) on the road to *Alexandria Troas*. Behramkale is the modern village built on the site of ancient *Assos*, some 240m (787ft) above the sea. The road passes through the village and heads steeply downhill to the ancient harbour, now a small resort known as **Iskele**. The traditionally restored hotels are usually full during the summer, but there are a number of small *pansiyon* in Behramkale.

Assos was founded by Greek Aeolian settlers in the tenth century BC. The ruins mostly date from the fourth century BC and the city wall is among the finest surviving examples of Hellenistic military architecture. It stretches for approximately 3km (1.8 miles) and is up to 14m (46ft) high in parts.

A footpath climbs above Behramkale to a converted Greek church which is built of ancient stones thought to have originated from the **Temple of Athena**. The temple is on the summit above and was built in 530BC. It is said to be one of the oldest surviving Doric temples in Asia Minor; the restoration is rather clumsy but the views from the temple terrace along the coast and to the island of Lesvos are magnificent. The foundations of the *agora*, a *bouleuterion* and a theatre are discernible on the steep slope below. Further west, an ancient paved road leads through the main city gate to the necropolis.

From Ayvacik the E24/550 continues south towards Izmir, and although the journey to Ayvalik is only 110km (68 miles) the road is mountainous and slow. Natural hot springs rise at the coastal village of Küçükkuyu and the **Kaplica Afrodit** is signposted on the left. Just past the village a yellow signpost points left to the Zeus Altar, 3km (1.8 miles) from the main road. The road passes the popular coastal resort of Akçay and the small town of Edremit and continues through olive groves to the turning right to Ayvalik.

Ayvalik, a busy fishing town and a centre for olive growing, is built around a wide bay, dotted with small islands. It was almost entirely populated by Greeks until the exchange of populations in 1923, and the Mediterranean-style houses and Orthodox churches still give the town a Greek atmosphere. One of the principal churches **Taksihyari-sah Kilise** is signposted on the right as the road enters the town, and is noteworthy for its frescoes. A causeway that links the small island of **Alibey Adasi** to the mainland is also on the right. Cunda is the main town on the island and there is a large but rather dilapidated church in its centre.

Ayvalik has a lively harbour and fish restaurants are clustered around the old customs house. The tourism office stands on the waterfront close to the jetty where small boats wait to take people on tours of the islands. There are a few hotels along the main promenade and many more at **Sarimsakli**, the beach resort 7km (4 miles) to the south. Buses to Sarimsakli leave from the main square every 20 minutes. In the early spring flamingoes can be seen on the marshy lands just before the resort. Sarimsakli has a wide sandy beach which stretches for about 4km (2.5 miles) and water-sport facilities are available.

There are panoramic views along the coast and out to the islands from the plateau to the south of Ayvalik, known as **Seytan Sofrasi**, the devil's table.

Route 3b — Ayvalik to Izmir

It is 63km (39 miles) from Ayvalik to Bergama and the journey takes less than an hour as the road is flat and well surfaced. Just south of Ayvalik, a Greek chapel is passed in a field on the right. Komili, the largest olive oil and soap factory in Turkey, is shortly afterwards. The road passes some salt lakes before **Dikili**, a popular coastal resort, on the right. After Ovacik, a centre for onyx-carving, the next left turn leads to Bergama.

Bergama is built on the classical site of *Pergamum*, 30km (18 miles) from the sea along the Bakir Çay river valley, known as the *Caicus* in ancient times. The modern day town has a long tradition of carpet making and is an important agricultural centre. The facilities for tourists are limited apart from a few restaurants along the main street. Most visitors stay outside the town either at the Tusan Motel on the E24 junction, or at the coastal resorts of Dikili and Çandarli.

The history of **Pergamum** really begins after Alexander the Great's death in 323BC and over the next few hundred years, it became one of the most influential and powerful kingdoms in Asia Minor. It later became the capital of the Roman Province of Asia.

The ancient ruins of the Acropolis and the Aesklepion are located on two separate sites. To see both sites, the museum, the basilica

Former Greek church in Ayvalik

The acropolis theatre at Pergamum

Inscription in the gymnasium, Pergamum

and the carpet shops in the town, takes a full day.

The **Acropolis**, perched 400m (1,300ft) above the town is the highest point of the ancient city. It is reached by a small winding road from the northern end of the main street where signs point up to the *akropol*. There is also a footpath that begins at the lower city and leads up past an agora, a gymnasium and the Demeter temple, to the summit. It is a long and steep hike and it is easier to take a taxi up and then walk down.

At the car-park there is a ticket office, café and toilet. A footpath leads up to the citadel through the city wall. The ruins of the theatre wall are on the left, and the flat open space next to it was originally a sacred precinct containing the Athena temple. Arrows painted on the rocks lead through a narrow vaulted passage to the top of the **theatre**. The seating drops at a spectacular angle to the stage, 36m (118ft) below, and there are excellent views out over the town.

The ruins of the famous **library** built by Eumenes II (197-159BC) lie on the north side of the sacred precinct. With a collection of some

200,000 books it competed in size with the Alexandrian library, prompting Ptolemy to stop papyrus supplies to the city. However this did not prevent the production of books at *Pergamum* as a local inhabitant named Hirodicus invented parchment. The library continued to rival that in Alexandria up until the reign of Cleopatra when Mark Anthony made her a gift of the Pergamene collection.

The footpath continues beyond the library to the **Trajaneum**, the largest temple in *Pergamum*, currently under major restoration by a German team. Most of the columns surrounding the temple have been re-erected and the vaulted substructure has been completely restored. It is made of impressive white marble and was built by Hadrian in honour of his predecessor Trajan. From the temple the path leads to the **arsenals** and the citadel walls. The north wall is particularly fine and there are splendid views across the river valley, where remains of an aqueduct can be seen. In Roman times water was supplied under pressure to the city by a lead-lined terracotta pipe from Mount Madradag, 45km (28 miles) away.

The lower city can be explored by descending the theatre and following the promenade, which forms the theatre stage, eastwards. The 250m (275yd) promenade runs between the **Temple of Dionysus** at one end to the **Zeus Altar** at the other. The Zeus Altar was transported to Berlin in 1878 and all that is left on the site is the base, surrounded by shady pine trees. From here an ancient paved road leads down to the middle and lower cities.

The **Red Basilica**, known as the Kizil Avlu, is at the northern end of the town, off Kinik Caddesi. It was first built by the Emperor Hadrian as a temple to the Greco-Egyptian god of medicine, Serapis, and Egyptian-style statues and Roman columns are scattered around the precinct. It was made into a basilica in Byzantine times and today there is a small mosque in one of the towers. The red brick walls which stand to a considerable height were originally clad in marble, but only the marble paving on the floor has survived. Below the altar, a steep passageway leads down to the Bakir Çay river, which flows under the building through a canal.

The **Archaeological Museum** is set back from the main street, opposite the bus station. It has an interesting but poorly labelled collection of statues and objects found in and around *Pergamum*. The statues of Hadrian and Trajan found in the Trajaneum temple are particularly notable and there is a scale model of the Acropolis as it would have appeared in Roman times.

The **Aesklepion** is 1km (0.6 mile) from the town centre, and is reached by a small road signposted on the right opposite the post office. The site was an important medical centre in Roman times and is named after Aesklepios, the god of medicine, who was popular in the fourth century BC when the precinct was first established.

From the ticket office, the footpath follows the Roman sacred way to the remains of the monumental gateway that leads into the precinct. The ruins are contained within a courtyard measuring 110m (120yd) by 130m (142yd). On the right are the foundations of the library and to the left is the circular base of the Roman **Zeus Aesklepios Temple**, built in the second century as a small replica of the pantheon in Rome. Steps lead down from the temple to another circular building, thought to have been used as a treatment room, connected to a sacred spring by an underground tunnel. The spring rises near a large plane tree in the centre of the courtyard. The slightly radioactive waters were an important part of the healing process and near the colonnade on the north side of the precinct there is a marble bathing pool. Beyond the colonnade there is a small theatre, with a seating capacity of about 3,500 people, set into a steep northern slope.

The E24/550 heads south of Bergama through dense olive groves. **Çandarli**, a small coastal resort located on the tip of a peninsula, is 41km (25 miles) from Bergama. The village is built on the site of *Pitane*, an ancient Aeolian city. There are no classical remains today but a well preserved fourteenth-century Genoese fortress stands on the hill overlooking the village. It is usually kept locked but the key is available from the *belediye*, the local council office, on the harbour front.

The E24/550 continues south past the industrial town of Aliaga, and the next right turn leads to **Foça**, an attractive seaside resort, 27km (17 miles) from the main highway. The village is built around two large bays with the remains of a Genoese fortress at the centre. *Pansiyon* and restaurants line the northern bay and there are beaches along the southern bay. More secluded beaches can be found along the coast road to Yeni Foça and some have basic camping facilities.

The E24/550 continues to Izmir, entering the city on a rather confusing one-way system. Konak, the city centre, is at the southern end of the bay.

The modern city of **Izmir** has a population of 1.5 million. It is the largest city on the Aegean coast and is a major port. High-rise blocks line the sweeping bay, and wide boulevards with palm trees splay out in all directions. The spacious recreation area near the city centre, Kültür Park, is the venue for the largest international trade fair in the east Mediterranean. It is held every year from 20 August to 20 September and during this period accommodation is often well booked. The wide selection of hotels and restaurants make Izmir a convenient base from which to visit the classical site of *Sardis*.

Horse-drawn phaeton in Izmir

Despite its twentieth-century appearance, Izmir has a long history. The earliest settlement, on the north side of the gulf, known as Bayrakli, dates from the third millennium BC but the present day site was founded when Alexander the Great built an acropolis on *Mount Pagus*, the modern Kadifekale, after being visited in a dream by Nemesis.

Konak is a good starting point for visiting the city. An ornate clock tower donated by the German Emperor Wilhelm II stands in the large plaza on the waterfront. On the hillside to the south of the plaza is the **Archaeological and Ethnographical Museum**. The museum, divided into two sections, is excellently displayed and well labelled. The ethnographical section contains an interesting collection of traditional crafts, ranging from felt-making to wood-block printing. In the archaeological section there is a vividly coloured Roman mosaic on the ground floor and a good collection of Greek and Roman statues made of bronze and marble. On the top floor, in the treasury room, there is a collection of coins and ancient gold funerary ornaments.

A pedestrian flyover leads from Konak to the bazaar area, past a small, tiled mosque dating from 1748. Anafartlar Caddesi winds through the **bazaar** to the old city quarter, where in a clearing among the closely packed houses, stands the Roman **agora**, built by Marcus

Manisa

Aurelius. Fallen blocks and decorative stones are scattered about the precinct, and on one side the marble columns are still standing. The whole courtyard is raised on a vaulted platform and in places it is possible to see down to the underground vaulting. The two great statues of Poseidon and Demeter that once stood in the centre of the market place are now in the archaeological museum.

The castle, **Kadifekale**, stands 160m (532ft) above the city on the site of the ancient acropolis and can be reached by *dolmus* from Konak. Little remains of the castle apart from its outer walls, but there are a number of tea-houses and restaurants, from where there are excellent views across the city and the gulf of Izmir.

Excursion to Manisa and Sardis

An excursion to the ancient site of *Sardis* can include a visit to the small Ottoman town of Manisa. The most direct route from Izmir is the 565 to Balikesir, but a more picturesque road, highway 250, leads from Menemen, north of Izmir, along the Gediz river to Manisa.

Manisa is a wealthy agricultural centre, located at the foot of the craggy peaks of Mount Sipylus. It is built on the site of *Magnesia-ad-Sipylum*, which was founded in 1190-80BC by a Greek colony known as the Magneti. Nothing remains of the ancient city as it was entirely destroyed by Tamerlane in 1390 and then again by a wayward dervish group in 1419. Sultan Murat II (1421-51) rebuilt the city and it was used as a training ground for the young princes throughout the Ottoman period.

Izmir Caddesi leads uphill from the tourism office to **Muradiye Cami**. The mosque is part of a complex, including a soup kitchen and a *medrese*, and was designed by Sinan in 1583-6 for Murat III. Inside the mosque the *mihrab* is finely decorated with Iznik tiles, and a staircase, hidden in one of the window recesses, leads up to the marble fretted balconies. The soup kitchen is now the **Archaeological Museum** and contains mosaics from *Sardis*, while the school is the **Ethnographical Museum**.

Sultan Cami is close by and was built in 1522 for Hafsa Sultan, mother of Süleyman the Magnificent. **Ulu Cami**, further up the hill, was built in 1366 on the site of a Byzantine citadel, and many of the old Byzantine and Roman stones can be seen in its construction. The *mimber* is original and dates from 1376-7.

The **Spildagi Milli Park** is above the town on the slopes of Mount Sipylus (1,517m/4,976ft). The road leading up to the park passes the mythical rock of Niobe, who according to legend asked Zeus to turn her to stone after she had lost all her sons. The 5,505 hectares (13,600 acres) of parkland is of great natural beauty and has a wildlife reserve containing bears, deer, mountain goats, vultures, eagles and pheasants. There are footpaths through the park, and the Manisa tulip, first imported to Europe in the seventeenth century, can be seen growing wild. Mountaineering expeditions up Mount Sipylus take place between 1 April and 30 November.

From Manisa, highway 250 is signposted to Turgutlu and Usak. About 7km (4 miles) from the town there is a carving of Cybele cut into a sheer rock face, set back from the road, on the right. It is believed to be a Hittite cult statue dating from the thirteenth century BC. At the junction with the E23, turn left, and follow signs to Afyon as far as the village of Sart. After crossing a stream, the ancient *Pactolus*, take the right turn, signposted to Sart Hrb, and follow a small road for 2km (1.2 miles) to a car park, next to the Temple of Artemis.

Sardis, capital of the Lydian Kingdom in the seventh century BC, became famous in the sixth century BC for minting the first gold coins. The gold came from the river *Pactolus* which runs close to the Temple of Artemis, and the river banks are now a popular picnic spot. The temple was built by Alexander the Great in 334BC on the site of an older temple dating from the sixth century BC. It was modelled on the vast *Didyma* temple and proved to be such an enormous project that building was still underway in the second century AD when the Romans took control, and finally had to be abandoned.

All temples dedicated to Artemis face west, and the footpath from the car park approaches the temple from the rear. The original entrance is at the far end of the building where two of the columns, built on the terrace in front of the temple, stand to their full height. The other columns only remain in sections, and only the base and foundation stones are left of the temple itself. A ruined Byzantine church dating from the eighth century stands at the south corner of the temple entrance.

About 250m (273yd) from the temple back towards the main road, a small footpath leads right to the Pyramid Tomb. The path continues on up past the tomb to the sparse remains of the acropolis, 300m (328yd) above the plain.

Back on the main road, a further kilometre from the turning to the temple, the remains of a Roman gymnasium and synagogue are visible on the left. The **gymnasium** façade has been reconstructed in a pinkish coloured stone and overlooks a large courtyard, surrounded by columns. Behind the façade there are a number of rooms, the largest of which contains a long bath.

The **Roman synagogue**, the largest yet discovered, runs along the southern side of the gymnasium and dates from the third century. The marble walls and floor mosaics inside the building have been restored, as has the courtyard outside. The altar, which stands in front of a wall shrine, has eagles carved on its base. The city obviously had a large Jewish population, as inscriptions such as 'shop of Jacob the Elder of the synagogue' have been found in the street of shops which lies between the synagagogue and the main road.

There is an ancient necropolis, known as **Bin Tepe**, near *Sardis*, and the main concentration of barrows is in the Gediz plain, about 4km (2.5 miles) further north.

Excursion to Teos and Çesme

Highway 300 heads west of Izmir along the Çesme peninsula to the popular coastal resort of Çesme. The classical site of *Teos* is on the southern coast of the peninsula, 50km (31 miles) from Izmir and can be reached by taking the left turn at Güzelbahçe to Seferhisar and Sigacik.

Teos was founded in 900BC by Ionians and was one of the most important and wealthiest ports on the Ionian coast. It originally stood on an isthmus with two sheltered harbours on either side, but with time the coastline has changed and the ruins are now some distance from the sea.

From the car-park the path leads to the **Temple of Dionysus**. The temple base is covered with tumbled columns and finely carved stones. The main frieze which once decorated the front of the temple is now in the Izmir Archaeological Museum. About 500m (546yd) along the path from the temple is a very overgrown **theatre** which dates from the second century BC. 500m (546yd) to the north-east of the theatre is the well-preserved Roman **odeion**.

Visitors who wish to swim should return to the village of Sigacik and follow the signposts for 2km (1.2 miles) to **Akkum** where there is a large sandy beach and some simple accommodation.

Çesme is a popular coastal resort for both locals and tourists. There are sports and recreation facilities available at the numerous holiday complexes, and at **Ilica** there is a thermal spa. Every June, during the Çesme Festival, there is a national pop contest, and the resort is very crowded.

The fourteenth-century **Genoese fortress** at the centre of the resort contains a museum, with exhibits ranging from Ottoman weapons, to artefacts from the nearby ancient site of *Erythrai.* Nearby is an Ottoman caravanserai, dating from 1528, now converted to a hotel. Day cruises to secluded beaches around the peninsula, and the daily ferry to Chios, depart from the modern marina.

Route 3c — Izmir to Kusadasi

The E24/550 heads south of Izmir on a fast dual-carriageway towards Aydin. Seventy-three kilometres (45 miles) from Izmir, the crenellated fortress at Selçuk (Efes) comes into sight.

The modern day town of **Selçuk** (Efes) is 5km (3 miles) from the ancient site of *Epheseus.* During the second millennium BC the citadel mound was the site of a Carian settlement, but it wasn't until the sixth century AD, when the harbours of *Epheseus* silted up, that Selçuk gained any importance, and a Byzantine town, known as *Ayasoluk* grew up around the citadel.

Most visitors choose to stay on the coast at the nearby resort of Kusadasi, but there are a number of *pansiyon* and small hotels in the town as well as a selection of restaurants, and there is a long sandy beach at **Pamucak**, 10km (6 miles) west of the town.

The **Archaeological Museum**, near the tourist office, is one of Selçuk's chief places of interest. It has an excellent collection of statues, carvings and mosaics from *Epheseus*, including a second-century bronze sculpture, *Eros and the Dolphin*, and a number of first- and second-century statues of Artemis Ephesia, the classical form of Cybele, the Anatolian goddess of fertility.

St John's Basilica is on the hill behind the museum and the road, which is signposted from the town centre, ends at a small car-park and ticket office. The **Gate of Persecution**, the sixth-century entrance to the citadel, lies to the right of the car-park and now leads into

Isabey Cami, Selçuk

the basilica. The basilica, which stands on the supposed burial place of St John, was built by the Byzantine Emperor Justinian in the early sixth century, with stones taken from the Temple of Artemision. Almost everything that is standing today has been rebuilt, as the basilica was totally destroyed by an earthquake in the fourteenth century. It is constructed in the shape of a cross, 110m (360ft) long and 40m (131ft) wide, and originally had eleven domes over the central nave. St John's tomb is in the main apse, surrounded by four small columns. In the north-west corner there are remains of a baptistry, and nearby is the treasury, and a chapel decorated with tenth-century frescoes.

The original Byzantine road can be followed from the Gate of Persecution past the basilica up to the **fortress**. The outer walls still stand to their original height and there are excellent views from the battlements across the cotton-growing fields to the long sandy bay of Pamucak. In the centre there are remains of a cistern and a small Seljuk mosque.

At the bottom of the hill, below the citadel, lies **Isabey Cami**, built in 1375. The architecture is very simple and the pink and grey granite columns supporting the two main domes are from the harbour at *Epheseus*.

ᴨ   The **Temple of Artemision** is in a marshy field, between Isabey Cami and the turning to *Epheseus*. It was built in 564-546BC as a sanctuary to Artemis, the fertility goddess, and originally had 127 columns each 20m (65ft) high. It was considered one of the Seven Wonders of the Ancient World, but a solitary column is all that remains today.

ᴨ   The classical site of **Epheseus** lies on the slopes of Bülbag Dag (ancient Mount Coressus) and Panayir Dag (ancient Mount Pion). The ruins date from Hellenistic and Roman times, but the history of the site goes back much further. The Ionians settled on the slopes of Mount Pion in the eleventh century BC, and it prospered under various rulers until the third century when the harbour began to silt up. The city was abandoned during the sixth century.

Epheseus is one of the best-preserved ancient sites in Asia Minor and a complete tour of the ruins takes at least 4 hours. During the summer it is best to arrive at opening time before the site is too busy and the sun gets too hot. There are two entrances, the main entrance is 3km (1.8 miles) from Selçuk, off the road to Kusadasi; the other is 4km (2.5 miles) from Selçuk off the road to Aydin. There is a large car-park at the main gate as well as souvenir shops, cafés and toilets. A roadway lined with spruce trees leads from the ticket office to the ruins.

The remains of the fourth-century church of **Haghia Maria**, also known as the Double Church, can be seen on the right. A path leads beyond the church to the overgrown walls of the **harbour gymnasium and bath complex**. This massive structure was built in the second century AD by the Emperor Hadrian, and later restored in the fourth century by the Byzantine Emperor Constantine.

The **Arcadian Way**, named after the Byzantine Emperor Arcadius who restored the street and installed lighting, is a marble-paved road 11m (12yd) wide and 500m (546yd) long which leads from the harbour to the theatre. The sea is now some 5km (3 miles) away and the harbour is marshland. The road is lined with columns and it is not hard to imagine the rows of shops in the shade of the fine colonnades either side. The **theatre**, built into the lower slopes of Mount Pion, looms ahead. It was started by the Roman Emperor Claudius in AD34-41 and finished in the reign of Trajan AD98-117. Building was still in progress when St Paul visited in AD54 from Tarsus and preached in the theatre. The riot recorded in Acts 19:23-41 occurred when St Paul, preaching his message 'there are no gods made with hands', threatened the trade of the silversmiths who earned their living making images of the pagan gods. The theatre, which seats 25,000 spectators, is still used during the Epheseus Festival, held every year in the first week of May.

From the courtyard in front of the theatre the **Marble Road** heads in a south-westerly direction towards the Celsius Library. Along the right side of the road, the low rusticated wall is the base of a long colonnade which forms one side of the first-century agora. The steps at either end allowed it to be used as a raised pavement.

The **Celsius Library** was built in AD114-17 in memory of Gaius Julius Celsius Polemaeanus, Roman governor of the province of Asia in AD106, by his son Tiberius Julius Aquila. Polemaeanus' sarcophagus is in the funerary chamber beneath the library and can be seen by looking through the slits in the back wall. The building has been completely restored and the excellent reconstruction of the ornamental façade gives a good idea of the former splendour of the city. Indeed, the façade was so admired by the Byzantines that a pool was built in front of the library in AD400 to capture the reflection.

To the right of the library there is a monumental gateway, the **Mazeus-Mithridates Gate**, which was built by two freed Roman slaves in the first century BC during the reign of Augustus. It leads into the **agora** which has some of the columns still standing around the edges and the remains of a water clock in the centre.

Curetes Street leads from the library uphill to the Magnesian Gate. The street has public buildings on the left and private houses on the right. The first public building is the **Scholastica Baths** which is on the corner opposite the library. It was built in the second century AD and restored by a Christian matron called Scholastica in the fourth century AD. There are numerous rooms, some with mosaics, others with underground heating. The pools are in the rooms to the east and a part of the building is believed to have been a brothel. The **Temple of Hadrian** is next to the baths. It was built in the second century AD and is decorated with finely carved reliefs.

About halfway up Curetes Street, a flight of steps on the right leads to some restored **Roman villas**. Visitors must buy a separate ticket to visit the villas. The interior walls of the houses are decorated with frescoes dating from the second century AD and the floors are patterned with attractive black and white tiles.

Curetes Street continues up the hill past a finely patterned mosaic pavement to the **Fountain of Trajan**. The fountain was originally two storeys high and had an enormous statue of the Roman Emperor Trajan, of which only the feet remain.

Beyond the fountain, after a series of broken columns, statue bases and pedestals, a road branches off right to the **Museum of Inscriptions**. The museum is housed in the vaults of the first century BC Temple of Domitian and contains a collection of stones bearing inscriptions which have been translated into German and Turkish only. The vast flat area littered with stones next to the museum is all

The Celsius Library, Ephesus

that remains of the state agora.

After returning to Curetes Street, the **prytaneum**, can be seen on the left. The building contained the perpetual flame in ancient Greek times, and it is one of the few prytaneum to have survived. The **odeion** is the next building on the left. It is built into the southern slope of Mount Pion and has seating for 1,400 people. The **Magnesian Gate**, set into the city walls, marks the end of the street.

Visitors can leave the site via the Magnesian Gate, or retrace the route to the car-park at the main gate. The road back to Selçuk from the Magnesian Gate passes the **Cave of the Seven Sleepers**, which lies up a small track on the left. The seven sleepers were said to have been persecuted Christians who hid in a cave and fell asleep for 200 years. They are supposed to be buried in the cave and a small church has been built in their memory.

Mereyemana is thought to be the place St John brought Mary to in AD37 and where she lived until her death in AD48. A modest church called **Panaya Kapulu**, dedicated to the Virgin Mary, was built in the fifth century and stands at the summit of Aladag (664m/2,178ft). The church was visited by Pope Paul VI in 1967, Pope John Paul in 1980, and a Greek Orthodox commemoration service is held here every year on 15 August. The site is signposted off the highway to

Aydin. The road winds up steeply for 4km (2.5 miles) to a car-park in front of the church.

Kusadasi is a thriving tourist resort, 20km (12.4 miles) south of Selçuk, on the E24/550. The coastline either side of the town is built up with holiday villages and camp-sites, all of which offer water-sport facilities. The road passes a large yacht marina at the northern end of the bay and follows the shore to the centre of the town. The main high street is lined with leather and carpet shops and the Ottoman caravanserai near the sea front, the Oguz Mehmet Pasa Kervansaray (1607-19), has been converted to an exclusive hotel. The small island, **Güvercin Adasi**, is linked to the shore by a 350m (382yd) causeway at the southern end of the bay and is a popular night-spot with a disco and restaurant built around the ruins of a fifteenth-century fortress.

In peak season up to six cruise ships a day call at the port for visitors to see Turkey and visit the three classical sites of *Priene*, *Miletos* and *Didyma* to the south, and *Epheseus* to the north. Daily ferries leave for Samos from the harbour and there are also day trips to **Kadinlar Plaji**, a sheltered sandy beach with a selection of hotels and *pansiyon*, 4km (2.5 miles) south of Kusadasi. Boats also run to **Kalamaki Milli Park** and to **Ahmet Beyli**, the site of ancient *Çlaros*. Kalamaki Milli Park can also be reached by road. Follow highway 515 along the coast and turn right to Davutlar, from where the park is signposted. Just before entering the park a yellow signpost on the left points to **Zeus Magarasi**, a large cave set back from the road. The park is scenically located on a peninsula, opposite the island of Samos, and covers an area of 10,985 hectares (27,133 acres). The land is wooded and rises up from the sea to the peak of Samsundag, ancient *Mount Mycale* (1,237m /4,057ft). There are two main beaches, Güzel Çamli on the northern side and Dipburun on the southern.

4

WEST MEDITERRANEAN COAST

T he region between Kusadasi and Antalya is one of the most popular stretches of coastland in Turkey. The Mediterranean summer is guaranteed to be long and hot, with an average temperature in July of 28˚C (82˚F), and the sea is a vibrant colour of blue. Beach resorts and holiday villages are found in almost every accessible cove and bay, and the main centres, Bodrum, Marmaris, and Kemer offer a wide selection of accommodation and good watersport facilities. Travelling generally takes a long time, as apart from the marshy flats around the Menderes river and Köycegiz Lake, the terrain is mountainous. However, only short distances are covered at a time as the route is punctuated with the classical ruins and attractive beaches that dot the shores of the ancient provinces of Caria, Lycia and Pamphylia.

If visitors intend to stop at all the points of interest, then at least 2 days are required for each stage of the route. The route is planned as a circular tour from Kusadasi: Route 4e leads inland past the interior lakes to the calcium springs at Pamukkale, then heads back to the coast at Selçuk. Visitors who wish to continue travelling south along the Mediterranean coast should join Route 6a at Antalya.

Route 4a — Maeander Plain

The ruins of *Priene, Miletos* and *Didyma* are all situated on the alluvial plain of the Büyük Menderes river, the ancient *Maeander*, in the most southern part of classical Ionia. They are well signposted and easily accessible from Kusadasi. Buses run to the inland town of Söke, from where *dolmus* leave for all three sites. Take a *dolmus* to Güllübahçe for *Priene*, Balat for *Miletos*, and Altinkum Plaji for *Didyma*. There is a wide range of accommodation at the beach resort of Altinkum Plaji, 5km (3 miles) south of *Didyma,* for visitors who do not wish to return to Kusadasi.

Priene lies 40km (25 miles) south of Kusadasi near the village of Güllübahçe, on the steep foothills of Samsundag, ancient *Mount Mycale.* The city was built by the Carian King Mausolus in 350BC and the site is quite unique in that it retains much of its early Greek character even though it was occupied by the Romans. It is also one of the earliest cities to have been designed on a grid-plan, an idea first introduced by the Greek city planner, Hippodamus.

From the car-park, a path leads up to the main gate in the city wall. At the first crossroads, the turning on the right heads towards the theatre, past the scanty remains of the upper gymnasium. The **theatre** was built in the third century BC and is the only building at *Priene* to have significant Roman additions. The Romans enlarged the seating capacity and added the bottom row of stone seats. The well-preserved stage buildings stand in front of the remains of a Byzantine church, from where a narrow path heads west to the **Temple of Athena**. The temple stands on a large man-made terrace and five of the thirty-four Ionic columns have been restored to their original height of 13m (43ft). The temple was designed by Pytheos, who was also the architect of the Halicarnassus mausoleum, under the auspices of Alexander the Great who oversaw a great deal of the building work when he arrived to liberate the city in 334BC.

The footpath continues west, between fallen columns and capitals, to a street of houses, built either side of a paved road. Most of the houses are designed around courtyards and originally had high narrow windows.

The **Sanctuary of Demeter** is directly above the houses, at the highest point of the city, 130m (426ft) above the plain. The remains are insignificant but there are excellent views over the ruins to the Menderes plain.

From the Temple of Athena, steps lead down to a street lined with statue pedestals and column bases. An excellently preserved **bouleuterion** is at the end of the street on the left. It was originally roofed and seated 640 people. On the right-hand side of the street lies the **agora**, which measures 128 by 95m (420 by 312ft) and would have been surrounded by shops and columns. An open market joins the north-east side but the whole area is now covered with broken columns and fragments of stone.

A paved road runs beneath the temple terrace and leads down to the former harbour. The remains of houses and shops lie on either side, in the shade of pine trees and oleander bushes. Near the bottom of the road is a large ruined building known as Alexander's house.

The road ends at the city walls, above the harbour which is now a large olive grove. A precarious path leads along the city wall to the lower gymnasium, which can also be reached by a better path leading from the ticket office.

The **lower gymnasium** stands 30m (100ft) above the plain on a solid outcrop of rock. The gymnasium baths are built on the west side of the courtyard and have a row of well-preserved stone basins with lion-head water-spouts. The room on the east side, with two column bases in the centre, is notable for the ancient graffiti on its walls. The remains of the **stadium** can be seen to the east, stones mark the starting blocks for the running tracks and some of the seating can be distinguished beneath the undergrowth on the north side.

Miletos is 22km (14 miles) south of *Priene*, in the marshy plain near the village of Balat. *Miletos* was probably first settled by Carians and Lelegians, but it first rose to importance in the eleventh century BC when the Ionians established a powerful trading centre.

The original Hellenistic **theatre** was enlarged by the Romans in the second and third centuries to a capacity of 15,000 spectators. The seats, built into the south slope of the hill, originally faced a small harbour, and some of the reserved place names can be seen on the third and sixth rows. The remains of the royal box, with its four columns, is in the centre. The theatre is entered by the original broad stairways at either side of the *cavea*. Vaulted passages run underneath the seating and provide access to each level of the theatre.

The remains of a Byzantine fortress stand at the top of the theatre and from here there are good views across the city. In the fields below are the remains of a circular building, formerly a **port monument**. The harbour mouth has been closed by an earth embankment as the area is still prone to flooding. At either end of the embankment, two stone-carved lions, about 2m (6.5ft) long, lie up to their flanks in mud.

The **Delphinion**, the largest temple in *Miletos*, is to the east of the port monument. Dedicated to Apollo, it was built in Hellenistic times, and is linked to the temple at *Didyma* by a colonnaded **sacred way**, the first section of which has been restored. The steps along the colonnades served as seating for spectators watching the religious processions pass along the sacred way. A well-preserved **bouleu-terion** stands at the southern end of this road. It is the oldest surviving building at *Miletos* and dates from 175-163BC. A pathway leads south past the **agora** to the **Faustina Baths**, built by Faustina II, wife of Marcus Aurelius, in AD161-180. The frigidarium is well preserved and has a statue of the river god, Maeander, at one end of the pool, and a lion at the other.

From the baths the track leads past **Ilyas Bey Cami**, a small deserted mosque, built in 1404 just before the Ottoman empire took

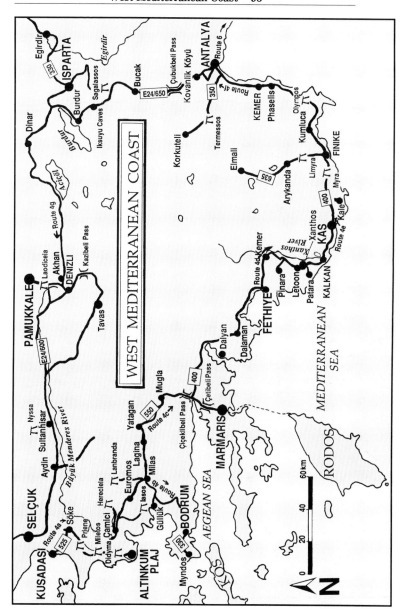

control. The finely carved portal and *mihrab* are decorated with fluid arabic calligraphy, and the lunettes above the windows are of fretted marble. The track leads back to the car-park in front of the theatre, past the half-submerged remains of the Roman **stadium** and a modest **museum** which contains a few locally found artefacts.

The ancient temple to Apollo at **Didyma** is 19km (12 miles) south of *Miletos*, in the centre of the village of Yenihisar. Excavations have shown that the site was used as a sacred precinct as early as the eleventh century BC, but was destroyed during the Persian invasions in 494BC. The ruins seen today date from the fourth century BC, after Alexander the Great's arrival in Asia Minor. The scale of the building was so immense that 600 years later the temple was still not complete.

The entrance is on the roadside, opposite a small car-park and a row of restaurants. The temple is raised on a platform of seven tall steps. The fourteen steps at the front lead up to twelve enormous column bases which form the pronaos, the porch in front of the temple. Ramps at either side lead down to the inner courtyard, known as the *cella*. The walls surrounding the courtyard are in excellent condition and around their base there is a collection of carved griffons and lyres which originally formed a frieze around the upper part of the walls. A flight of steps leads up from the courtyard to a platform that looks out over the pronaos.

The remains of a **stadium** run along the east side of the outer wall of the temple. The steps of the temple platform served as seating, and are covered with ancient graffiti. At the eastern end of the track there are nine stone blocks which originally held starting posts.

The carved head of Medusa, which was part of the temple façade, sits beneath the stairway at the entrance to the site.

Altinkum Plaji is a busy resort with two large sandy beaches. The sea front is lined with hotels, *pansiyon*, camp-sites and restaurants, and water-sport facilities are available.

Route 4b — Lake Bafa to Bodrum

The E24/550 follows the winding contours of Lake Bafa which is roughly 20km (12 miles) long and 9km (5 miles) wide. It used to be joined to the sea and was known as the Gulf of Lade, but the change in coastline, brought about by the silt from the Menderes river, has left it a freshwater lake.

The ancient site of **Herecleia** can either be reached by hiring a boat from one of the camp-sites at the lake edge, or by following the small road from the village of Çamici, a few kilometres east of the lake. The ruins are 12km (7 miles) from the main road, picturesquely situated on the northern shore of the lake, at the foot of Besparmak

Dag, ancient *Mount Latmos*. The settlement, originally called *Latmos*, was founded by the Carians and only later changed its name to *Herecleia*. In the third century BC, Lysimachus constructed a vast wall, 6.5km (4 miles) long, around the city, and during the Roman period a number of fine buildings were erected. During the Byzantine era, Christians sought shelter on the many small islands and reedy inlets around the lake, and the numerous remains of monasteries and churches date mostly from the fourth century.

Just before reaching *Herecleia* there is a small promontory jutting into the lake with the remains of a **Byzantine fortress**. The ruins are reached by following the path across the field to the steps cut into the rock that at one time supported the city wall. At the end of the promontory, below the castle walls, rectangular tombs are carved into the flat rocks at the lake edge.

The village of Kapikiri is built on top of the ancient ruins of *Herecleia* and although villagers have used many of the ancient stones to build their own houses a few monuments have survived. The **Temple of Athena** is one of the best-preserved buildings, dramatically located on a high rocky outcrop overlooking the lake. A small path alongside the school on the left of the main street passes through the playground, originally the agora, and heads uphill to the temple site. The temple is Hellenistic and is built in antis, which means there are no surrounding columns. The walls are excellently preserved and the stonework is exceptionally fine.

From the village square at the end of the street, a path leads off right to a small Roman **theatre**. The theatre has not been excavated and the ruins are easy to miss as they are surrounded by olive groves and fruit orchards.

The ruins of a monastery are on the tiny island, joined by a causeway to the village harbour, and boats can be hired to visit other ruins in the lake.

The E24/550 heads south from Çamici towards Milas, between two ranges of hills, the Labada Dag on the right and the Besparmak Dag on the left. The road climbs up, passing through a short unlit tunnel, and then descends into the broad flat plain surrounding Milas. At the village of Selimiye a yellow sign points left to Zeus Tapinagi, one of the six best-preserved temples in Asia Minor. It originally stood just outside the city walls of ancient **Euromos**, and is all that remains of the city. Sixteen fluted columns with beautifully carved Corinthian capitals still support part of the ancient architrave. A number of the columns are unfluted, probably because the work on the temple was never completely finished.

A few kilometres south of *Euromos* and about 12km (7 miles) before Milas, a yellow signpost points right to *Iasos*.

Lake Bafa

The remains of **Iasos** are 17km (10.5 miles) down a small road which crosses the plain and then climbs up a range of hills. At the top of the hill there is a domed water cistern and there are magnificent views across the marshy plain to the sea beyond. The ruins are on the coast next to the modern day village of Küren. On approaching the village, a Roman burial tomb is passed on the right, built in the style of a temple with finely carved Corinthian columns. The interior is used to house a collection of locally excavated Minoan and Mycenean pottery.

The village, **Küren**, stretches along the shore as far as the ancient harbour where there are a couple of *pansiyon* and restaurants at the water's edge. The ruins of *Iasos* lie on the small headland opposite, connected to the mainland by a narrow isthmus. The Carian King Mausolus enclosed the city within a 2km (1.2 mile) defensive wall in the fourth century BC, but the remains are largely unexcavated and are covered in olive groves. A ruined **Byzantine fortress** stands on the top of the hill, while the **theatre** is on the sea-facing slope and can be recognised by its fine outer walls. Near the theatre are the remains of a **Roman villa** with a black and white patterned floor. The ruins of the harbour defences can be seen near the mouth of the bay.

Milas is a busy agricultural town in the heart of an important

The Temple of Zeus, Euromos

carpet making region. It stands on the ancient site of *Mylasa*, the first capital of the Carian kingdom, on the foothills overlooking the plain of the Sari Çay river.

To the west of the town centre, **Gümüskesen**, a small first-century replica of the *Halicarnassus* mausoleum, stands in almost perfect condition. It has a pyramidal roof supported on finely carved Corinthian columns. There are also several mosques in the town dating from the Mentese period. **Ulu Cami**, situated near the river, was built in 1378 using stone from ancient *Mylasa*. The pink marble of **Firuz Bey Cami,** built in 1394, also originates from the classical site.

Bodrum is built on the site of the ancient city of *Halicarnassus*, founded by Dorians, and lies 48km (30 miles) west of Milas on highway 330. Thirteen kilometres (8 miles) from Milas there is a signpost on the right to the small resort of **Güllük** where there are some simple hotels and boats can be hired to reach *Iasos*. The road continues along the peninsula past numerous coastal resorts before descending into the bay of Bodrum.

Bodrum is one of the most popular resorts on the Mediterranean. The relaxed European atmosphere attracts wealthy Turkish holiday-makers as well as foreign tourists, and the town abounds in hotels, *pansiyon*, restaurants, bars, discos, fast-food cafés and shops. Bodrum comes alive after dark as during the day most people leave town for the surrounding beaches. Bars and discos open late and stay open until the early morning. The harbour is filled with row upon row of yachts and *gulet*, traditional wooden schooners. Boats ferry people to the beaches around the peninsula and also on longer cruises along the Mediterranean coast.

The **Castle of St Peter** is now a museum and contains a good collection of artefacts found on the sea-bed and in ruined vessels, dating from the Bronze Age up until the Byzantine era. The castle is surrounded by a moat and has five towers. The **British Tower** is in the southern corner and has the coat of arms of Edward Plantagenet and a relief of St George and the Dragon. The **French Tower** stands at the highest point in the centre of the castle, overlooking the bay of Gokova to the island of Kos. The **Chapel of the Knights** in the outer bailey was used as a mosque in Ottoman times and has been well restored. The castle is the venue for the Bodrum Art and Culture Festival every September.

There are no beaches in Bodrum itself but there are regular *dolmus* and boats to the sandy bays around the headland to the west. **Gümbet**, the nearest beach 3km (1.9 miles) away, is overcrowded in the summer but has wind-surfing, diving and other water-sport facilities. Further around the coast are **Bitez** (8km/5 miles), and the traditional boat-building centre **Ortakent** (10km/6 miles). Boats leave the harbour around 11am and return between 6 and 7 in the evening. Longer cruises, *mavi-tur*, take at least 2 days, and call at *Knidos*, on the Datça peninsula and Gümüsluk, the site of ancient *Myndos,* which can also be reached by road. The ruins lie submerged in the sea on the opposite side of the headland from Gümüsluk.

Route 4c — Bodrum to Marmaris

Highway 330 retraces the route to Milas, from where an excursion to the mountain-top site of *Labranda* can be made. The ruins have an exceptionally scenic location, but at least 2 or 3 hours should be allowed for the excursion as the site is 14km (8.5 miles) from the main road up a steep and unsurfaced track. The turning is signposted off the Milas to Izmir highway, just north of the town.

The ruins of **Labranda** are at the head of a high valley, overlooking the plain of Milas. A small footpath leads up to the ruins from the left-hand side of the road. A village stood on top of the ruins until the site was excavated by a Swedish team in 1969. The guardian, who shows visitors around the site, lives in the only remaining house. *Labranda* was a sanctuary to Zeus, founded by Queen Ada, the younger sister of King Mausolus, in the fourth century BC. Like

Didyma there was a temple oracle and large processions would climb the 12km (7 miles) sacred way from *Mylasa* to partake in the religious festivities.

A well-preserved banqueting hall (Andron House) stands directly above the guardian's house. It is one of the finest surviving examples of its kind. The double walls, built for insulation, stand to a considerable height, and the doorway and some of the windows are still intact. The **Temple of Zeus** stood on the terrace opposite. Nothing remains apart from the foundations and a great many tumbled column drums. A row of columns forming the **north stoa** stand on the hill above, and just beyond them is an excellently-preserved **royal tomb,** containing five sarcophagi.

Below the temple terrace a broad flight of twenty-three stone steps lead to the south gate. The remains of a **Byzantine church** are at the bottom of the steps and to the east there are the ruins of a first century **Roman baths**. The columns standing in the orchard to the left surround a pool that at one time held the fish used by the oracles to predict the future. The mountain spring which used to fill the pool now provides Milas with drinking water.

The fortress, **Beçin Kale** is 5km (3 miles) south of Milas on the road to Oren, off highway 330. The castle is perched high on the edge of a rocky crag, above the village of Mutluca. The site has been inhabited since the second millennium BC and served as a religious sanctuary in classical times. The classical site lies unexcavated and nothing remains to be seen, but the Byzantine fortress is well preserved. The Mentese Turks held out inside these castle walls for a whole year against the Ottoman army in 1390. Ahmet Gazi, the last of the Mentese emirs, was killed when the fortress fell to Sultan Beyazit I, and his burial chamber is in the **medrese** next to the fortress. The *medrese* was built in 1375, and is still attended by local women who regard the tomb as a shrine. The rags on the nearby trees have been tied there for luck.

A flight of steps leads to the castle gate and passes between two defence towers. Just inside the entrance, on the right, is a 30-40m-(100-130ft-) deep well and the entrance to the underground dungeons. The centre of the castle is occupied by a few deserted houses and the remains of a Byzantine church. There are good views from the outer walls across the red-earthed plain of Milas.

Highway 330, signposted to Mugla, climbs up into wooded hills. Just beyond the village of Eskihisar, a yellow signpost points right to Lagina Hrb, the site of ancient *Stratoniceia*. The sparse ruins are 9km (5.5 miles) from the main road and are not really worth visiting. At Yatagan, a mining town, the road joins highway 550, a busy road crossing the plateau to **Mugla**. The town was the capital of the

Waterfront, Marmaris

Mentese Turks in the fourteenth century and has some attractive architecture dating from that time, as well as some reasonable hotels.

After Mugla, the road climbs up to the village of Kizilagaç and crosses the Çiçeklibeli Pass (775m/2,542ft). The views from the summit are spectacular, mountains stretch into the distance and the blue bay of Gökova lies far below. The descent is slow and winds around a series of hairpin bends for about 14km (8.5 miles), but the road is wide and well surfaced. At the bottom, Marmaris is signposted to the right, along a road that climbs up to the Çetibeli mountain pass (510m/1,672ft) before descending through pine and oleander to Marmaris. Just before reaching the resort the turning to *Knidos* and Datça is signposted on the right.

Marmaris is a popular coastal resort and centre for yachting. It is located in a deep bay protected by offshore islands and promontories on either side. The situation is ideal for small boats and the harbour front is lined with *gulet* and yachts. Cruises in the deep blue water of the Mediterranean, *mavi tur,* are very popular and are always fully booked in peak season. Reservations should be made well in advance.

There is a well-sheltered sandy beach at one end of the bay, but it gets very crowded in the summer and most people take day boat

Theatre at Knidos

trips from the nearby quay to the **Loryma peninsula** where water-sport facilities are available on most of the beaches, or to the small islands in the bay of Marmara. The Greek island of Rodos (Rhodes) lies off the Turkish coast, close to Marmara. Boats regularly make the 3-hour crossing during the summer.

Marmaris has good shopping, with a pedestrianised bazaar area that sells all manner of souvenirs, leather, carpets and onyx, as well as natural sponge and honey, specialities of the region. Accommodation and restaurants are in plentiful supply, both in the town and along the shore on either side. In the summer season everything stays open late, and bars, restaurants and discos are open until the early hours of the morning.

The land to the west divides into two narrow peninsulas: the Datça peninsula to the north and the Loryma peninsula, part of ancient *Rhodian Peraea*, to the south. A poorly-surfaced and winding road leads along the Datça peninsula, locally known as Resadiye Yarima-dasi, to the small town of **Datça**, 87km (53 miles) west of Marmaris. The ruins of *Knidos*, at the tip of the peninsula, can be reached by either boat or minibus from Datça.

Knidos, built around a double harbour, was founded by the Dorians in the fourth century BC. They moved here from Datça to take advantage of the well-placed, natural harbour. An ancient paved road with the original steps leads from the Marmaris highway to the scanty remains of the **Sanctuary of Demeter**. Just beyond there is a theatre built into the east facing slope of the acropolis mound. A second theatre, near the south harbour, is the better preserved of the two. A path leads up behind the fish restaurants clustered around the harbour to the foundations of the circular **Temple of Aphrodite**, famous at one time for the statue of Aphrodite made by Praxiteles in 350BC. Very little remains of the temple and the statue has been lost, although Roman copies exist. However, there are fine views along the coast.

Route 4d — Marmaris to Fethiye

From Marmaris, visitors must retrace their steps to the Bay of Gökova, where highway 400 leads right to Fethiye. Sixty-three kilometres (39 miles) from the turning, the road passes Köycegiz , a small town with a selection of simple hotels, *pansiyon* and camp-sites, on the shore of Köycegiz Lake. A little further along highway 400 a yellow signpost points off right to *Kaunos*.

Dalyan is a small village built along one side of the Dalyan Çayi river, close to the ancient site of *Kaunos*. A group of spectacular **Lycian tombs** are carved into the cliff-face on the opposite side of the river. Fish restaurants line the quayside at the centre of the village, while small *pansiyon* and attractive hotels are built at the waterside on either side of the village. Mosquitoes can be a problem here in the summer and before booking into a hotel, visitors should check that the windows have mosquito nets. The wooden boats at the quayside belong to a cooperative which operates tours of the river and the ancient ruins of *Kaunos*, and also takes visitors out to the long sand spit beach at the mouth of the river.

A full boat tour starts at the hot springs near Köycegiz Lake, and then follows a meandering course down the river through the thick reeds and bamboos towards *Kaunos*. A system of gateways, constructed across the river, catch sea bass and grey mullet as they return to the sea after spawning in the lake.

A **Carian fortress** marking the acropolis of *Kaunos* comes into sight on a hilltop on the right. The boat pulls in at a wooden pier, from where a footpath leads uphill, past a **Byzantine church** and a large **baths complex**, to the **theatre**, the best-preserved building on the site. From the theatre, there are views to the sheltered port below, now filled with reeds. The area next to the port is under excavation and contains a **nymphaion**, a monumental fountain dedicated to Vespasian.

The boat continues for a further 3km (1.8 miles) beyond the ruins to the coast where there is a 6km (3.7 miles) sand spit. There are a few fish restaurants around the landing stage, but otherwise the beach is deserted. A road leads to the opposite end of the beach from the centre of Dalyan, marked by signposts to **Bogazici Plaj**. The coast here has recently been designated as a nature reserve in order to protect the rare loggerhead turtles that breed here.

Highway 400 continues south of Dalyan through the village of Ortaca to Dalaman where the airport is signposted on the left. The road then climbs steeply for 10km (6 miles) passing the village of **Inlice** where there are some tombs carved in the cliff-face on the left. The road then twists back down to the coast, and there is a right turn to **Katiranci**, a lovely beach in a deep-sheltered bay. It is very popular with Turkish families in the summer and there is a camp-site in the forest just behind the beach. The road climbs a final range of mountains before descending into the bay of Fethiye, where a yellow signpost indicates the local museum to the right of the road.

Fethiye does not hold the same charm as the other Mediterranean resorts, as the town is divided by a busy road and it lacks a proper centre. The yacht marina is at the eastern end, surrounded by the best hotels and most expensive restaurants. The cheaper hotels and restaurants are in the town centre. The nearest beach is 3km (1.8 miles) to the west, at **Çalis**. However, it is an uninspiring stretch of sand and most visitors head across the mountains to Ölü Deniz, otherwise known as the Blue Lagoon.

Fethiye is built on the site of ancient *Telmessos* but all that has survived of the city are the **Lycian tombs.** The most impressive tombs are carved in the rock face above the town and date from 350BC. Other free-standing tombs are dotted around the town and mainly date from the fifth century BC. The largest one is in front of the *belediye*, the local council hall, and there is another just outside the post office.

The town is overlooked by the remains of a **crusader castle** built by the Knights of St John. It is in very poor condition, but offers good views across the bay of Fethiye, known as the gulf of Glaucus in ancient times.

Ölü Deniz lies 15km (9 miles) from Fethiye. *Dolmus* regularly ply back and forth between the resort and Fethiye, on the small winding road that leads over the hill from the west end of the town. At the summit there is a right turn signposted to **Karmylassos,** also known as Kaya, a deserted Greek town. The houses are spread along the slopes of three hills and the town was populated by Greeks until the exchange of populations in 1923. Today the buildings are slowly falling down and the frescoes in the small chapels and two main basilicas have been defaced. A narrow and winding road continues

The long shingle beach at Ölü Deniz

beyond Kaya, over the hills, to **Gemile**. A small island with the ruins of a Byzantine monastery lies just offshore. Locals hire out their fishing boats to tourists who wish to visit the island. Boats can also be hired from Ölü Deniz.

The bay of **Ölü Deniz** with its long shingle beach is lined with *pansiyon* and hotels. Water-sports equipment can be hired along the beach but the main attraction is the beautiful lagoon at the west end of the bay. A fee is charged for entry into the area around the lagoon where there is a car-park, changing cabins, showers and snack-bars.

Route 4e — Fethiye to Kas

Ancient Lycia extends south along the coast from Fethiye to Antalya and the remains of about forty Lycian cities have been so far identified by archaeologists. Highway 400, signposted to Antalya, heads inland, west of Fethiye. At Kemer visitors who do not wish to tour the Lycian coast can continue inland on the newly built highway 350 to Korkuteli. Highway 400 follows the lush Xanthos river valley due south, where 49km (30 miles) from Fethiye, a yellow signpost points right to *Pinara*. A rough track winds steeply up for 6km (3.7 miles) to a parking area.

π   **Pinara** is one of the largest cities in Lycia and the ruins, spread

A quiet bay near Ölü Deniz

over a wide area on either side of a broad valley, involve visitors in some strenuous walking. The guardian usually guides tourists around as the ruins are overgrown and the path is not always clearly marked. A sparkling mountain river flows through the centre of the valley, at the foot of a steep rocky crag which is peppered with rock-carved tombs. The summit of the crag, which lies 600m (1,968ft) above the river bed, was the site of the original city, but only the ruins scattered along the foot of the cliff are worth visiting. There is a group of beautifully carved **Lycian tombs** dating from the fourth century BC with reliefs of figures on the pediments, close to the river. Further north the path climbs up to the ruined **Temples of Artemis and Apollo** from where the well-preserved Greek theatre, built into the hill on the other side of the valley, can be seen.

Highway 400 continues south and heads uphill from the hamlet of Gölbent to a right turn signposted to *Sidyma*. The remains of this Lycian city are scanty and do not really warrant the 12km (7 miles) detour from the highway. Further along the main highway, another right turn leads to *Letoon*, a sanctuary dedicated to Leto, 4km (2.5 miles) from the main road. A small road leads through the village of Kumluova to the car-park.

Letoon has been identified as the place in Greek mythology where Leto found refuge, following her persecution for being the mistress of Zeus, and gave birth to Artemis and Apollo. There are three temples which lie alongside one another, next to the car-park. The first is dedicated to Leto and dates from the second century BC. The second, which is considerably smaller, is dedicated to Artemis and dates from the fifth century BC. The third temple is dedicated to Apollo and contains the only surviving Lycian mosaic. It depicts a bow and arrow, which represents Artemis, and a sun and a lyre, which represents Apollo.

The remains of a **Byzantine basilica** lie behind the temple ruins and to the right a **monumental fountain** is partly submerged in water. The **theatre** lies to the north of the temples. It is entered through the original vaulted tunnel and inside the seating is well preserved. The sixteen stone-carved theatrical masks over the northern entrance should not be missed.

The ancient Lycian site of **Xanthos** lies a few kilometres south of *Letoon*, close to the village of Kinik. As highway 400 enters the village a track leads off left up to the ruins.

Xanthos was a principle Lycian city from the fifth century BC until the Roman invasion in the first century AD. Most of the ruins seen today are Roman and the **theatre**, which lies directly next to the car-park, dates from the second century. The pile of stones in front of the theatre is all that remains of the stage buildings which originally stood two-storeys high, but the seating and the back wall are in very good condition.

Two **pillar tombs** stand above the theatre; the one on the left is a typical fourth-century Lycian tomb which, unusually, has been raised on a pedestal, the other dates from 470BC and is known as the Harpies Tomb after the creatures carved around the top of the north and south sides. The original reliefs were removed by Charles Fellows in the nineteenth century along with the Nereid monument, and presented to the British Museum in London.

The piece of land jutting out over the Xanthos river valley behind the theatre is the site of the **Lycian acropolis.** The whole area is covered in low-lying walls that outline a series of rooms thought to be the **royal palace**. The path passes by a large rock-hewn water cistern and the foundations of a temple, to the **royal terrace** which overlooks the river at the tip of the promontory.

Opposite the car-park, the large flat area strewn with stones is the agora. Nearby stands a large **monolithic stone** that used to support a tomb. It dates from the fifth century BC, and has the longest Lycian inscription yet discovered. A path leads behind the car-park to a large **Byzantine basilica** which has a very fine geometrically patterned mosaic floor. The track continues up to the **Lycian necropolis** on the eastern slope of the hill. On the summit of the hill there are the scant remains of the **Roman acropolis**.

Highway 400 continues south of *Xanthos* to a right turn marked by a yellow signpost which leads to **Patara**, 6km (3.7 miles) from the main road. This is the birthplace of St Nicholas, the legendary Santa Claus, and St Paul embarked from here to Rome. The ruins of the ancient city are gradually being buried by sand drifting along the 30km (18 mile) beach, and the former harbour has filled up with marshland. The city was founded in the sixth century BC and was an important trading centre throughout the Roman and Byzantine periods, but was deserted in the fifteenth century when the harbour finally silted up.

The remains are spread over a fairly wide area and although the terrain is flat, the marsh and thick undergrowth make walking difficult. The **monumental gateway** to the city is passed on the right, just before the ruins of the baths. Further along the road a footpath leads from a lay-by on the right, to the theatre. Although the **theatre** is half-full of sand, the seating is well preserved and there is a long, second-century inscription on the front wall. A small **Corinthian temple** stands on a low mound about 500m (1,600ft) north of the theatre. The walls are about 10m (33ft) tall and the doorway is exquisitely carved. On the hilltop behind the theatre there is a rock-carved water cistern, 8m (26ft) deep, and the views across the dunes to the sea are spectacular. The Roman **Granary of Hadrian** can be seen across the marsh, north-east of the theatre.

Highway 400 passes through the small town of Yesilköy and then climbs steeply through olive groves and pine forests, before dropping down to the coast at **Kalkan**. As with so many of the villages on the Aegean and Mediterranean coasts, Kalkan had a Greek population until 1923. Many of the houses are Greek in style and the mosque on the waterfront is a converted church. The village has been carefully renovated to accommodate tourism, with just a handful of newly-built hotels overlooking the yacht marina and a selection of fish restaurants around the harbour. *Pansiyon* are tucked away in side streets and the main thoroughfare is lined with small shops selling *salvar*, the traditional baggy pants worn by Anatolian peasants, carpets, crafted leather and jewellery. There are two pebble beaches to the left of the bay but a fresh mountain spring gushes into the sea making the top surface of the water very cold. Other beaches can be reached by hiring a boat from the harbour.

Highway 400 twists and climbs along the rocky coastline between Kalkan and Kas. The road crosses a dramatic gorge at **Kapitas** where a sandy cove can be reached by steps down the cliff side.

Further along the road, a yellow sign marks the **Mavi Magarasi**,

Pillar tombs, Xanthos

the Blue Cave, which is a steep clamber down from the roadside and can only be entered by swimming, but inside the cavern, the water is an exceptionally deep blue colour. The last stretch of road before Kas winds along a protected inlet, opposite a long, thin peninsula.

Kas is built around a deep, sheltered bay, originally the ancient harbour of *Antiphellus*. The harbour is now filled with boats, while the bay is lined with night-clubs, bars, discos and restaurants. Large hotels and holiday villages expand further along the coast every year, and in the summer almost every house is open as a *pansiyon*. The beach consists of a narrow strip of sand to the west of the town, but boats make day-trips out to other beaches.

The **Lycian necropolis** and a well-preserved theatre, 2km (1.2 miles) west of the town, are all that remain of the ancient site. The theatre is set back from the road on the right in a picturesque setting amid olive groves. The necropolis is behind the theatre on the top of the hill. One of the largest remaining tombs is built in the style of a house and stands 5m high. It dates from the fourth century BC and a frieze carved around the inside of the walls depicts twenty-four women.

There is a cluster of tombs carved in the rocky cliff-face above Kas and a few typical Lycian tombs also stand in the town. One is near the

Lycian rock-cut tomb at Kale

harbour and another is on the road leading up the hill.

Tickets for boat trips to **Kekova** are sold at the quayside in Kas, and several boats leave every morning, returning in the early evening. During the day the boat stops to allow people to swim, and calls at various coves and villages on the way.

The ruins of *Kekova* lie under the water along the edge of an island which has the remains of a Byzantine church in a sandy cove at one end. Diving is strictly prohibited as the site has never been excavated, but the stone-carved steps and walls can be seen clearly from the boat.

Kale, the small village on the mainland opposite, is a popular stopping place for lunch and has several modest fish restaurants built along the quayside, near some partly submerged Lycian tombs. A crenellated **fortress** dominates the hilltop above. It was built in the Byzantine era on the ancient acropolis of *Simena*. Some of the Hellenistic walling remains and in the centre of the fortress there is a small rock-hewn **odeion** with a seating capacity of 300 people.

Carved relief above Lycian rock tomb, Myra

The village of **Uçagiz** lies beyond Kale on the site of ancient *Teimiussa*. Little remains of the city apart from the Lycian tombs that stand half-submerged in the water, to the east of the harbour.

Route 4f — Kas to Antalya

Highway 400 climbs steeply up into the mountains behind Kas to the village of Yavi, where a path is signposted left to the Lycian city of **Kyenea**, 2km (1.2 miles) from the main road. It is a steep 45-minute hike and the remains are sparse, but it is a spot of great natural beauty and there are some finely-carved sarcophagi in the necropolis.

The highway continues across a high plateau passing through several small villages. After Bavazlar the road winds up and down over mountain peaks to Gürses, where it begins the long and winding descent to the alluvial plain surrounding Demre. A fine Roman tomb resembling a temple stands on the road junction at the foot of the mountains.

Demre is a busy agricultural town situated about 6km (3.7 miles) from the coast. It has little in the way of accommodation or restaurants, but it is worth stopping by to visit St Nicholas' Church and the Lycian ruins of *Myra*.

Entering Demre from the direction of Kas, take the right turn marked by a yellow signpost to **Myra** and follow the small road for 1km (0.6 miles) to the parking area. A footpath leads from the carpark to the theatre, built at the foot of a high crag. The cliff-face is honeycombed with rock-carved tombs that were built to resemble houses and have windows, doors and log-cabin-style roofs.

The Roman **theatre** was built in the second century and is one of the largest in Lycia, with a diameter of 150m (492ft). The structure is very well preserved. The grand vaulted stairways and entrances, which were used by the audience and would have contained shops, are virtually intact and only a part of the stage buildings have collapsed.

A well-trodden but precarious footpath leads up to the tombs from the theatre entrance. Some of the tombs have Lycian inscriptions above the doorways and a few are decorated with carved reliefs.

The **Church of St Nicholas** is marked by a yellow signpost to Baba Noel, from the central crossroads in Demre. St Nicholas was the Bishop of *Myra* in the fourth century and was well known for his kindness to children, virgins and sailors. The church, built on the site of a third-century Byzantine church, was rebuilt in the sixth century and heavily restored in the eleventh. It contains St Nicholas' sarcophagus, but not his mortal remains as they were taken to Bari by pirates in 1087. Much of the building is like a museum, filled with Byzantine stonework and mosaics. The main part of the church is still used for the services held here on St Nicholas' Day, 6 December, and the semi-circular choir stand has been rebuilt in the main apse.

Andriake, *Myra*'s ancient harbour, is near a popular beach 6km (3.7 miles) from Demre. Follow the main coastal road west from the town, then take the small road on the left, across the marsh, towards the sea. Just before the beach, the road passes **Hadrian's Granary** on the left. A small footpath leads to a building which has eight large rooms and a small relief of Hadrian and Faustina above the central door.

The road continues across the marsh to a car-park where there are several tea-houses and a restaurant. The beach is sandy and the water is shallow, and basic camping facilities are available.

The journey from Demre to Finike takes little over half an hour. A flat road follows the long, empty beaches east, before heading inland across a marsh. It returns to the coast and then winds along an attractive coastline to Finike.

Finike stands on the site of ancient *Phoenicus*, of which nothing

Lycian sarcophagus tomb, Limyra

The Olympos river valley

remains. Today the town is a shipping centre for the locally grown oranges and tomatoes, and there is a small industrial port to the west of the town. Hotels and *pansiyon* line the sandy beach to the east and provide a good base from which to travel inland to the two Lycian sites, *Limyra* and *Arykanda*.

Limyra lies 7km (4 miles) inland from Finike on highway 635, the road to Elmali. At Turunçova, *Limyra* is signposted down a wide road on the right. At the village mosque, fork right and continue for a further kilometre to the theatre on the left of the road. Founded in the fifth century BC, *Limyra* was a wealthy Lycian city, but the only major building left standing is the **theatre** which dates from Roman times. The seating is in very good condition, as are the vaulted entrances, which are now closed off to store excavation material. The only remnant of the Lycian city is the vast **necropolis** on the hills above the theatre. The tombs date mainly from the the fourth century BC and some are carved with beautiful reliefs. A footpath, marked with red dabs of paint, leads up from the tea-house underneath the mulberry trees at the roadside. This is also the best way to reach the **heroon**, although it is signposted from the theatre. The path to the heroon leads to the right of the necropolis to a high terrace overlooking the plain of Finike. It was originally a religious sanctuary, but a rock-carved base that once supported a tomb and a few foundation stones are all that remain. Locally excavated statues are displayed in a room built at the back of the platform.

The site of **Arykanda** is approximately 25km (15 miles) inland from *Limyra*. Highway 635 continues uphill, between high mountains, along the ancient *Arycandus* river valley. Fork right to Çatallar and follow the signs past the village for appoximately 2km (1.2 miles). A stony track leads from the right-hand side of the road to the ruins. There is no car-park and vehicles must be left at the roadside.

The city was founded in the fifth century BC and was inhabited until the nineteenth century. The substantial remains of the ancient city, high in the Beydag mountains, are very scenic. The ruins of the **acropolis** are on the right of the track. A number of small rooms can be distinguished with underground heating in places.

An impressive **baths complex** is on the hillside to the left and contains three main rooms, each with a large window, overlooking the valley. The hypocaust system is evident in many places and there is an attractive marble pool in the last room.

There is a street lined with sarcophagi above the baths, and further up the hill is the **agora.** This unusual market-place is sunken, and has raised walkways on three of its sides, the fourth side being open to the panoramic view. In the back wall of the agora a columned doorway leads into the well-preserved **bouleuterion**.

Continue up the hill to the **theatre**. The stage building has been partly restored and the seats have attractively carved supports. Above the theatre, at the highest point of the city, lies the **stadium**. Only the terrace and a few seats are visible, but the view down across the city and to the distant mountain peaks is ample reward for the steep climb.

Before returning to Finike, visitors may wish to refresh themselves in the sparkling waterfall 100m (109yd) up the road from where the cars are parked at the start of the path.

Highway 400 follows the coast from Finike across a plain to Kumluca, an unattractive town built around a busy crossroads. Turn right to Antalya and start the very steep ascent up into the **Beydag mountains**. The road climbs up one hairpin bend after another through pine forests. As the road starts the long descent the other side, there is a yellow signpost which points to *Olympos* and soon after it a second sign which points to both *Olympos* and Çirali. Although the second road is not as well surfaced, it is the more direct route of the two, and enables visitors to reach both sites.

The site of **Olympos** lies 7km (4 miles) from the main highway down a steeply winding road. At the bottom of the hill take the right fork and park at the small camp-site and restaurant near the beach. Walk along the beach to the right, as far as the river, and follow its course inland. The ruins are hidden in the thick undergrowth on either side of the river and have never been excavated. They can be hard to find, but the beautiful valley with its oleander bushes and reeds is really the main attraction. On the south bank of the river is the **theatre**, the **baths complex** and the **Hellenistic quayside**. The acropolis lies on the top of the steep hill on the north side of the river, but very little remains of it.

The **Chimera**, described by Homer as a fire-breathing monster: 'in front a lion, behind a serpent, in midst a goat', was slain by the hero Belerophon with the help of his winged horse Pegasus. It has been suggested that the burning gas issuing from the rock at Çirali, north of *Olympos*, might have been the origin of this legend. Apparently it used to be more impressive, and a sanctuary to the god of fire, Hepaistos, was built here in ancient times.

From *Olympos* a small road heads east along the coast past the Çirali *pansiyon*. Follow the gravel track, bearing left wherever there is a choice, for 3km (1.8 miles), until it peters out in a wood of pine trees. A path, marked by red dabs of paint on the rocks, leads up the south slope of Tahtali Dag (2,366m/7,760ft), ancient *Mount Olympos*, to the flame. The climb takes about 25 minutes. At the top there is a big ash-covered hill with a number of flames issuing from small holes in the ground.

The concrete platform at Tünektepe near Antalya

Highway 400 continues past the turning to *Olympos* and descends to the coast. The first right turn after the village of Tekirova is signposted to **Phaselis**, founded in the seventh century BC by colonists from Rhodes. The ancient ruins are in a park 2km (1.2 miles) from the highway. Inside the park there is a shop, a café and toilets. A track leads for 1km (0.6 miles) from the car-park to the ruins. At weekends this is a popular picnic spot and can be quite crowded.

The ruins are picturesquely located on a thin peninsula around three harbours. A **colonnaded street**, lined with statue pedestals and the remains of shops, links the north-eastern bay to the south-western bay. The middle bay, the main **harbour**, is the smallest of the three and the ancient harbour mole can be seen just below the surface of the water. On the left of the paved road are the remains of a **baths complex** and a sign points to a small **theatre** which is largely unexcavated. The remains of Hadrian's Gate are at the end of the road and the south-western bay lies just beyond.

Kemer lies to the right of highway 400, roughly 10km (6 miles) from *Phaselis*. It is a modern resort which offers one of the widest selections of recreational facilities on the Mediterranean and has over fifty good hotels as well as holiday centres such as Club Mediterranée and Club Robinson. The beaches on either side of the yacht

Beach at the foot of the Beydag mountains, in the coastal Sahil Milli Park near Antalya

marina are excellent, but the resort lacks the bustle and atmosphere of other Mediterranean towns and in winter it shuts down completely.

From Kemer the road climbs through dense pine forests to **Beldibi**, the site of a prehistoric cave dwelling where local pottery sherds have been radio-carbon dated to the seventh millenium BC. The highway then passes through two tunnels, both of which are unlit. After the second tunnel a yellow road sign indicates the entrance of the Akyarlar Caves.

The final stretch of coast before Antalya is a national park area known as the Sahil Milli Park. The scenery is outstanding and numerous attractive pebble beaches lie just off the road. On the edge of the plain surrounding Antalya another yellow signpost marks a turning on the left to **Tünektepe**. A small road winds precariously up a mountain for 7km (4 miles), with hairpin bends all the way. At the top there is a vast concrete platform and a hotel is being built on the cliff edge. The views over the plain around Antalya and the Beydag mountains are stunning.

Highway 400 continues west of Tünektepe along the gulf of Antalya, past an industrial port and a long pebble beach known as Konyaalti, to the city at the eastern end of the bay.

Antalya is the provincial capital and one of the largest cities on the west Mediterranean. The old part of the city is built on an outcrop of red rock 40-50m (130-165ft) above sea level, overlooking the wide bay. In recent years the traditional Ottoman housing has been restored and the renovation of the harbour has won several awards. Clean and cheerful *pansiyon* can be found in almost any street, and souvenir shops selling meerschaum, leather, jewellery and carpets line the main thoroughfares. At the commercial centre of the city there is a colourful bazaar, and regional specialities including white cheese, fresh fruit jams and tall jars of pickles are sold in the local shops.

The main sites of interest can be visited in the space of an afternoon. The earliest historical remains date from the second century BC when King Attalus II of *Pergamum* established *Attaleia* as an important naval base. There are also considerable remains from the Seljuk era which ruled from 1207 until the Ottoman conquest of Antalya in 1391.

A **clock tower** stands on one side of Cumhuriyet Meydani, the central square. It is in fact part of the original city wall, and the fluted minaret to the west, known as **Yivli Minare**, is one of the oldest Seljuk buildings in Antalya. It was built by Sultan Keykubad in the thirteenth century. Steps lead down from Cumhuriyet Meydani to a small garden around the minaret and a path leads to **Alaeddin Cami** which also dates from the thirteenth century. The monumental tomb next to the mosque was added in 1377. The path continues through the gardens to a whitewashed building covered by red-tiled domes. It was built as a dervish convent in the eighteenth century and now houses the **Güzel Sanatlar Muzesi**, the Fine Arts Museum.

From the clock tower, Uzun Çarsi Sokagi heads down the hill, past the **Tekeli Mehmet Pasa Cami** on the left, another Seljuk mosque, to the old city quarter. **Kesik Minare**, Broken Minaret, is surrounded by Ottoman houses in the middle of the old quarter. It is built on the foundations of a fifth-century basilica. The harbour, to the west of the old quarter, is lined with restaurants and cafés and boats can be hired from the quayside.

Hadrian's Gate, on Atatürk Caddesi, is a magnificent monumental gateway, erected in AD135 in honour of the emperor. It has a triple arch and is built of white marble, ornately decorated with rosettes and flowers. **Karaalioglu Park**, the municipal gardens at the end of Atatürk Caddesi, extend to the cliff edge, from where there are good views over the bay. The remains of a Roman tower, known as

Hidirlik Kulesi, on the cliff, is thought to have been used as a lighthouse.

The **Archaeological Museum** is on the main highway to the west of the city. It contains a rich collection of archaeological finds from the area, covering a vast spectrum of history ranging from palaeolithic to Ottoman times. The exhibits are well displayed and have informative labels in English. The collection of Greek statues from *Perge* is particularly outstanding.

Antalya is a convenient base from which to explore the surrounding region and there are a number of good beaches on either side of the city. Topçam Plaj is a pebble cove, west of Tünektepe, and has a camp-site amid the pine trees behind the beach. Lara Plaj, 12km (7 miles) east of the city, has a selection of comfortable hotels and water-sport facilities are available. To the east of Antalya there are some impressive waterfalls formed by the icy rivers flowing down from the Taurus mountains. **Düden Selale** is one of the most popular, plunging over the cliffs into the sea 10km (6 miles) east of the city.

In September Antalya hosts the Akdeniz International Song Contest, and in October the Golden Orange Film and Arts Festival. In the winter a ski resort opens at **Saklikent** on the northern slope of Mount Bakirli (1,750-1,900m/5,740-6,232ft), which is 50km (31 miles) north-west of the city.

Route 4g — Antalya to Selçuk

The E24/650, a well-surfaced dual carriageway, is signposted from Antalya, along Vatan Bulvari, to Isparta and Burdur. As the road leaves the city, a turning is signposted on the right to the **Düden Basi Selalesi**, (9km/6 miles), the Upper Düden Falls. Eleven kilometres (6.8 miles) from Antalya, the Korkuteli road, highway 350, leads off left to the **Termessos Milli Park**. Follow the road for 23km (14 miles) before branching left again to the park entrance.

The national park surrounding the ruins of **Termessos** is an area of great natural beauty and covers 6,702 hectares (16,554 acres) of forested, mountainous land. From the main car-park a track continues up the mountainside, ancient Mount Solymus, for 8km (5 miles) to a small parking area near a spring. The site has never been fully excavated and its exact origins are unknown, but a people called the Solymians are supposed to have founded the earliest settlement. The remains mostly date from the Roman era when the city was at its peak of importance, and the ruins seem to have lain untouched since the city was abandoned in the fifth century.

The upper parking area lies next to the remains of **Hadrian's Gate**, which originally led into a small, columned temple. The footpath begins at the opposite side of the car-park and roughly follows

Antalya harbour

the **King's Way**, the main road leading up to the city. Some of the ruins along the path are labelled, but are not really worth stopping for. A lot of fallen stonework comes from the triple defence wall that once surrounded the city.

The path divides near the top of the hill and the left-hand fork leads to the **gymnasium and baths**. A large stone building with many rooms runs along one side of a flat exercise area with stone steps for spectators. Despite its large size, the building is gradually disappearing beneath the undergrowth. Far more impressive is the **theatre**, which is further uphill to the south. Although it is modest in size and could only seat about 4,200 spectators, it has the most dramatic setting, perched on the edge of a rocky outcrop some 1,500m (4,920ft) high. It is Greek in style and the well-preserved seating looks out over a spectacular landscape.

The **agora** is behind the theatre, but is completely ruined and all that is left is a flat terrace strewn with stones. On the south side of the agora is a well-preserved **bouleuterion**, with finely carved exterior walls. The bouleuterion is surrounded by four temples. The **Temple of Zeus Solymeus** is the best preserved and stands west of the bouleuterion, while the other three are to the south-east. The **Artemis Temple** has a well-preserved doorway, the inscription on

Hadrian's Gate, Antalya

which names Aurelia Armasta as the founder. The other two are in poor condition and only the bases can be seen. On the north side of the agora there are five deep water cisterns carved from the rock, and a **heroon** nearby is also rock-carved.

The footpath continues uphill through the **necropolis** to the highest point of the city. Ancient sarcophagi lie scattered in great numbers all over the hillside. They are all shapes and sizes and have some beautifully carved decorations and inscriptions. A fireman's **watch-tower** stands at the very summit of the hill. A solitary fireman lives here with his family during the summer to watch for forest fires. Should one be spotted, the forestry commission is notified on a wind-up telephone. The tower looks over a magnificent panorama in all directions.

Karain is a prehistoric cave at the foot of the mountains north of Antalya, to the left of the E24/650. The small road passes through the carpet-making region of Dösemealti (Yeniköy) and crosses a fertile cotton-growing plain. After 13km (8 miles) a turning is marked on the left and the site is a further 5km (3 miles) down this road. The cavern lies to the left of the car-park, at the foot of Mount Cadir. A footpath climbs steeply up the hill, behind a small museum which contains a collection of objects excavated at the site.

Returning to the E24/650 the road heads towards the mountains. Just before the road starts to climb, a right turn is signposted to **Kovanlik Köyü**, a carpet-making village with a cooperative that deals exclusively with the regional (Dösemealti) carpets.

The E24/650 makes a steep ascent to the Çubukbeli Pass (925m/3,034ft) and onto the high plateau, known as Turkey's Lake District. The highway follows the Seljuk caravan route that linked Konya to Antalya. The **Incirhan caravanserai** is marked by a signpost shortly before Bucak, and lies 6km (3.7 miles) from the main road. Shortly after the turning to the caravanserai, another yellow sign points left to the ruins of the Roman city of **Kremna**.

After Bucak, the road divides and travellers must decide whether to continue via Isparta or Burdur. The Isparta route is more pictur-esque and passes close to Egirdir, the most beautiful of the inland lakes, but the Burdur route is more direct.

Highway 685, signposted to Isparta, is a narrow and winding road climbing steeply up to Aglasun, where a yellow signpost directs visitors to the ruins of **Sagalassos**. A track winds up into the mountains for 7km (4 miles). The city, important in Roman times, has a good theatre and necropolis and is in an attractive setting. The highway then continues over the Koruglubeli Pass (950m/3,116ft) to the plain surrounding Isparta.

Isparta takes its name from the Spartan Greeks who originally

Shop selling rose products, Isparta

founded the city. The town had a large Greek population until 1923, but it has grown rapidly in recent years and little remains from its past. The recent prosperity of the town derives from its carpet industry and its pre-eminence as a centre for rose growing. Isparta carpets are of poor quality and copy floral Persian designs. However, Isparta merchants deal in carpets from all over Turkey and supply many of the carpet-makers with their wool. Rose products are sold all over the town and range from essances and oils to Turkish Delight and rose candy. A **museum** is located on the outskirts of the town and has an interesting collection of antique carpets and ethnographical exhibits.

Egirdir is 34km (21 miles) east of Isparta on highway 330. The

Fishing boats on Egirdir Lake

Theatre at Hieropolis, *Pamukkale*

Cascading calcium deposits at Pamukkale

town is built on the shore of **Egirdir Lake** which covers an area of
517sq km (199sq ft) and is surrounded by apple orchards. The scant
remains of a Seljuk fortress stand at one end of the town, and **Hizir**
Bey Cami, built in 1275, marks the centre. The theological school
built next to it is now a shopping area called **Dünderbey Carsisi**.
There are no other buildings of historical interest, but the lake is very
scenic. A causeway stretches out from Egirdir and connects two
small islands to the mainland. There are several *pansiyon* around the
shores of the islands and a ruined Greek church stands in the middle
of the larger island.

The main attraction of taking the route via Burdur, apart from
saving time, is to visit the **Iksuyu Caves**, signposted at the roadside
just before Burdur. Thirty-five kilometres (21 miles) past Burdur, the
highway merges with the road from Isparta and follows the E24/625
across the plateau to Denizli. At **Akhan**, a small village just before
Denizli, there is a thirteenth-century Seljuk caravanserai on the right
of the road. A kilometre beyond Akhan, a yellow signpost points right
to Laodikya and Pamukkale.

A couple of kilometres along the Pamukkale road, a narrow track
leads left to the ruins of **Laodiceia**. The city was destroyed by Turks
in the thirteenth century and very little remains to be seen today apart

from an overgrown stadium dating from the reign of Tiberius (AD79), a baths complex and the remains of two theatres. It is perhaps better known as the site of one of the Seven Churches of the Apocalypse.

A small road climbs the white ridge of cascading calcium deposits to the spa resort of **Pamukkale**. It is always busy during the summer and the growing number of hotels using the hot spring water (33°/91°F) leaves less to flow across the travertines each year. The resort is built on the site of ancient **Hieropolis** and the Pamukkale Motel is built around the original sacred pool which is strewn with ancient columns and stones. Rooms should be booked well in advance throughout the tourist season.

The ruins of *Hieropolis* are scattered over an area of 2 or 3 kilometres. At the car-park the remains of the baths, a gymnasium and a library have been made into a **museum**. A small road climbs the hill behind the Pamukkale Motel, passing the **Temple of Apollo**, built over a cave which exudes poisonous fumes (now blocked off), to the **theatre**. The theatre, carved into the slope of Mount Caldag, is both large and well preserved, and offers good views across the Büyük Menderes plain towards Denizli.

Further ruins are strewn along either side of the road that leads north across the plateau from the car-park. A triple-arched Roman gateway, the **Gate of Domitian**, built in the first century AD, marks the end of the city and a ruined **Byzantine basilica** lies nearby. Beyond the gate is the necropolis, one of the most extensive and best preserved in Asia Minor.

Denizli is a busy city laid out along modern palm-lined boulevards. There is nothing of particular interest to visit in the city but there is a fairly wide selection of hotels and restaurants.

The fastest route from Denizli to Selçuk is along the flat Menderes river valley on the E24/600. However, to visit the ancient city of **Aphrodisias** head south of Denizli on the minor road to Tavas, across the Akdag mountains and the Kazikbeli Pass (1,200m/3,936ft). The site is signposted to the left of the road at Geyre, about 35km (22 miles) after Tavas.

From the car-park and café, a footpath leads to the **museum**, where there is a fine collection of white marble statues from the site. The footpath continues due south to the **theatre**, which is built into the hillock on the left. It seats 10,000 people, and the remains of the royal box can be seen in the centre of the lowest row of seats which all have carved backs. Dolphins decorate the ends of each row and some seats in the upper rows are inscribed with place names.

The **agora** in front of the theatre is paved with the local blue-grey marble and has the foundations of a circular fountain in the centre and a row of columns along one side. Nearby are the remains of the baths, also made of the local marble. The path climbs to the site of the Bronze Age acropolis on top of the hill. In the valley below, the row of columns that can be seen through the poplar trees marks the site of the **north agora**. This agora, which stretches between a monumental gateway and the Portico of Tiberius, is closed for excavation. The **Baths of Hadrian**, west of the north agora, were built in the second century AD and have six main rooms supported by vaulted sub-structures. The footpath continues to the second-century **odeion**, where several of the seats have carved lions' feet, and the remains of a Byzantine palace, thought to have been used by the Bishop.

The **Temple of Aphrodite** is passed on the left. It was built in the first century BC but was converted to a basilica in the fifth century. The footpath then crosses a track to the **stadium**, the best preserved in Asia Minor. It is 227m (745ft) long and could seat 30,000 spectators. The twenty-six rows of seats are in good condition and the original vaulted entrance ways at either end of the arena are intact. The track leads back to the car-park from the stadium, passing the ruins of the **Tetrapylon**, a monumental gateway, on the left.

From Aphrodisias the E24/600 is reached by following the minor road north-west for 38km (23 miles). Head west along the E24/600 to the village of Sultanhisar, where a yellow road sign indicates the turning to **Nyssa**. The ruins lie either side of a steep rocky gorge 3km (1.8 miles) from Sultanhisar.

The ancient city of *Nyssa* is believed to have been founded by the Seleucids in the third century BC. It was deserted in the fifth century when Tamerlane led the Mongol invaders through the region. The gorge is straddled by a **Roman bridge** and the ancient *Thymbus* river flows far below. A finely-preserved **theatre** stands next to the car-park. It has well-preserved stage buildings decorated with carved reliefs depicting dancing satyrs, musicians and gods. The river passes underneath part of the road in front of the theatre through an ancient **tunnel** about 100m(328ft) long, 8m (26ft) wide and 5m(16ft) tall. A narrow track heads uphill from the car-park to the **bouleu-terion**. Set in the middle of an olive grove, it is built of fine marble and has twelve rows of seats.

From *Nyssa* the E24/600 continues across the flat plateau to Aydin and then follows the course of the Menderes river through the hills down to Selçuk (Efes).

5
TRANS-ANATOLIA

The Anatolian plain is a high plateau surrounded by mountains, 1,000m (3,280ft) above sea level. Route 5 crosses from one side to the other, from the Uludag mountains in the north, to the Taurus in the south. Most of the plateau landscape is arid and barren as winters are harsh, and summers are hot and dry. The land is grazed by sheep and goats. The only regions of cultivation are around the major towns and cities. Konya, the largest city on the route, is one of the main centres of agriculture.

Most of the roads crossing the plateau are built in straight lines following the paths of ancient caravan routes. Although the roads are fairly narrow, the surfaces are reasonable and there is very little traffic, so distances can be covered fairly quickly.

Each section of Route 5 can be covered in a day, although visitors may want to spend longer in Kütahya to make an excursion to the ruins of *Aizanoi*, or at Karaman, to visit the mountain-top churches of Bin Bir Kilise. At Silifke, visitors can either join Route 6e to travel east along the coast, or Route 6d to travel west.

Route 5a — Bursa to Kütahya (map A, p131)

Follow the signs to Ankara on highway 200 from Bursa, across the plain and over a spur of the Uludag mountains to **Inegöl**. The town centre is on the right and the **Ishak Pasa Kervansaray**, built in the early Ottoman period, stands on the ancient caravan route from Bursa to Konya. The local dish, Inegöl *köfte*, grilled meat-balls, is served in most of the restaurants along the main street of the town.

After Inegöl, a yellow signpost points right to **Oylat**, a natural hot spa, 12km (7 miles) up a small mountain road. Highway 200 then climbs up through hills to Bozüyük. Five kilometres (3 miles) beyond the town, highway 650 leads off right to Kütahya. The road is poorly surfaced but the countryside is attractive and 22km (13.6 miles) before reaching Kütahya, a thermal spa resort, the **Ilica Kaplicalarasi**, is signposted 4km (2.5 miles) to the right.

Kütahya is situated on the Anatolian plateau, 945m (3,100ft) above sea-level, on the site of ancient *Cotyaeum*. It reached the height of its importance in the eighteenth century when it superseded Iznik and became the centre of ceramic production. The tradition of pottery-making lives on and workshops continue to reproduce

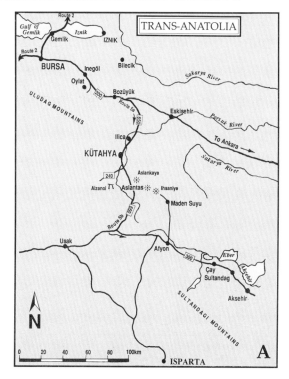

the Ottoman designs, in fluid blue, green, turquoise and red glazes, on coarse white clay. There are numerous pottery shops in the town and it is possible to visit the workshops to see the pottery being made.

An ornamental fountain, made of a large Kütahya vase, marks the town centre and yellow signposts lead along Cumhuriyet Caddesi towards the castle. At the end of the street on the right there is an Ottoman theological school called the **Vacidiye Medresei** (1314). It houses the local museum which has a good collection of ceramics dating from the Bronze Age to the Ottoman era, and an ethnography section with a collection of *kilim,* traditional costumes, and local embroidery. **Ulu Cami**, next to the museum, was built by Yildirim Beyazit in 1410. The marble columns which were added when the mosque was restored come from *Aizanoi*.

A yellow sign points uphill, past the mosque, to **Kossuth Evi** and **Kütahya Kalesi**. Lajos Kossuth (1802-1894) was a Hungarian socialist who travelled around Turkey and lived in Kütahya from

1848-9. His house has been converted to a museum and the rooms are furnished in the original style.

The road continues up the hill to the castle, built in the fifteenth century on the site of an earlier Byzantine fortress. The remains are not very impressive but there are fine views over the town.

The classical site of **Aizanoi** is 60km (37 miles) south-west of Kütahya and can be reached by taking a bus to Çavdarhisar. Follow highway 650 south for 11km (6.8 miles) to the turning on the right to Usak and Gediz, highway 240. A narrow road climbs up and down rolling hills to the village of Çavdarhisar where a yellow sign marks the turning on the right to the site.

The impressive remains of the **Temple of Zeus** come into sight from the bridge crossing the ancient *Rhyndacus* river. Two sides of the temple remain completely intact giving a vivid impression of how the temple must have looked when it was built in AD150. The janitor holds the keys to the oldest part of the temple which is the vaulted chamber beneath, built as a sanctuary to Cybele in 300BC. The site of the **agora**, in front of the temple steps, is scattered with fragments fallen from the temple pediment. One of the finest pieces shows the head of Medusa.

To the north-west of the temple there are remains of a second-century **Roman baths and gymnasium**, a **stadium** and a **theatre**. The stadium lies between the theatre and the temple. The running track and the banks of seating on either side are clearly visible, but unexcavated. The theatre has a seating capacity of 20,000 and there are reliefs of animals among the tumbled stones in the orchestra.

Route 5b — Kütahya to Konya

(map A, p131 and map B, p134)

Highway 650 heads south of Kütahya through pleasant undulating countryside. In 1922 this area was the scene of some decisive battles fought between the Greek and Turkish forces in the War of Independence. About 40km (25 miles) from Kütahya the turning right to Izmir, highway 615, leads to most of the battlefields: **Zafer Tepe Abidesi** (29km, 18 miles), **Sehitligi Sancaklar Mehmetcik Aniti** (30km, 18.6 miles), **Dumlupinar Abidesi** (41km, 25 miles). A further 25km (15.5 miles) along highway 650, the **Anit Kaya Sehitligi** war monument is passed on the left.

Afyon is set in a flat plain at the foot of an imposing outcrop of black basalt rock, topped by a ruined castle. Literally translated *afyon* means opium, and the modern town is the centre of Turkey's opium-poppy cultivation. While the opium extracted from the plant is used to produce medicines, the seeds are widely used locally, on bread and pastries and even on *lokum*, Turkish Delight. The modest range

Medusa and the Temple of Zeus, Aizanoi

of accommodation and restaurants in the town makes Afyon a convenient stopping place for visitors.

The castle, **Afyon Karahisar**, is within easy walking distance of the centre of town, but the ascent is something of a scramble. The outcrop of Karahisar was fortified as long ago as the second millennium BC when the Hittites built their fortress, *Khapanuma* here. Renamed *Akroenus* in the classical period, it became an important Seljuk stronghold in the thirteenth century. The castle summit is 226m (741ft) above the town, and the steep footpath passes cisterns and rock-cut basins before entering the walls through the original fortified gate. The remains at the top are not very impressive but there are good views across the town.

Afyon fell to the Ottomans in 1428 and **Imaret Cami**, in the town centre, was built shortly after their conquest. It is one of the finest mosques in the town and is connected to a nearby *medrese* and public baths. The Seljuk **Ulu Cami** is much older. It was built in 1272 and has the large flat roof supported by numerous columns which is

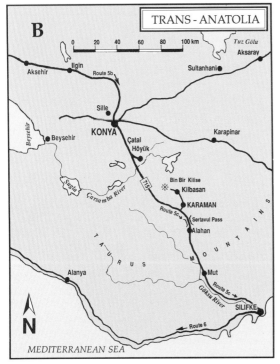

typical of the era. The local **museum**, on Kurtulus Caddesi, has exhibits tracing the history of the region, from the Early Bronze and Hittite periods, through to the Roman and Byzantine ages.

Afyon was the westernmost point of the Phrygian empire in the eighth century BC. Just over 50km (31 miles) to the north of Afyon, two rock-carved Phrygian monuments, **Aslantas** and **Aslankaya** stand in the middle of a desolate countryside. A good road is signposted as far as the village of Maden Suyu, then a rough track leads to Ihsaniye, from where it is a matter of searching and asking as there are no further signposts. *Aslankaya*, dating from the sixth century BC, is the more impressive of the two.

Highway 300 follows the route of an ancient caravan trail from Afyon to Konya. After 20km (12.4 miles) the hot springs of **Sifali Kaplicalari** are passed on the left.

The road continues east, past the turning to Dinar and Denizli, to the richly cultivated foothills of the Sultandagi mountain range. The fields either side of the road are all farmed by hand and it is quite common to see in everyday use wooden ploughs and carts that would be seen in museums elsewhere. Lush fruit orchards surround the small rural villages and at the sleepy town of Çay there is a ruined caravanserai.

The lakes of Ebergölu and Aksehirgölu lie in the plain to the left of the road. At Sultandag the Seljuk caravanserai, **Ishakli Han**, dates from 1250.

Craftsman at work in one of Kütahya's many pottery workshops

Ulu Cami, Kütahya

Aksehir was the most important stopover point on the caravan route and has the remains of a very early caravanserai which was built in 1216. The town is built on the site of a Byzantine city known as *Philomelium*. There are no Byzantine remains but the town is well known today as the burial place of Nasrettin Hodja, the thirteenth-century Turkish humorist. Yellow signs lead from the centre of the town to **Nasrettin's tomb** which is surrounded by a large cemetery.

East of Aksehir the landscape becomes gradually less hilly. At the town of Ilgin the **Ilgin Kaplicalar**, a large caravanserai and thermal baths, is signposted down a small road on the right. After Ilgin the road leaves the foothills and enters the vast cultivated plateau which surrounds the city of Konya.

Konya is 1,016m (3,332ft) above sea level, on the southern edge of the Anatolian plain. The site was originally settled by the Hittites in 1500BC, but the thirteenth century AD saw the city at its peak of importance and the city was endowed with many fine buildings.

Today, Konya is undergoing a rapid industrial expansion, and suburbs of factories and worker-housing spread further into the plain around the city every year. Carpet-making is one of Konya's oldest industries, and it too is experiencing something of a revival. Most Konya carpets are made in the outlying villages and retailed through the umpteen shops in the city centre. There is a fairly good selection of hotels and restaurants in the city centre. However, Konya has a reputation for piety and during the fast of Ramazan it can be difficult to find food during the day.

Alaeddin Tepesi is the ancient mound of the acropolis, believed by the Phrygians to have been the first place to emerge after the Flood. The Seljuk mosque, **Alaeddin Cami** lies at the top of the mound, but it is unfortunately shut for restoration and it is best seen from the road below. It was designed by a Damascan architect in 1150 but it wasn't until 1220 that the building was completed. Inside are the tombs of several Seljuk sultans. On the slope below the mosque are very scant remains of **Alaeddin Palace**, covered by a concrete shelter.

The **Karatay Medrese** lies across the road from the palace. It was originally built as a school of astronomy, physics and maths in 1251 by Celalettin Karatay. Today it houses an excellent collection of Seljuk tiles originating from the Alaeddin Palace and also a thirteenth-century summer palace Kubadadad, which originally stood on the shore of Beysehir Lake. The *medrese* has a very finely carved portal and contains the tomb of Karatay in the chamber at the far end. The main room is covered by a large dome, decorated with beautiful Seljuk tiles. Originally it was open to the sky and served as an observatory. Water trickled into the pool in the centre of the room along the stone-carved channels seen in the floor.

Walking around the base of Alaeddin Tepesi in an anti-clockwise direction, **Ince Minare Medrese**, a religious school built in 1258, is passed on the right. It has an elaborately carved portal, decorated with bands of bold Arabic lettering, typical of the baroque Seljuk style, but the interior is being restored and the building may be shut.

Konya's other main sights are all located at the far end of Alaeddin Caddesi, which leads from Alaeddin Tepesi to the Mevlana. The bazaar area fills the side streets on the right about half-way down Alaeddin Caddesi. **Aziziye Cami**, built in a highly ornate baroque style, is in the centre of the bazaar. It was constructed in 1894 and its minarets with their enclosed balconies are very distinctive. **Selimiye Cami**, built in 1558 by Sultan Selim II, is at the end of Alaeddin Caddesi in front of the Mevlana.

The **Mevlana** is easily recognised by the dazzling turquoise-tiled roof that stands above the tomb of its founder, Celaleddin Rumi (1207-73). Rumi founded the Sufist sect of whirling dervishes in

Afyon, the centre of Turkey's opium-poppy cultivation

Konya in 1244. The sect was banned in 1925 and the Mevlana is now open as a museum, although it is also widely visited by Islamic pilgrims, and skirts and scarfs are issued to visitors who are not dressed appropriately. The entrance leads into a courtyard which is paved with eighteen flagstones, representing the mystical number of the sect, and has a *sadirvan* in the centre.

The mausoleum contains the tombs of Rumi's father, son and other prominent dervishes, as well as Rumi himself. The tomb is protected behind a silver grill and is covered by an exquisitely decorated cloth, embroidered with Arabic script. The other rooms house the treasures and relics of the dervish order, including their instruments, costumes and illuminated manuscripts. A semi-practising sect of dervishes still exists and the whirling ritual is performed in the largest of the rooms, the *semahane*, every December.

There are two other museums in the city. The **Archaeological Museum** is on Larende Caddesi, south of Alaeddin Tepesi. It contains ancient pottery and tools from the neolithic site of Çatal-höyük as well as a notable collection of third-century Roman sarcophagi. The carpet museum, the **Köyünoglu Muzesi**, is about a kilometre south-east of the Mevlana on Topraklik Caddesi. It is a relatively new museum and large areas of the building are empty, but the top floor has an interesting collection of old carpets and kilims.

The dazzling turquoise-tiled roof of the Mevlana, Konya

Sille is a small village built on the site of a Byzantine hermitage, 10km (6 miles) north-east of the city. On arriving at the village a left turn, just before the bridge, leads to the **Church of St Helen**, which is built on the site of an earlier Byzantine church. The remains date from the seventeenth century but the frescoes were restored in the nineteenth century. The ornately carved wooden rood screen, pulpit and balustraded galleries give an idea of the former splendour of the church and the size of the Greek congregation that used to live in the village. The military rather dominate the village now, and many areas are sectioned off, but some of the hermits' caves and rock-carved dwellings on the surrounding hills are still accessible.

Route 5c — Konya to Silifke (map B, p134)

Highway 715 is signposted to Karaman and Mersin. At the village of Içericumra, 32km (20 miles) south of Konya, a yellow sign points left to Çatalhöyük. This major neolithic settlement is near the village of

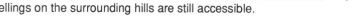

Cumra, 24km (14.9 miles) from the main highway. There is little to actually see, but excavations have uncovered sophisticated tools and artefacts dating from the seventh millennium BC, as well as wall paintings. It is thought to be the one of the most ancient cities in the world, and most of the discoveries are now in the Ancient Civilisations Museum in Ankara.

The road continues across the plateau to the Taurus mountains, where the land becomes more fertile and cultivated. The high peak in the distance to the left is Karadag (2,288m/7,505ft).

Karaman is a small agricultural town with a few simple hotels and restaurants. It takes its name from the Karamanoglu tribe who made it the capital of their emirate at the beginning of the fourteenth century. The Karamanoglu formed the most important emirate to emerge immediately after the collapse of the Seljuk empire. It ruled much of the land east of Konya up until 1466 when Mehmet II incorporated it into the Ottoman empire. The town, aware that it has some of the finest examples of Karamanid architecture in Turkey, has spent the last few years carefully restoring its monuments.

A narrow track leads up to the **Karamanid citadel** which overlooks the town. The large towers at each of the four corners are well preserved and the inner keep is entered by the original gate-house. An open-air theatre has been built inside the castle walls, and popular Turkish artists perform here once or twice a month during the summer. Directly below the castle walls is the fourteenth-century mosque, Eski Cami.

Hatuniye Medrese is on the main road that leads into the town from the castle. It was built in 1382 as a religious school and has an attractively carved portal. The **Archaeological Museum**, behind the *medrese*, has an interesting and well-displayed collection of local archaeological finds. The earliest objects date from 5000BC and come from the neolithic settlement at Canhasan, 13km (8 miles) north-east of Karaman. The museum also has a small ethnographical collection. **Ibrahim Bey Imaret**, further along the main street, is an Islamic foundation and contains a mosque, a school, a monumental tomb and a library. At the far end of the main street there is another religious complex. It was built in 1370 as a dervish convent and contains the tomb of Rumi Celaleddin's mother. The convent was closed in 1926 and now functions as a mosque, known as Aktekke Cami.

Bin Bir Kilise, literally translated 'a-thousand-and-one churches', is the site of a Byzantine monastic centre, high in the Karadag mountains, 44km (27 miles) north of Karaman. It is said that every hill-top in the region has a church on it, which may not be as fanciful as it sounds, and the site is awaiting excavation. There are two main sites visited today, both have been severely plundered for stone, but the natural beauty of the setting is part of their attraction.

Highway 42.27 crosses the railway and heads north of Karaman across the plain to the Karadag mountains. After Kilbasan, a right fork leads to Dinek where yellow signs mark the road on the left climbing up to the village of **Maden Sehir**. In the village a track leads off right, passing a tomb on the left. One of the best preserved and largest churches, Bir Noya Kilise, lies to the right of the track. It was abandoned in the seventh century when Arabs invaded, but revived in the ninth century before it was destroyed in the eleventh century. It has lain deserted ever since.

A track continues up into the mountains from Maden Sehir to Üçkuyu. The official janitor lives in the village of Deyle and will accompany visitors for the last 8km (5 miles) up to Üçkuyu which are especially steep and poorly-surfaced. A large lake can be seen over the mountain edge on the right after Deyle and the views are spectacular. On approaching Üçkuyu ruined churches and tombs can be seen on the rocky summit above. The best-preserved church in the village is converted to a mosque, now disused, others lie in various states of collapse all around the hill top.

Highway 715 is marked by road signs to Mut and Mersin from Karaman, and the road passes through gently undulating, but bare countryside, to Gökçe Çamligi, a picnic area set in a pine forest. The road then climbs steeply for 10km (6 miles) to the Sertavul Pass (1610m/5281ft) where there is a tea-house with spectacular views from the summit.

Just over the pass, is the **necropolis** of Alahan, with its clusters of simple tombs carved in the cliff-face. The turning to the Byzantine monastery, **Alahan**, is on the left, opposite a tea-house.

A steep winding track leads up the mountainside for 2km (1.2 miles) to the monastery which is perched at the head of the valley. Steps lead from the car-park past some monk's cells, across a paved courtyard, to the **first church**, which dates from the end of the fifth century. The archangels, Gabriel and Michael, are carved on either side of the entrance and inside the nave is lined with Corinthian columns with stone carved pews around the apse. The left side of the church is entirely hewn from the natural rock, and on the right there is a small chapel.

The path continues to a **baptistry** which has an attractive cruciform font. The path then joins a stone-carved road which leads past four grand tombs in the rock face, to the **main church**, which is built out of a honey-coloured stone on a raised platform and dates from the sixth century. It is excellently preserved and has three doors in the façade, each of which is decorated with beautiful stone car-

Karamanid tomb, Karaman

vings. Inside, there are narrow aisles on either side of a central nave; the left-hand aisle is hewn from the rock as are some of the column bases. Tall columns support the partially collapsed, domed ceiling.

Highway 715 winds down a picturesque valley for 18km (11 miles) to the small town of **Mut**. A ruined **castle** stands on the hill above the town and **Laal Pasa Cami**, an attractive mosque is in the town centre. The mosque was built in 1444 and has a high stone dome and two monumental tombs joined to one side. There are a couple of restaurants along the highway but the accommodation available is poor.

Highway 715 crosses a barren stretch of land to the wide, flat river valley of the Göksu river, where the countryside becomes greener. The valley gradually closes in with high cliffs rising on either side. The scenery around the village of Kargicak is exceptionally beautiful. The road winds high along one edge of the canyon, then crosses the river, passing the spot where Frederic Barbarossa, leader of the fourth crusade, drowned. As the road leaves the valley gorge, Silifke and its castle come into sight on the left.

Alahan Monastery

6
EAST MEDITERRANEAN COAST

A fter crossing the Pamphylian plain the east Mediterranean is dominated by the Taurus mountains which reach down to the coast forming deep protected bays with secluded sandy beaches. In ancient times the region between Alanya and Silifke was known as Rugged Cilicia. The road winds endlessly up and down, making even short distances long journeys, but the route is dotted with Crusader castles and classical ruins, and the scenery is spectacular. By contrast the area around Mersin and Adana is completely flat. Formerly the Cilician plain, it is now known as the Çukurova, and is the centre of cotton growing. There are few historical remains in the Cilician plain, the coasts are lined with factories and ports and the holiday homes of residents of the two big cities, Adana and Mersin. The rich agricultural land is intensively farmed and produces up to three harvests a year.

The temperatures on the coast rise towards the east, and rainfall decreases. The average annual rainfall in Adana is 611mm (23.6in) as compared to 1,000mm (39.4in) in Antalya. Summer droughts are a common problem in the eastern region and agriculture depends on good irrigation.

Chapter 6 follows directly on from Route 4f and is divided into six routes, each of which can be covered in a day. Longer should be allowed for Route 6d and 6e as the area around Silifke is particularly rich in historical remains and there are a number of good beaches. Adana is at the end of Route 6f and from here it is possible to fly to Istanbul, or continue inland on Route 9.

Route 6a — Antalya to Side (map A, p146)

The E24 coast road to Mersin and Adana, leaves Antalya along Cetin Kaya Caddesi. The turning left to **Kursunlu Selalesi** is 12km (7 miles) from Antalya. The waterfall is set in a forested park with picnic facilities, 8km (5 miles) from the main road. The waterfall is torrential in winter, but less impressive in the summer.

The ruins of **Perge** are reached by turning left at the village of Aksu, 13km (8 miles) from Antalya. The site lies in the flat plain, 3km (1.8 miles) from the village, at the foot of a rocky hill. The original site, founded in the first millennium BC, was built on the hill summit, but by 188BC when the Romans took control, the city had moved to its present location. The Roman emperor Trajan endowed the city with some of its grandest buildings, many of which remain standing.

The **Roman theatre** is on the left of the road before the main site. It is well preserved and has an attractive frieze along the stage building which depicts the story of Dionysus, the god of wine. The **stadium** lies close to the theatre on the opposite side of the road. It is one of the best-preserved in Asia Minor and is 234m (768ft) long. The seating is built over barrel-vaulted substructures which on the east side served as shops. All that remains of the monumental gate which formerly stood at the southern end of the stadium are the broken pieces of finely carved stone displayed in the arena.

The car-park is slightly further along the road, next to the **main city gate**, which is flanked by two round towers. These are the oldest structures on the site and date from the Hellenistic era. Inside the gate there is a horse-shoe shaped area with niches set in the walls that once held statues of Roman emperors and city patrons. Most of these statues have been found and are on display in the Antalya Museum. Planca Magna, the priestess of the Artemis temple and a prominent citizen of *Perge*, built the large gate at the far end of the courtyard in AD122. It was built in imitation of the Hadrian's Gate in Antalya and had three grand doorways.

From the gate, a **paved road**, 300m (984ft) long and 20m (65ft) wide, leads towards the acropolis. A water channel runs down the centre of the street and the broad pavements on either side are lined with the remains of shops. The large Roman **baths complex** on the left has a semi-circular pool in the central chamber and a rectangular pool in the end room. The **agora** is on the opposite side of the street to the baths and can be recognised by the column bases which stand around the courtyard on all sides. It was built in the fourth century and has the remnants of a circular fountain in the centre.

The E24 continues across the plain to a turning on the left signposted to **Siliyon**. The city stands on the flat-topped hill, visible

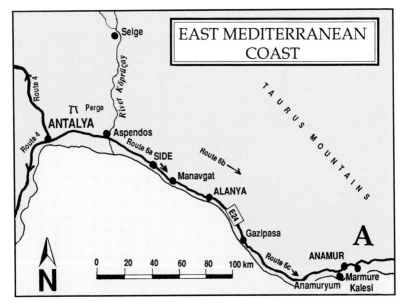

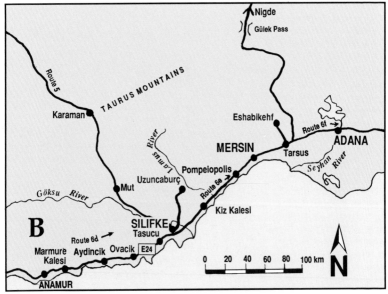

Roman remains at Aspendos

in the distance to the left, 8km (5 miles) from the main road. The site has never been fully excavated, and the terrain is rough, though there are a number of well-preserved Hellenistic buildings scattered on the hilltop and the slopes below.

Thirteen kilometres (8 miles) further along the E24 another sign on the left points to *Aspendos*. The road follows the banks of the Köprüçay river, the ancient *Eurymedon*. A right fork leads to a thirteenth-century **Seljuk bridge** crossing the river while the main road continues straight ahead to Belkis. The road ends at a car-park, shortly after the village.

Aspendos was once an important sea-faring city, but is now some 12km (7 miles) from the coast. It was originally founded in the first millennium BC, but the only major structure left standing is the **Roman theatre**. The city came under Roman rule in 190BC but the theatre was not constructed until the reign of Marcus Aurelius (AD161-80). It is the best-preserved Roman theatre in Asia Minor. The high enclosing walls stand to their original height, as does the stage building, all that is missing are the statues that stood in the many niches around the theatre. Vaulted galleries, lit by narrow slits cut in the stone, lead around the back of the theatre on two levels. The seating has been rebuilt in many places as the theatre is put into use during Antalya's Akdeniz International Song Contest.

The only other remains at *Aspendos* are on the **acropolis** which can be reached by following the footpath over the hill behind the theatre. The acropolis was once contained within a wall that had three monumental gateways, but little has survived the passage of time. The flat area marking the agora at the top of the hill has the ruins of a monumental fountain, and the remnants of a council hall lie to the north.

The turning to **Selge** is a further 17km (10.5 miles) along the E24 on the left. The ruins are 55km (34 miles) from the main road, but the poor road surfaces make it a long excursion and it may be better to join one of the jeep tours that regularly leave from Side. The site is high up in the hills in the **Köprülü Kanyon Milli Park**. The park covers an area of 36,000 hectares (88,920 acres) and the canyon, which is up to 400m (1,312ft) deep in places, stretches for 14km (8.7 miles). The ruins are unexcavated and most visitors come for the setting rather than the historical remains.

The E24 continues past fields of cotton and citrus orchards to the small village of Peri, where a signpost points right to Side, on the coast 4km (2.5 miles) from the highway. There are several turnings off the winding road to Side which lead to holiday villages, motels, camp-sites and beach clubs along the big sand beaches either side of the resort. Visitors must leave their vehicles outside the resort in the car-park near the ancient theatre as the main street is pedestrianised.

Side was originally founded in the first millennium BC by a colony of Aeolian Greeks. In recent years a busy resort has grown up around the ancient site and the ruins create a romantic setting for the many restaurants and *pansiyon*. Cars are prohibited from entering the village as the roads are narrow and crowded with holiday-makers. The main street, lined with souvenir shops and restaurants, leads downhill to a small harbour. The narrow lanes leading off either side of the main street are clustered with *pansiyon* and however busy the site looks it is always possible to find a room. Discos and bars come to life about nine o'clock, and the shops selling carpets, leather, beach-wear, jewellery and onyx stay open until midnight. The beaches either side of the resort are sandy and water-sports facilities are available. The beaches close to the town are strewn with chunks of marble from the ancient city.

The **Roman baths** at the top of the hill have been made into a museum and are filled with sarcophagi, statues and stone-carved fragments from the site. The second-century Roman **theatre**, across from the museum, is unusual in that it is not built into the side of a hill. Instead, the outer wall is constructed out of a series of arches which

*The Roman
theatre at Side*

*Attic sarcophagus,
third century AD,
Side museum*

Kale pansiyon, *Side*

support the seating. It is the largest theatre in the region and could seat a crowd of 15,000.

The E24 continues east to Manavgat where a left turn is sign-posted to **Selale**, a popular waterfall, 4km (2.5 miles) from the main road. The river is broad and shallow and the falls are not very dramatic. A restaurant set under the trees in the surrounding park serves the river trout.

Route 6b — Manavgat to Alanya (map A, p146)

The E24 heads through cotton and maize fields to the coast, where it passes a number of camp-sites before reaching the turning left to **Alarahan**. The road winds for 9km (6 miles) along the Alara river valley to the foot of a steep rock. A Seljuk **caravanserai** sits on the right of the road. It has a finely carved portal and is built around two courtyards, one with outdoor sleeping quarters that were used during the summer, and another with fireplaces for use during the winter.

The steep pinnacle of rock with the remains of a Seljuk **fortress**

Brick-making in Alanya

perched high on top can only be reached by a hard, hour-long climb. The footpath leads from the end of the road past greenhouses and vegetable plots to a hole in the side of a rock-cut tunnel that leads up to the castle. The lower part of the tunnel, now collapsed, led to the river and allowed the defenders to draw water and so resist a long siege. The upper section is well preserved and 135 steep steps lead up to the lower gate-house. The path continues up more steps carved in the natural rock to the middle gate. The upper gate-house can only be found by clambering over the steep rocks on the west side of the peak where a small arched door leads into the inner courtyard. Inside, there is a vaulted chamber, a large cistern, and a rewarding pano- rama along the Alara valley to the coast. Visitors planning to make the ascent to the summit should take a torch for the tunnel and plenty to drink.

The E24 continues along the coast past long, deserted beaches as far as the Ulas Dinlenme Park where the holiday developments around Alanya begin. The motels and holiday villages which are built on the sandy beaches all have swimming pools and water-sport facilities.

Alanya is a busy resort town built in the shelter of a rocky promontory on the ancient site of *Coracesieum*, a Cilician pirate stronghold which held out against the Romans until 65BC. A crenellated fortress marks the top of the promontory and dates from the Cilician settlement, but it was largely rebuilt in 1222 by the Seljuk Sultan Keykubad who added 6.5km (4 miles) of defensive walling.

The main streets in the town are lined with shops selling leather clothing and souvenirs. At the harbour, where a few exclusive hotels are built, boats can be hired for tours of the caves dotted around the promontory, including the **phosphorescent grotto**. One of the largest caves, **Damlatas** is on the small sandy cove on the west side of the promontory. The air in the cavern has an exceptionally high humidity and is said to be good for sufferers of asthma and bronchial complaints. The ceilings and walls are covered in stalactites and stalagmites, and even if you are not suffering from an illness, the cool air is very pleasant. A **museum** is close to Damlatas and contains a modest collection of archaeological finds ranging from the Bronze Age to the Ottoman era.

The Red Tower, **Kizil Kule**, stands on the edge of the peninsula overlooking the harbour and was built in 1226 by the Seljuk Sultan Keykubad. Stairs lead up the tower from where there are good views of the double defence walls that snake along the eastern slope of the peninsula. The tower, now open as a museum, has been fully restored to its original height of 35m (115ft) and has five storeys. On the ground floor there is a display of looms, carpets and Ottoman artefacts, and on the first floor a collection of Seljuk and Ottoman wooden doors.

The Selcuk **dockyards** are just south of the tower and can be reached by following the footpath along the bottom wall. The dockyards were built in 1227 when Alanya was the headquarters of the Seljuk navy, and the plaque over the main door is dedicated to Alaeddin Keykubad: 'King of the two seas'. A small mosque lies to one side of the entrance and a guard's room to the other. Inside, there are five long bays, still filled with water, covered by vaulted ceilings.

The castle is 2.5km (1.5 miles) up a steep and winding road signposted from the town. The ruins of the Seljuk city cover the slopes around the citadel and a yellow signpost indicates the **bedesten**, the Seljuk bazaar, and **Suleymaniye Cami** to the right of the road.

The road continues up the hill, past the defensive walls to the carpark. Nothing remains of the Seljuk palace which once stood inside the citadel, but there is a ruined Byzantine church dating from the sixth century and a number of water cisterns. The turreted walkways along the top of the walls offer spectacular views along the coast in both directions.

Route 6c — Alanya to Anamur (map A, p146)

The E24 traverses the last of the coastal plain 25km (15 miles) east of Alanya and then starts to climb into the mountains of Rugged Cilicia. Forty-five kilometres (28 miles) from Alanya the road drops down to Gazipasa, a small town with a few simple hotels. Basic camping facilities are available on the long shingle beach 3km (1.8 miles) from the town and a handful of restaurants and tea-houses are clustered round the parking area next to the beach.

The next 85km (53 miles) to Anamur cross a particularly steep range of mountains where one hair-pin bend follows another and most of the drive has to be made in the lowest gear. There are no filling stations on the way so drivers should leave Gazipasa with a full tank of fuel. The road is very panoramic and children stand at the side of the road selling bananas and fruit to the passing traffic. The road descends for 10km (6 miles) into the plain around Anamur, where a yellow sign indicates the right turn to *Anamuryum*.

Anamuryum, an important city in Roman and Byzantine times, has lain deserted since the Arab attacks in the seventh century AD. The oldest remains to have survived date from the third century AD when the city was at its height of prosperity, but most of the site is Byzantine. *Anamuryum* lies 2km (1.2 miles) from the main highway, next to a long shingle beach. The beach is quite deserted and there is nowhere to buy drinks or refreshments but there is a fresh water well at the car-park. Camping on the beach is strictly prohibited.

The hillside behind the beach, which looks like a deserted village, is the **Byzantine necropolis**. The tombs, made of small stones, are mostly in the form of a single chamber with a niche at one end, and some are decorated with frescoes. The largest and most beautifully decorated tomb is kept locked and it is necessary to find the janitor to open it.

A Roman **theatre** lies at the east end of the necropolis. It is completely overgrown but it is just possible to distinguish the curved shape of the seating. On the slopes above the theatre are two well-preserved **aqueducts**, while below the theatre on the opposite side of the road, is a large **Roman baths**. The floors are covered with mosaics, but these have been covered with sand to help preserve them.

Sections of the defensive wall which once surrounded the city can be seen on the rocky promontory at the western end of the beach. It is difficult to climb up to the walls but there is a pleasant footpath along the bottom of the promontory to the modern lighthouse.

Anamur is a further 7km (4 miles) east along the main highway from *Anamuryum*. It is primarily an agricultural town that doesn't receive very many tourists and there are only a few simple hotels and

Mamure Kalesi near Anamur

restaurants. However, the beach resort at Iskele is more popular and has a variety of *pansiyon* and motels. There is a frequent *dolmus* to Iskele from the main square in the centre of Anamur. A yellow sign in the main square marks the road to the **Kösebükü Astim Maga-rasi**, a group of caves 10km (6 miles) from the town.

 Mamure Kalesi is an impressive fortress on the coast 16km (10 miles) east of Anamur. The castle was constructed by crusaders and later restored by the Ottomans in 1840, but the site was occupied by a fortress as far back as the third century. It has passed through many hands and at various points in history was held by the Armenians, the Kings of Cyprus and the Karaman Turks. The outer walls have been completely restored and thirty-six towers defend the sea and land faces. The land side is also protected by a deep moat, now full of frogs and terrapins. The entrance to the castle passes by a tall, fourteen-sided tower which overlooks the two grassy courtyards inside the walls. In the middle of the right-hand courtyard stands a small Ottoman mosque that is still in use. A sentry-walk leads from the tower along the top of the walls.

Route 6d — Anamur to Silifke (map B, p146)

The E24 follows the coast past the few hotels clustered around

Truck loaded with cotton, Silifke

Marmure Kalesi, to Pullu, a camp-site run by the forestry commission. Shortly after the village of Çubukköyagi a yellow sign points left to **Softa Kalesi**, an Armenian fortress in a romantic setting, high on the rocky crag to the left of the road. A steep, winding track climbs for 2km (1.2 miles) to the castle ruins.

The terrain east of the castle is extremely mountainous and the road climbs endlessly up and down from dizzy peaks to sheltered bays. At the village of Aydincik there are a few *pansiyon* and restaurants around the harbour, and a holiday village and camp-site at the far end of the bay. After Büyükeceli the road winds up through beautiful pine forests, the Karayar Orman, before the big descent to Ovacik where there is a camp-site and hotel on the beach. The coast from here, being less steep, is dotted with holiday villages and small resorts.

Tokmar Kalesi, one of the many crusader castles along this coast, is 3km (1.8 miles) up a steep, rough track on the left, 25km (15 miles) before Silifke. Shortly after the small resort of Bogsak there is another ruined castle, **Liman Kalesi**, reached by a narrow track along the promontory on the right. The road continues past **Tasucu**, a busy commercial port 10km (6 miles) before Silifke, from where ferries run to the Turkish Republic of Northern Cyprus. There is a good selection of accommodation around the port and along the beaches either side, and most visitors to the region stay here rather than in Silifke.

Silifke is a quiet agricultural town, surrounded by citrus orchards, along the banks of the Göksu river, the ancient *Calycadnus*. It stands on the ancient site of *Seleucia-ad-Calycadnum*, which was founded in the third century BC by Seleuceus Nicator. The castle on the hill overlooking the town was built by the Byzantines in the seventh century on the site of an early acropolis. It was later restored and used by the Crusader Knights of St John. In 1190 the third crusade was brought to an abrupt end, almost under the castle walls, by the unexpected death of their leader, Frederic Barbarossa, who had a heart-attack and drowned in the *Calycadnus* river. The exact location is marked by a memorial plaque 10km (6 miles) north of the town on the road to Mut.

A 2km (1.2 miles) winding road leads up to the **castle** from the centre of the town. On the lower slopes of the castle hill, to the left of the road, there is a huge rock-hewn cistern, **Tekir Ambari**. In one corner a stone spiral staircase leads down to the bottom of the pit.

At the top of the castle hill the road ends at a restaurant and tea-house, built in the shadow of the walls, with splendid views over the town. Inside the castle, which has never been excavated, the large courtyard is filled with tumbled stone, but the wall, complete with twenty-three towers, is quite well preserved and contains numerous chambers and passages.

Aya Tekla, the site of a Byzantine basilica, is on a hilltop to the west of the town. From the town centre, follow Inönü Caddesi past the remains of the **Temple of Zeus** and the local **museum** to the E24. The basilica is signposted 2km (1.2 miles) to the west up a small road on the right. The road ends at a parking area next to the ruins of an apse. This is all that remains of the basilica dedicated to St Thekla, which was built in AD476.

The ancient ruins of **Diocaesarea** lie 28km (17 miles) north of Silifke at the village of Uzuncaburç. The road is well signposted from the town and can be reached by public transport, details of which are obtainable from the tourism office on Atatürk Meydani. The signposts lead across the Göksu river over the original Roman bridge, built by the Governor Octavius Memor. A narrow road climbs up the rocky valley to the village of Demircili, on a plateau top 7km (4 miles) from Silifke. The village is built on the ancient site of *Imbriogon*. Nothing much remains of the city, but there are six well-preserved **Roman tombs** built in the style of classical temples, five of which are easily accessible from the road. The first is on the right of the road set into the natural rock with a well-preserved roof and four fine Corinthian columns. The next tomb, three storeys high, can be reached by crossing the field on the left from the big bend in the road. The remains are not very impressive, but the pair of mausolea just to the north are in a very good state of repair. One contains sarcophagi with reclining figures and lions carved on their lids. After the last mausoleum on the right, the road climbs through pine forests and rocky mountains to Imamli, where yellow signposts are marked to Uzuncaburç.

The road becomes increasingly steep and winding as it approaches Uzancaburç and a 16m- high (52ft-) **mausoleum** stands on the summit (1,203m/3,946ft) to the left of the road. The tomb is Hellenistic and a sliding stone door, which was originally hidden beneath the facing stone, leads into the burial chamber.

The road passes through the village of Uzancaburç to a parking area, which lies close to the Roman **theatre**. The theatre is almost invisible from the car-park as it is set into the hill below the level of the road. It was built in the second century AD and could seat 2,500 spectators. A **monumental gate** with five columns and Corinthian capitals, that used to support busts of the Roman emperors, marks the entrance to the city. The colonnaded road that leads to the **Temple of Jupiter** was once part of a major highway that stretched for 40km (25 miles) to *Korykos* on the coast.

The temple lies within the walled precinct on the left of the colonnaded road. It was built in 295BC by Seleuceus I and is one of the oldest known Corinthian-style temples in Asia Minor. Many of the columns are still standing and the area is littered with beautifully carved stone fragments. During the Byzantine era it was converted to a basilica and a wall was built between the columns to form the apse.

The **Temple of Tyche**, built in the first century, stands at the end of the street. The five columns left standing are carved from single pieces of Egyptian granite and still support the original capitals and architrave.

Returning to the corner of the precinct surrounding the Temple of Jupiter, a road leads left to the city gate and passes through the scant remains of the wall to the village. The tall **tower** standing on the hill above the village was originally part of the city wall. The five-storey tower stands to its original height of 22.30m (73ft).

A signpost points from the centre of the village to the **necropolis**, where there are a great number of tombs carved in the rocky sides of a valley, as well as many free-standing sarcophagi with carved decorations.

Route 6e — Silifke to Mersin (map B, p146)

From Silifke follow the signs to Erdemli and Mersin across the cultivated plain to the coast. **Susanoglu** is one of the most popular holiday resorts along this stretch of coast and has several camp-sites and private beaches. The road continues along the coast, through the seaside village of Akyar, to **Narlıkuyu**, a small fishing village with a few restaurants surrounding a rocky bay. There is a tiny museum in the village built on the site of a **Roman baths**, of which nothing remains except the fourth-century mosaic depicting *The Three Graces*, with the inscription: 'Poimenio found the waters of this bath agreeable'. Opposite the turning to Narlikuyu, a yellow sign marks the road that leads uphill for 3km (1.8 miles) to **Cennet and Cehennem**, Heaven and Hell.

The two vast chasms of Cennet and Cehennem are steeped in legend and local visitors still regard the site with a certain superstition, tying rags and pieces of plastic onto the branches of trees for luck, or to ward off evil spirits. The chasms were formed when the roofs of immense underground chambers, created by a subterranean river, collapsed. The city of *Paperon* was built around the chasms in Roman times, but the only remains on the site are a few scattered Byzantine ruins.

Cennet is the chasm nearest the car-park. It is 70m (230ft) deep, and the pit is 250m (820ft) long and 90m (295ft) wide. Four hundred and fifty-two steps descend into the pit and a footpath leads into the vast cavern at the southern end. The chapel in front of the entrance to the cavern was built in the fifth century and dedicated to the Virgin Mary. It was restored in the thirteenth century by Armenians.

Inside, the cave is quite dark and guides wait with paraffin lamps to lead visitors around. As the path descends, the temperature drops, and a tea-house shrouded in the swirling blue smoke of the paraffin lamps is a convenient spot to acclimatise. The river heard thundering in the distance is believed to be the ancient *Styx*, the legendary gateway to the underworld, *Hades*. In the winter the river fills the lower part of the cave, but in the summer it recedes, although the path is still wet and slippery.

The chasm of **Cehennem**, 100m north-east of Cennet, is 120m (394ft) deep. Unlike Cennet it is impossible to enter the chasm as the sides are too sheer and steep. Legend has it that the one-hundred headed monster, Typhon, was imprisoned here before being buried underground.

Carved tombs in the necropolis at Kanlidivane

A track leads from the car-park to the **Wishing Cave**, a series of inter-connected underground caverns with impressive stalactites, stalagmites and calcite curtains. A spiral staircase leads 18m (59ft) below ground from the newly-built tourist complex at the top of the hill, from where a well-lit, but slippery footpath makes a circular tour of the main chambers.

The E24 continues to wind along the coast to the small resort of **Akkum**, where there are camp-sites on the beach and a selection of *pansiyon* along the road. Just past Akkum, is another resort, **Kiz Kalesi**, named after the castle 850m (929yd) offshore. The castle can be reached by taking one of the small fishing boats that leave from the harbour. It was originally built to defend the ancient port of *Korykos* and legend has it that the daughter of King Korykos lived on the island to avoid being poisoned by a snake as prophesied at her birth. However, the princess did not escape her fate and was bitten by a viper concealed in a basket of grapes sent from the mainland. The castle walls and the eight towers are in good condition and were constructed in the thirteenth century.

Another **castle** is built on the shore opposite, at the eastern end of the bay. The first fortress to be built on this site was Roman. The castle seen today, built in the twelfth century, uses many of the original stones and Roman inscription stones set into the walls on either side of the main gate. Inside, hidden beneath the undergrowth, are the remains of three chapels built by the Byzantines, Armenians and crusaders.

Little is left of the ancient city of **Korykos**, founded in the seventh century BC, but ruins are spread over a vast area, stretching for up to 3km (1.8 miles) east of Kiz Kalesi. There is an extensive **necropolis** in the valley opposite the land castle. It is not easy to walk around the necropolis as there are no footpaths, but a fine tomb, carved with a headless warrior and dating from the fourth century BC, can be seen from the roadside.

East along the E24, the ruins of two large Byzantine basilica and sections of an aqueduct which supplied water to *Korykos* from the ancient *Lamus* river, are passed on the left-hand side of the road before reaching Kumkuyu. A yellow signpost points left to the ancient site of *Kanlidivane*, 3km (1.8 miles) from the main road.

Although *Kanlidivane* dates back to the Hittites, the ruins are mostly Roman and Byzantine. During this period the city was known as *Kanytelis* which literally translated means Blood City. It has been suggested that it got its name from the sacrifices made in the enormous pit in the centre of the city.

About 300m (984ft) before reaching the site car-park, a small earth track leads off left to the **Roman necropolis**. There are nine impressive tombs cut high in a south-facing rock face each with carved figures above the entrances.

The pit which dominates the site of *Kanlidivane* lies alongside the car-park, and is about 90m (295ft) long, 70m (230ft) wide and 60m (197ft) deep. The original stone-carved stairway leads to the bottom although the undergrowth makes it difficult to reach the two rock-reliefs that are carved on the walls inside. The best carving, which depicts six figures, is directly below the high tower on the edge of the pit. The other, on the north-west wall is obscured by undergrowth.

The city ruins lie around the sides of the pit. The 17m (56ft) **tower** on one side was part of the Hellenistic city fortifications, while the **basilica** on the other is just one of four Byzantine basilica in the city. 200m (656ft) north of the pit there is a well-preserved **temple-style tomb** and a number of finely-carved sarcophagi.

The coast is less attractive east of Kumkuyu and a fast road leads through a string of holiday developments built along the flat beaches all the way to Mersin. At Limonlu the road crosses the ancient *Lamus* river, the boundary between Rugged Cilicia and the Cilician plain, and at the suburb of Mezitli a yellow sign points right to **Viransehir**, the site of ancient *Pompeiopolis*.

The city was originally founded by colonists from Rhodes in 700BC who called it *Soloi*, meaning sun. It was renamed *Pompeiopolis* by Pompei who completely rebuilt the city in 64BC after capturing it from Cilician pirates. The city was flattened by an earthquake in AD527 and only a few columns remain along the **paved road** which leads to the ancient harbour. Some of the columns are carved with the portraits of the city's benefactors and have fine Corinthian capitals.

After Viransehir the road passes through an industrial suburb to the port of **Mersin**, the largest city on the east Mediterranean. Mersin is the capital of the province of İçel and is one of the oldest continuously inhabited settlements in Asia Minor with origins going back to neolithic times. A Hittite fortress has been located on the hilltop 3km (1.8 miles) from the city at Yumuktepe. However, the oldest buildings in Mersin today date from no earlier than the nineteenth century and there is little to attract tourists apart from a good selection of accommodation and restaurants.

Route 6f — Mersin to Adana (map B, p146)

The E24/400 is signposted to Tarsus and Adana. The traffic through the industrial outskirts east of Mersin is heavy, but once out of the city there is a good dual-carriageway across the plain to Tarsus.

Tarsus stands on an ancient site which dates back to the early Hittites in the fourteenth century BC. Classical Tarsus was a seafaring city, originally located on the edge of a lake, connected to the sea by a navigable river. The modern town is sprawled out along a faceless high street, and the hotels and restaurants are very mediocre, but it is worth a brief visit to see the few historical monuments that have survived.

A monumental Roman arch, known as **Cleopatra's Gate**, stands at the eastern end of the main street. The inscription stone next to it, is a proclamation of the independent status of Tarsus, and dates from AD222-235. **St Paul's Well** supposedly marks the apostle's birthplace. The well, set in a small courtyard, is about 100m (109yd) north of the centre of town.

In the centre of the town a yellow sign indicates the road leading to the remains of a Roman temple, **Domuktas Roma Tapagi**. The temple is surrounded by narrow streets and houses and it is best found by looking for the high wall that encloses it.

A small road leads up into the hills to the Islamic shrine of **Eshabikehf**, 13km (8 miles) from the town. The shrine is visited by pilgrims on their way to Mecca and a large mosque has been built here.

Leaving Tarsus in the direction of Adana, a Byzantine bridge, built during the reign of Justinian, is passed on the left.

Adana is the fourth largest city in Turkey and is located in the heart of the rich agricultural land of the Cukurova plain, 40km (25 miles) east of Tarsus. For such a large and wealthy city Adana has a surprisingly rural atmosphere. Donkeys and carts mingle with the traffic and a fleet of old fashioned Skoda wagons provide *dolmus* services around the city. There is nothing of particular historical interest to see, but the general atmosphere is lively, and there is a wide choice of accommodation available. Most restaurants serve the regional speciality, Adana kebab, spicy minced meat on a skewer served with pitta bread and salad.

The Seyhan river, east of the city, is crossed by two busy bridges carrying traffic bound for Syria. The southernmost, known as **Tas Köprü**, was built in the second century AD by the Roman emperor Hadrian, and later restored in Byzantine times by Justinian. The museum, signposted as the **Bölge Müzesi** from the town centre, is to the left of the modern bridge, Girne Köprü. There are two parts to the museum, an archaeological section and an ethnographical section. The earliest archaeological finds date from 7000BC, and the locally found Hittite pottery, decorated with animal motifs, is particularly notable. The ethnographical section traces the history of the local nomadic tribes up until the present day.

7
BLACK SEA COAST

F ewer tourists visit the Black Sea Coast than the Aegean and Mediterranean, as there are few classical ruins and the climate is wet. It rains almost every day, especially in the eastern Black Sea, and the summer season is short with an average temperature of 20°C (68°F) in July. The sea temperatures never get very high and the strong currents and undertow make the coast dangerous to swim in many places.

The beautiful, verdant landscape is one of the biggest attractions of the region. Deserted sand beaches are backed by the hazelnut covered slopes of the Black Sea mountains. The mountain peaks, often shrouded in mist and swirling clouds, get steeper and higher towards the east. The highest peaks at Rize are about 4,000m (13,120ft). The mountains drop dramatically into the sea leaving only a narrow coastal strip where development of any kind is almost impossible. Most of the towns are built on the flat lands around the mouths of the region's major rivers: the Sakarya, the Kizilirmak and the Yesilirmak.

Route 7 is divided into five sections, each of which can be covered in a day although visitors will probably wish to spend longer in Trabzon. Cruise ferries carrying cars run regularly between Istanbul and Trabzon, calling at Sinop and Samsun. Driving can be very slow in the mountainous areas and visitors may wish to forfeit the scenic drive along the coast, either for the ferry, or for the E5, the fast inland road from Istanbul to Samsun. It is possible to join Route 10 from Samsun, or head inland on Route 8 from Trabzon.

Route 7a — Istanbul to Sile (map A, p166)

Sile is 75km (46.5 miles) from Istanbul on highway 020. The narrow and hilly road is signposted off the E5 at Üsküdar. Pine forests and lush vegetation cover the hills and a number of barbecue-style *mangal* restaurants are passed at the roadside. Approaching Sile a yellow signpost points left to **Kumbaba** where there is a motel and camp-site on the beach.

Sile is a small coastal village with a busy fishing industry and a tradition in making cheesecloth. The village is divided by a steep river valley. A harbour lies at the centre, protected by a rocky promontory with the remains of a Genoese watchtower, and high cliffs and long sandy beaches stretch either side. There is a selection of fresh sea-food restaurants behind the beach in Sile, and hotels and *pansiyon* are dotted along the cliff-tops. At **Aglayan Kaya**, 2km (1.2 miles) east of the village, beyond the lighthouse, there are camp-sites and rooms for rent in family homes. Great care should be taken swimming from the isolated beaches around Aglayan Kaya as the currents can be dangerous. It is safer to swim from Sile or Kumbaba where there are lifeguards on duty.

Route 7b — Sile to Amasra (map A, p166)

The small coastal road east of Sile is indicated by a road sign to 'sahil'. It climbs up and down steep hills covered in hazelnut trees to the fishing village of Yesilcay which is built around a sandy bay. While the new coastal road is still being built between Sile and Amasra it is necessary to make a diversion inland from Yesilcay to Kandira and Adapazari before rejoining the coast.

Adapazari, the capital of the Sakarya province and a well-known centre for oil-wrestling, has a few hotels and restaurants along the main street, but nothing else of interest to the visitor. Highway 650 follows the Sakarya river from Adapazari to the coast at Karasu. The road then runs along the coast past long sandy beaches through Akçakoca to Eregli.

Eregli is a small industrial town built on the site of ancient *Hereclea-ad-Pontus*, thought to have been founded by Megarian colonists in the sixth century BC. There are no ancient remains but a few stones from the Byzantine settlement can be seen in the park at the centre of the town. A Byzantine grotto, 2km (1.2 miles) east of the town centre, is reached by a narrow track signposted from the road to **Cehennem Agzi Magaralari**. The track follows the river and the grotto, also known as the Cave of Heracles, is on the right. The cave has been identified by some as the legendary spot where Heracles descended into Hell to bring Cerberus, the monstrous dog which guarded the underworld, up to Eurystheus. The sections of mosaic on the cavern floor date from the time when the grotto was used as a Byzantine church. Small entrances above the cave lead further underground to other grottoes which fill up with water after rain. Other Byzantine relics can be seen in the **Atatürk Kültür Sitesi**, a small museum on the main street of the town.

Until the new road is complete, the journey from Eregli to Amasra follows a scenic but poorly-surfaced mountain road. At the coal mining town of Zonguldak the road heads inland towards Devrek and climbs through forests of sweet chestnut trees to Sapaci Tünel, a 568m (1,863ft) unlit tunnel. At **Bartin** many of the original timber houses still stand. The town is built on the Roman site of *Parthenium*, which was linked to Amasra by a Roman road built in the reign of Claudius.

The road continues through green fields and hazelnut orchards, up onto the summit of a coastal headland above Amasra, then winds down to the shore past the remains of a small **Roman theatre** in the middle of a graveyard, surrounded by garden allotments.

The site of **Amasra**, former *Sesame*, was founded by colonists from *Miletos* in the sixth century BC. It is a peaceful fishing village with a small woodcraft industry and is built around an ancient Roman harbour. The village has a few simple *pansiyon* and restaurants, and the tourism office helps visitors find rooms in private homes if necessary. There are considerable Roman remains in the town, and the local **museum**, housed in a nineteenth-century naval school on the harbour wall, contains fine Roman statues as well as a collection of traditional crafts and ethnography.

The **citadel**, on the hill above the town, is entered through a fifteenth-century gateway, known as **Büyük Liman Kapisi**. A Byzantine bridge leads to another gate with attractive vaulting. The citadel wall dates from Roman times although it was later restored by the Genoese. A **Byzantine church** now a mosque, called Fatih Cami, stands just outside the east gate. A weather station now stands on the summit of the citadel hill from where there are excellent views along the coast.

Route 7c — Amasra to Sinop (maps A+B, p166)

The road from Amasra to Sinop is one of the least travelled stretches of coast in Turkey, and although the road surface is poor the landscape it passes through is outstanding. The highway, marked by road signs to Sinop, heads east along the coast and climbs up and down a series of steep valleys with deep coastal bays and long deserted beaches. The beach at Karamanlar is particularly good, and at Kapisu a traditional boatyard, making wooden fishing boats, lies behind the beach.

After **Cide**, the site of a former Roman harbour, the road dips violently up and down before making a final dramatic descent to

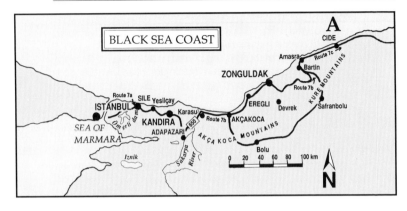

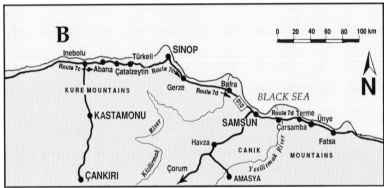

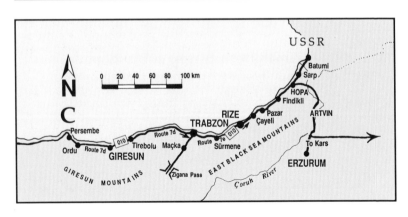

The Black Sea coast

Inebolu, in the coastal bay of the Ikiçay river valley.

The terrain east of Inebolu is less mountainous and the road follows the coast to the tiny resort of **Abana** where there is a 5km (3 mile) stretch of sand beach. From Türkeli, another simple resort with a big beach, the road heads inland through cherry orchards and then across rolling fields of grain to the narrow peninsula at Sinop. The road enters the town through the original city wall.

Sinop, at the northernmost tip of Turkey, was founded as a Milesian trading colony in 770BC, and there are historical remains from all periods of the town's history. The city wall, built by the Seljuks, is made with stones from earlier buildings and completely surrounds the town. The best section stretches from the harbour across the neck of the peninsula, to the coast on the other side. It has several fine gates and towers and the sentry walk can be followed from the **clock tower** to the main city gate, **Kale Burç Girisi**.

The local **museum**, signposted from the clock tower, stands next the Deniz Sehitleri Park which contains the remains of an ancient **temple to Serapis**. Only the base of the temple remains, and the best pieces of stonework and columns are displayed around the museum.

A road continues uphill from the museum to **Balatlar Kilisesi**, the site of the seventh-century Byzantine citadel. The courtyard, inside the walls, is very overgrown and the buildings are in ruins, but the church has frescoes depicting saints, angels and members of the palace staff, although most of them are badly damaged.

Alaeddin Cami, a Seljuk mosque built in 1214, lies off Sakarya Caddesi in the centre of the town. The mosque was restored in 1322-61 by a local emir whose monumental tomb stands in the courtyard joined to one side. The theological school attached to the mosque, **Pervane Medrese**, is still in use.

A small road, signposted to **Karakum**, leads 3km (1.8 miles) east of the town to the tip of the peninsula where there is a small resort on a sandy beach. An Ottoman fortress, **Pasa Kale**, is passed on the way to the resort. It was built in 1850 and is still in use by the military, but visitors are free to walk around.

Route 7d — Sinop to Trabzon (maps B+C, p166)

Highway 010 follows the coast through the small fishing town of Gerze, after which it winds up and down mountain valleys to the Güzelçay river and the flat coastal plain around the mouth of the Kizilirmak. The road crosses the Kizilirmak river into the town of Bafra, and passes through the tobacco-growing plain to the industrial suburbs of Samsun.

Samsun is the centre of the tobacco industry in Turkey and is the largest port on the Black Sea. There is a good selection of hotels and restaurants available, but otherwise the city holds little to attract the visitor. The ancient site of *Amisus* is a few kilometres north-west of the modern city, at Kara Samsun. It was founded in the seventh century BC by Greek colonists, and renamed *Aminsus* by the Byzantines. Samsun, the Seljuk name for the city, was kept after the old town was destroyed by fire in 1425 and moved to its present site.

The **Archaeological Museum** on the south side of the plaza in the city centre, houses a few relics from the Roman city *Amisus*, including a fine mosaic depicting the four seasons.

Atatürk began his campaign of resistance, which led up to the War of Independence, in Samsun. The day commemorating his arrival in the city, 19 May 1919, is now a national holiday. The equestrian statue of Atatürk stands in the centre of the plaza.

Highway 010 continues across the flat plain bordering the coast to **Ünye**, which is a busy market town with a few hotels and restaurants along its sandy beach. A pleasant excursion can be made from the town to **Caleoglu Castle**. Follow the signs inland to 'kale' along the road to Akkus and Niksar, for 6km (3.7 miles) to the left turn signposted to Kaleköy. The village of Kaleköy lies at the foot of the castle hill and a well-marked footpath leads steeply up from the village square, past a Roman rock tomb on the left carved high in the cliff face. The path continues up to the outer walls, passing through the original gateway into a small courtyard. Further up the hill a steep tunnel, to the right of the inner gate, leads underground down forty-four rock-hewn steps. Another tunnel, on an even larger scale, can be found near the summit of the rock. It has over 400 steps and leads steeply down through the centre of the rock to the river in the valley below. The tunnels, which allowed the fortress to survive a lengthy siege, were probably built by the Pontic king, Mithridates in the first century BC. The peak of the summit is reached by a wooden ladder, and the view from the top is superb.

Four kilometres (2.5 miles) east of Ünye, a yellow signpost points right to **Tozkoporan Magarasi**, a small rock-cut tomb with two simple chambers. The track follows the Cevizdere river, past a cement factory, and the tomb is on the right.

The highway continues along the coast through Fatsa and Bolaman to **Yason**. A track leads out onto the promontory to the left of the road where there is a church. It is Armenian in style and was last restored in 1868, but the site of the church is much older and originally had a temple dedicated to the cult of Jason. During the second century it was also a Roman fish-farm and vague outlines indicate where the fish-pools once stood.

The road follows long sand beaches, dotted with occasional camp-sites and hotels, to **Persembe**, an attractive fishing town with a simple range of accommodation.

Cotorya, founded in the sixth century BC, is 18km (11 miles) east of Persembe, just before the town of Ordu. A ruined citadel is all that can be seen today, but the city is remembered for having given refuge to Xenophon's army of 10,000 in 402BC. **Ordu** is the provincial capital and centre of the hazelnut industry. An eighteenth-century Armenian basilica is above the turning to **Boztepe**, a hilltop tea-gardens.

The coastal road continues east of Ordu along sand beaches through the small coastal resort of Güzelyali, to Giresun.

The main road into **Giresun** passes an Armenian church, now a mosque called Kumyali Cami, on the right. The town is spread around the foot of a large hill, the site of a **Byzantine castle**. Not much is left of the castle, apart from the outer walls, and the hilltop is now the town's park and contains a tea-gardens and a restaurant. There are fine views from the walls to the island of **Büyük Ada**, ancient *Aretias*, said to have been one of the stopping places on Jason's search for the Golden Fleece. Of *Cerasus*, the ancient site at Giresun, very little remains.

Highway 010 continues along the coast through the town of Kesap, where the ruins of a Genoese castle, **Andöz Kalesi**, stand on a high rocky outcrop on the right.

Tirebolu, a small town built around a twin bay, has a camp-site and some simple accommodation, and the remains of a fourteenth-century Genoese castle stand in the east bay.

Bedrama Kalesi, another Genoese fortress, is signposted inland along the road to Torul. The castle defends the Dogankent river valley, a strategic pass crossing the Black Sea mountains. The turning is indicated 1km (0.6 miles) east of Tirebolu.

At Açakkale, a thirteenth-century Byzantine **fortress** stands on a promontory, surrounded by vegetable plots and tobacco fields. The walls are 20m (65ft) high in places and there is a fine defence tower.

Highway 010 continues along the coast and Akçaabat is the last town before reaching Trabzon.

Trabzon has a long and illustrious history dating back to the first millennium BC, when a Greek trading colony, *Trapezus* later known as *Trebizond* was founded on the site. It is built around two deep river gorges, crossed by elegant stone viaducts. The old city stands on the high ground between the two gorges, encircled by the original citadel wall, while the modern centre and the commercial port lie further to the east. The modern city centre is at Park Meydani, a busy square filled with tea-gardens and surrounded by hotels and restaurants.

Üzün Yollu, the main shopping street in the city, heads west of Park Meydani towards the citadel. As the road starts to slope downhill, **St Ann's Church**, now Küçük Ayvasil Cami, can be seen in a side street on the left. It was built in the seventh century and is the oldest surviving church in Trabzon. The **bazaar** area, in the side streets to the right of Üzün Yollu, has a lively atmosphere and local crafts, such as silver filigree and woven silver jewellery, can be found. Two of the original bazaar buildings, **Tas Han** and **Vakup Han** are still in use today.

At the end of Üzün Yollu a bridge crosses the Tabakhane Deresi, the east gorge, to the citadel walls. **Panaghia Chrysokephalos Church**, now a mosque called Fatih Cami, is at the centre of the citadel and is the burial place of four of the Comnene emperors. The church is most impressive if entered through the vaulted porch and hallway on the west side. It is built in the shape of a cross, and on either side of the central apse are remains of marble mosaic panels. The structure has been altered to accommodate a *mihrab* and the frescoes on the walls have been covered with plaster.

Sehit Refik Caddesi leads due east of Fatih Cami up a steep hill. *Dolmus* heading for Bahçecik or Ceza Evi run up and down the hill, and save walkers the steep climb. The ruins of the **Comnene Palace** are on the right next to a small mosque called İç Kale Cami. They are surrounded by ramshackle housing and only parts of the outer wall

Atatürk Square, Trabzon

and a tower, believed to have been the chapel, remain standing. The
views across the gorge to the **Church of St Eugenios** on the far side
and the monastery above are excellent. St Eugenios was the patron
saint of *Trebizond* as well as its protector against invasion. The
church was built in 1351 for the wedding of the Emperor Alexius III,
but the saint let the city down for it was here that Mehmet I held the
first moslem prayer service to be made in Trabzon in 1461. It has
served as a mosque ever since and is now called Yeni Cuma Cami.

From Fatih Cami, the Zaganos bridge heads due west of the
citadel walls to **Gülbahar Cami**, the first Ottoman mosque to be built
in Trabzon. It was constructed at the end of the fifteenth century for
Gülbahar, the Comnene princess married to Sultan Beyazit, and her
mausoleum stands next to the mosque on the left.

Aya Sofya Church, now a museum, is one of Turkey's finest
Byzantine monuments. It is situated on a high terrace overlooking the
sea, 3km (1.8 miles) west of the city. The church was originally built
in 1204 but it was altered in the 1250s by Manual I, who added the
three porches on the north, south and west sides. The outer walls are
attractively decorated with stone-carvings, and although the south
door is now used as the main entrance, it is best entered through the
west porch.

The restoration work undertaken by a British team in 1957 has brought back to light some beautiful fresco work inside the church. The figure of Christ Pantocrator encircled by the apostles and adoring angels painted on the central dome is partly effaced, but the frescoes depicting Christ's miracles in the narthex are among the finest examples of Byzantine painting. A grey stone tower stands in the rose gardens surrounding the church on the north terrace. It was built in 1427 by Alexius IV as a bell tower, but also served as an observatory.

 A short excursion can be made from the city to **Kizlar Manastiri**, the remains of the Theokephastos Convent, on the hillside, 3km (1.8 miles) north of the city. *Dolmus* marked to Boztepe run up the hill towards the convent from Park Meydani. The exact origins of the convent are unknown but it is believed to have been used by the Comnene princesses. The site is enclosed within a high wall and the warden who lives nearby holds the key to the gate. Inside, the area is entirely overgrown, but many parts of the building are well preserved. A **belfry**, covered with a dome, supported on four columns is passed on the right. The **church** is at the back, partly hewn from the natural rock, and it is just possible to discern the fifteenth-century frescoes beneath the layer of black soot. A nineteenth-century **chapel** stands next to the church and contains the earlier rock niche tomb of Andronikos, son of Alexius III, who died by falling from a palace window. On the hillside above, the small domed roof supported by four columns, decorated on the inside with a painting of the Pantocrator holding the Bible, is the **tomb of Constantinos** (1830-79), a Greek metropolitan.

Atatürk Köskü, where Atatürk stayed for 3 days when he visited Trabzon, is a short excursion from the city centre. The house lies on the steep slopes of Soguksu hill, 4km (2.5 miles) north-west of the city. Soguksu was a popular suburb with the Greek bourgeoisie in the days of *Trebizond* and a number of grand houses were built on the slopes. Atatürk Köskü is typical of its era with its art-nouveau furniture and decor. It is set in a pleasant garden surrounded by pine forests.

Route 7e — Trabzon to Hopa (map C, p166)

Highway 010 continues east of Trabzon along the coast, at the foot of the hazelnut plantations which cover the mountainsides. There are no historical remains along the route apart from a ruined thirteenth-century fortress on a promontory at Arakli.

As the coast curves northwards after Sürmene, the landscape changes. Rain clouds bank up along the slopes of the Black Sea mountains, producing overcast skies and frequent rainfall. This warm but wet climate is ideally suited to the tea plantations that cover the steep slopes of all the mountains. Tea-processing factories surround the small towns and line the roadside around Rize, the centre of the tea industry.

East of Rize the mountains become even steeper and cables run up the slopes to bring the harvested tea down to the roadside. Five kilometres (3 miles) past Pazar a road leads up into the mountains for 22km (13.6 miles) to the beautiful mountain village of Çamlihemsin. **Zil Kale**, a turreted fortress surrounded by thick forests, lies 12km (7 miles) south of Çamlihemsin, at the foot of the Kaçkar mountains. The range is popular with hikers and climbers and mountain guides can be hired in Çamlihemsin.

Highway 010 continues along the coast, crossing the swiftly flowing Firtini Çayi river, to **Hopa**, an insignificant town which most visitors only pass through on their way to Artvin, or the Soviet border, 22km (13.6 miles) away. A border crossing has recently been opened between Turkish Sarp and Soviet Batumi. Visas and permits should be applied for well in advance.

There is a regular *dolmus* service from Hopa to **Artvin**, a picturesque town located on a steep mountainside 457m (1,500ft) above the Çoruh river valley. The town has a good hotel which is a suitable base from which to visit the lush alpine valleys and the deserted Georgian churches of the region. The main core of churches is found between Savsat and Tortum, high on the mountain peaks on either side of the Çoruh and Imerhevi valleys. Others are hidden away in tiny mountain hamlets and have been converted to mosques, while some lie in ruins in the middle of nowhere and are only accessible on foot or by jeep.

The Georgians are an ancient Christian people and their language, now only spoken in the most remote villages, is related to Caucasian. Their church architecture is influenced by both Byzantine and Armenian styles. Most of the churches that have survived, date from between the tenth and the twelfth centuries, and range from small chapels to extensive monastery complexes. The region can be toured in two separate excursions. The first, south of Artvin along the Çoruh valley, on the road to Yusufeli, takes in the churches of **Ishan**, **Bana**, **Hahuli**, **Vank**, **Dört Kilise** and **Barhal**. The second tour, north-west of Artvin, follows the Imerhevi valley on the road to Savsat, and visits **Dolishane**, and the more remote churches of **Opiza**, **Porta**, **Tbeti** and **Yeni Rabat**.

It is possible to continue over the Black Sea mountains on a tortuous but picturesque route to Kars, via Ardahan, or to Erzurum via Tortum. Otherwise visitors should return to Trabzon and join Route 8a to tour the east of Turkey.

8
THE EAST

The eastern part of Anatolia covers the highest plateau in Turkey, lying 2,000m (6,560ft) above sea-level. Over-grazing and soil erosion have turned most of the area into a virtual desert, and the severity of the climate makes any sort of cultivation difficult. Some areas are covered by snow for 9 months of the year, and it is quite normal for winter temperatures to drop to at least 10°C (50°F) below freezing. In the summer the sun parches the land and drought is a serious problem.

The region used to be part of ancient Armenia, but the Armenian people were deported in World War I and today the population is mainly Kurdish. The areas close to the Soviet border are heavily guarded by the military, and some of the monuments or roads along the frontier require special permission to visit.

Not many tourists visit the region and it is quite normal to be followed around by a crowd of children, or to have people stop in the street and stare. Tourist facilities have really only developed around the main historical attractions and in the largest eastern Anatolian city, Erzurum. Finding places to eat in the more rural areas can sometimes be a problem. It is advisable to check the food before ordering as it is often not refrigerated and flies are in abundance. Sis kebab is the standard fare in most places, but there are a number of regional dishes worth looking out for such as *otlu peynir* a herb cheese, and *lahma* an unleavened bread baked in a wood-fired oven.

Route 8 is divided into six stages and each section can be covered in a day. Most of the roads are fairly well surfaced except over high mountain passes where they are usually unmetalled. When driving through rural villages extra care should be taken as children often rush out into the road without looking, and some may throw stones for want of anything better to do.

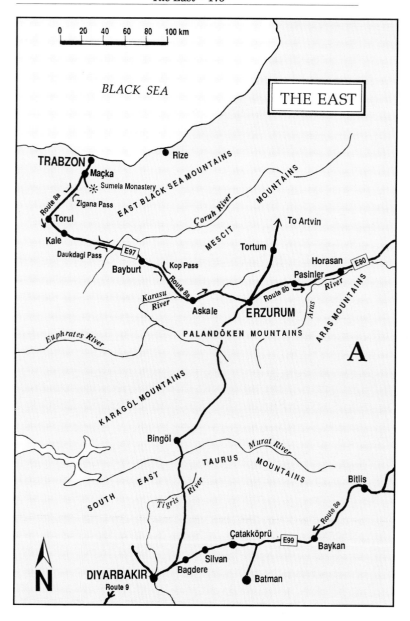

Route 8a — Trabzon to Erzurum (map A, p175)

The E97, signposted to Erzurum, leads inland from Trabzon to the lush Degirmendere river valley, following the ancient caravan route to Bukhara. After the small town of Maçka a left turn is marked by a yellow signpost to **Mereyemana**, the Sumela Monastery. The narrow road winds alongside the sparkling Altindere river through a spectacular alpine valley to the monastery, 47km (29 miles) from Trabzon. The road ends at a fee-paying car-park near an outdoor *mangal* restaurant next to the river.

Sumela Monastery is perched on a rocky ledge, 1,200m (3,900ft) above a richly forested valley. Often shrouded in cloud and obscured by the sheerness of the rock, it is difficult to see from below. But a half-hour climb up a zig-zagging path from the car-park brings it into full view. Near the top the original aqueduct supplying water to the monastery can be seen on the left, and at the end of the path a flight of steps leads up to the ticket office. The monastery lies beyond, in the shelter of a vast overhanging cliff.

The monastery is said to have been founded by the Byzantine emperor, Justinian. In 1349, Alexius III Comnenus came to the monastery to be crowned Emperor of Trebizond. The monastery was in use until the Greek deportations in 1923, when it was burnt down and the treasures, including the Icon of St Luke and an extensive ancient library, were lost.

The tall façade on the edge of the precipice, formerly the monks' **dormitories**, dates from the nineteenth century. Opposite the dormitories, carved into the rock face, are a series of small cells and prayer niches, some of which have the remains of frescoes. The main **church**, a little further along, is entirely hewn from the natural rock, and the frescoes covering both the inside and outside walls were painted in the eighteenth and nineteenth centuries. There are more rooms and cells at the end of the terrace, and below the dormitories are the original stone latrines.

It is possible to take a different route back to the car-park by forking right just after the ticket office. The ruins of **St Barbara's Convent** are passed on the left and there are good views looking back towards the monastery. The path descends through a forest of spruce and rhododendron to the rushing river below. A bridge crosses over the river and a track leads along the bank back to the car-park.

The E97 winds up from Maçka, between the Horos and Zigana mountains, to the Zigana Pass, 2,025m (6,642ft). The views from the restaurants in the small village of Hamsiköy and from the summit at Zigana, are stunning. The road winds down the southern face of the mountains to the town of **Torul**, and the change in the landscape is dramatic. The lush green pastures and the cool damp air of the Black Sea are replaced by a dry, yellow landscape and burning hot sun.

The road follows a wide and fast flowing river through a valley to Gümüshane, named after the local silver mines which were exhausted some 200 years ago. The town used to have a large Greek population, but after the exchange of populations, Gümüshane started with a clean slate and built the faceless town seen today.

The landscape becomes increasingly arid approaching the village of Tekkeköy, where a dervish shrine, recognised by its conical-shaped roof, stands in the graveyard next to the road. The next town, **Kale**, is built in the shadow of a Byzantine fortress which gives the town its name. The outer walls are in good condition and the ruins can be reached by a track on the left. From Kale the E97 makes a gradual climb up to the Daukdagi Pass (1,875m/6,150ft) and then crosses a deserted plain to Bayburt.

Bayburt is a rural outpost set in a dusty landscape, overlooked by the crumbling fortifications of a castle. The Çoruh Nehri river flows through the centre of the town and a couple of very simple hotels and eating places have balconies overhanging the muddy-coloured water. The women, almost camouflaged, cover themselves with a coarse woven shroud, known as *ihram*. These cloths, woven in natural hand-spun wool, have simple embroidered motifs and are available in the local shops.

A clock tower marks the main square and to the south is **Kebir Cami**, recognised by its distinctive minaret which is decorated with turquoise tiles. The mosque was built in 1225 and has recently been restored with authentic timbers.

The **castle**, originally built by the Armenians, was reconstructed by the Byzantine emperor, Justinian, then by the Bagratids, and most recently by the Ottomans. A small road leads up the hill from the north end of the town to a car-park beneath the main gate. Only the outer walls remain, as the castle was largely destroyed in 1828 by the Russians. There are good views across the town to the hilltop opposite where there are two green-coloured tombs.

From Bayburt the E97 follows the Musat Deresi river to the tiny village of Maden, from where a long ascent is made up to the Kop Dag mountains. The road surface becomes increasingly pot-holed as it approaches the Kop Pass (2,305m/7,560ft) at the summit. The road down the other side is under reconstruction, but the surface improves once it reaches the wide river valley leading to Askale. There is a large military base just outside Askale where the road joins the E23 from Ankara. The Black Sea mountains finally recede into the distance and the Karasu river valley, a tributary of the Euphrates, leads into the flat basin surrounding Erzurum.

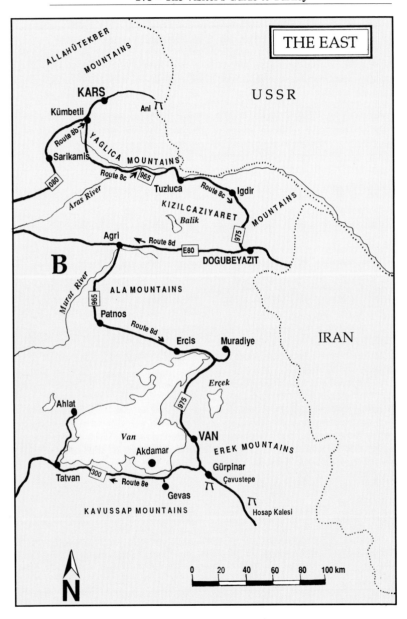

Bayburt town square

Erzurum lies in a shallow basin 1,853m (6,078ft) above sea-level, surrounded by high mountains. The high altitude makes the temperatures cool even in the summer and a light jacket or sweater is needed in the evenings. The city is a stopover point for lorry drivers on the main transport route to Iran and there is a good selection of hotels and restaurants available.

The city's name is derived from the Arabic, *Arz Er Rum*, Land of the Romans. Nothing remains of either the Roman city, or the Byzantine city, known as *Theodosiopolis*. The earliest historical monuments date from the time of the Mongol invasions in the eleventh century. Other buildings date from the Seljuk and Ottoman periods.

Yakutiye Medrese, in the city centre, was built in 1310 by Mongol invaders and named after the grandson of Genghis Khan. The chunky proportions of the tiled minaret and the bold stone-carving indicate a Persian influence. The carved relief on the left side of the portal, depicting two lions beneath a tree with an eagle on top, is particularly striking. Unfortunately, the interior of the building is closed.

Lala Cami is set in the shady gardens directly behind Yakutiye Medresei and is a typical sixteenth-century Ottoman mosque. It was built in 1563 shortly after the Ottoman conquest of Erzurum.

Cumhuriyet Caddesi leads east of Lala Cami to **Ulu Cami**, originally built in 1179, but extensively restored in 1957. It is designed on a rectangular plan, and the large pyramidal dome in the centre of the building is decorated with stylised stalactite carving.

Çifte Minare, built as a theological school, stands to the east and takes its name from the pair of tiled minarets on either side of the main portal. It was built in 1253 under the Seljuk ruler Alaeddin Keykubad II. The courtyard inside is cross-shaped and is surrounded by students' cells and arcades of decorated columns. The lecture hall is at the far end and the Hatuniye turbe, the mausoleum of Keykubad II's daughter, lies underneath it.

A group of three monumental tombs, known as **Üç Kümbetler**, are 300m (328yd) due south of Ulu Cami. The grandest of the three belongs to an early Turkish ruler, Emir Saltuk and is built of decorative red and white stone.

The **fortress** at Erzurum sits on a mound close to the centre of the city, and was originally constructed by the Byzantine emperor Theodosius in the fourth century. It was later rebuilt by the Seljuks and the outer walls are in good condition. Inside there are several cannons, and the tower originally built as a Seljuk minaret in the eleventh century has been converted to a clock tower.

The **bazaar** area is downhill from Lala Cami along the left hand fork. **Rüstem Pasa Han** is one of the most interesting of the market buildings and is a centre for craftsmen working the local stone, *oltu tasi*, a form of jet. To explore other parts of the bazaar, continue downhill and bear right. There is a large agricultural section where the thick felt coats worn by shepherds can be seen for sale.

The local **museum** is a 20-minute walk south of Cumhuriyet Caddesi on Pasalar Caddesi. It contains fragments of mosaics from a church at Gümüshane as well as an impressive collection of Urartian drinking horns and Hellenistic alabaster vases, with local costumes and weaving looms in the ethnographical section.

Route 8b — Erzurum to Kars

(map A, p175 and map B, p178)

The E80 heads east of Erzurum across a dry barren plateau to Pasinler where a crenellated fortress lies to the left of the road and a thermal spring, Kaplicalar, is signposted on the right. A thirteenth-century bridge, the Çoban Dede Köprüsü, crosses the river at Köprüçay. It is 128m (420ft) long and has six pointed arches.

Kars is signposted from Horosan where the E80 forks right along highway 080. The road crosses the plain for 28km (17 miles), and then follows a rocky river valley, passing through beautiful pine forests and grassy vales to Sarikamis, a dull town dominated by a large military base. The road makes the final ascent up onto the Kars plateau where hardy brown sheep graze on the rugged steppeland. The first of many Armenian churches to be seen in the region lies in a field on the right at Kümbetli, a few kilometres before reaching Kars.

Kars lies at an altitude of 1,768m (5,800ft), roughly 25km (15.5 miles) from the Soviet border. It has a rather bleak atmosphere even in the summer when the snow has melted and the sun is shining. Due to the harsh climate and the lack of agriculture, carpet-making is one of the main industries in the region. Most of the carpets are transported directly to the west, but there are a few outlets in the town. Facilities for tourists are limited, even the best hotels are substandard and visitors in search of comfort are recommended to stay in the motel at Sarikamis.

Kars was originally an Armenian town built on the slopes beneath the fortress. Nothing remains of the Armenian city, but the **Church of the Apostles**, built in 932 during the Bagratid era, stands near the river at the foot of the citadel. Now used as a timberyard, it is built of a coarse basalt stone and takes its name from the stylised carvings of the twelve apostles around the outer drum. **Tas Köprü**, an Ottoman bridge, crosses the river to the **fortress** seen ahead. It is built of the same coarse basalt as the church and dates from the Seljuk era. It was extensively rebuilt by the Ottomans and is still in use and only open to the public at weekends.

The only other thing left to do in Kars is to apply for permission to visit the site of *Ani*, the ruins of a deserted Armenian city on the Soviet border. The application is a straightforward routine: passport and car registration documents are first taken to the tourism office on Lise Sokak, and then to the police headquarters, the Emniyet Müdürlügü, where the permission document is drawn up.

The site of *Ani* is marked by yellow signposts from Kars. Twenty-five kilometres (15 miles) from the town, permits and passports must be shown at the *jandarma*, and cameras have to be left here as photography at *Ani* is forbidden. There are no postcards, but rather poor quality photos can be bought from the snack stall at the *jandarma*.

The ruins are a further 10km (6 miles) down the road and lie in the strip of no-man's land between Turkey and the USSR. A guard

Carved relief on Yakutiye Medrese, Erzurum

accompanies visitors from the last military post just outside the village of Ocaklar as the frontier is heavily guarded.

The original site of **Ani** dates back to an ancient Armenian settlement founded in the pre-Christian era, but the ruins seen today mainly date from the ninth century. The site is entered through the main gate set in the original fortifying wall, which was built around 964. The ruins lie spread over the promontory bounded by the deep ravines of the Arpaçay and Alaca Çayi rivers. The remains of ten churches and one mosque are all that are left standing amongst the piles of rubble and broken red stone. A footpath leads visitors around the main churches starting with the eleventh-century **Church of the Redeemer** of which only a section remains. **St Gregory's Church**, built in 1215, is better preserved and is decorated with beautiful frescoes depicting the life of Gregory the Illuminator. The tenth-century **Cathedral of Ani** is also well preserved and is one of the largest surviving Armenian churches in Turkey. A Seljuk mosque, **Menucer Cami**, is built on the edge of the Arpaçay ravine, and the

Harvesting near Kars

citadel, now out of bounds, can be seen on the peninsula jutting into the gorge below. The remains of the **Marco Polo Bridge** lie slightly to the left. The **Great Church**, or the Church of Gagik I, is the next major building. It was constructed in 1001 on an unusual circular ground plan with tall columns which once supported a high dome.

On the way back to the entrance the footpath follows the edge of the Alaca Çayi river gorge where cave-dwellings, which date from the chalcolithic age, can be seen carved in the rock face.

Route 8c — Kars to Dogubeyazit (map B, p178)

There are two possible routes from Kars to Dogubeyazit. The quickest is via Horasan and Agri on the busy E80 to Iran; the quieter and more scenic route follows the Soviet border on highway 965.

Highway 965, signposted to Igdir and Tuzluca, leads off left just after the village of Kümbetli. The road crosses a plateau and makes a gradual climb up to the Pasli Pass (2,020m/6,625ft). Steep hairpin bends follow one after another down from the pass to a sparse rocky valley where a yellow signpost points left to **Yunt Mas Tas Cagiri Magari**, the site of palaeolithic caves. A steep track winds up to the village of Camuslu, from where the ascent up into the mountains must be made on foot.

At Kagizman the road joins the flat bed of the Aras river which gently winds between the bare gullied slopes of the Yaglica and Kizilcaziyaret mountains. At Tuzluca there are salt mines in the cliffs behind the town and it is possible to climb up into some of the salt caves. As the Soviet look-out posts come into sight past Tuzluca, across the Aras river, the road passes within 2km (1.3 miles) of the Soviet Socialist Republic of Armenia.

Igdir is an unremarkable town set in a barren windswept landscape. It may be of interest to visitors that the people here are Shi'ite Moslems and not Suni as in the rest of Turkey. The road heads due south of Igdir and gradually ascends into the foothills surrounding Mount Ararat. After climbing to an altitude of 2,200m (7,216ft), the road crosses the plateau to Dogubeyazit.

 The dormant volcano of **Mount Ararat** (5,165m/16,941ft), locally known as Agri Dag, last erupted in 1840. The summit is popularly believed to be the resting place of the legendary Noah's Ark, and excavators continue to search the lava peak for its remains. In the summer hiking groups make the 3-day climb to the ice-capped summit, but this can only be done with official permission from the Turkish ministry in Ankara, and when accompanied by an approved guide. The travel firm Trek Travel based in Istanbul with a branch office in Dogubeyazit, specialise in climbing expeditions and arrange the necessary papers, but bookings should be made well in advance.

Dogubeyazit is a small town, 35km (21.7 miles) from the Iranian border on the vast plateau at the foot of Mount Ararat. There are a number of hotels and restaurants along the main street which cater for the tourists who come here to visit the nearby eighteenth-century Isak Pasa Palace.

Although Dogubeyazit is now an insignificant town, it had a population of some 250,000 during the Seljuk era. However, in a reprisal for the Kurdish uprisings in the 1930s, the old city was destroyed and abandoned, and only scant remains are left scattered on the hill slopes below the Isak Pasa Palace.

Isak Pasa Palace, the only monument to Dogubeyazit's former days of glory, sits high on a terraced spur, 6km (3.7 miles) east of the town. The architecture of the palace is unlike any other in Turkey, and shows the diverse influences of Persian, Armenian, Georgian, Seljuk and Ottoman-baroque styles. It was commissioned by a wealthy Kurdish vizier, Isak Pasa, in the eighteenth century, and is built around three main courtyards.

A tall decorative portal leads into the spacious outer courtyard which is linked to the smaller, inner courtyard by a second portal. The granaries, store houses and guards' lodgings are on the left, and Isak Pasa's **mausoleum** is on the right. The mausoleum is octagonal and the sides are covered with beautiful carvings. A flight of steps leads down to an underground chamber which contains the tombs. A doorway to the right of the mausoleum leads to the *selamlik*, a series of rooms which originally had balconies looking out over the valley. On the other side of the valley a small Ottoman mosque and the ruins of a Urartian castle can be seen. A vaulted passageway leads from the *selamlik* to the palace **mosque**.

A third portal leads into the **harem**, where there is a splendid **banquet room** decorated with black and white chequered stone. The arcades either side of the room allowed the women of the harem to be kept discreetly out of sight. The corridors surrounding the banquet room lead to a number of bedrooms each with its individual fireplace. The **kitchen** is on the left side of the banquet room and has a boiler room and baths at one end.

Route 8d — Dogubeyazit to Van (map B, p178)

The E80, marked by signposts to Agri from Dogubeyazit, is a fast, busy highway. The road crosses the plain to the **Diyadin Kaplicalari**, a thermal springs, on the left, 37km (23 miles) west of Dogubeyazit.

At Agri follow the signposts to Van, on highway 965, along the scenic course of the Murat Nehri river, a tributary of the Tigris, to Tutak. A poorly-surfaced road then climbs over a range of dry, yellow hills to a large plateau where the town of Patnos is passed on the right and the snowy peak of Süphan Dag (4,434m/14,543ft) looms ahead.

From Ercis there are splendid views of **Lake Van**, one of the highest altitude lakes (1,650m/5,412ft) in the world and the largest in Turkey, covering an area of 3,764sq km. Highway 965 traces the northern shore, which is dotted with small beaches, and then crosses inland for 30km (18 miles) before rejoining the lake edge at Van.

Van, 6km (3.7 miles) from the lake edge, is 1,720m (5,642ft) above sea-level. The town attracts a fair number of tourists and there is a reasonable selection of hotels and restaurants along the main street, Cumhuriyet Caddesi. The numerous carpet shops in the town sell the well known Van *kilim* as well as Iranian flat-weaves. Van is also known for its aromatic herb and garlic cheese, *otlu peynir*, which is often eaten for breakfast. Among the peculiarities of the region is the Van cat with its long, white fur, different colour eyes and reputation as a good swimmer.

The present town was built in 1918 and there are no historical buildings, but the local **museum** is quite good and has an excellent collection of Urartian jewellery, as well as antique *kilim* work from Van and Hakkari. The town is best used as a base from which to visit the surrounding area which has many sights of interest. The tourism office at the southern end of Cumhuriyet Caddesi organise day

Mount Ararat, a dormant volcano

Isak Pasa Palace, Dogubeyazit

Detail of carved portal, Isak Pasa Palace, Dogubeyazit

excursions, which include Van Castle, the Armenian church on Akdamar Island, the Urartian fortress at Çavustepe and the seventeenth-century citadel at Hosap.

Van Castle lies 3km (1.8 miles) west of the town on the sheer rock mass known as the Rock of Van. The outcrop is 1.8km (1.1 miles) long and 120m (394ft) wide, and stands above the scattered remnants of old Van, which was founded by the Armenians on the ancient Urartian site of *Tusba*. It was totally devastated at the start of the century and only the partially collapsed remains of two sixteenth-century mosques, Kaya Celebi Cami and Hüsrev Pasa Cami, and a few monumental tombs, are left standing amongst the debris.

A footpath, marked from the small café at the base of the rock, leads up to the remains of the Urartian citadel which dates from the eighth century BC. The footpath climbs some ancient rock-carved steps to the **tomb of King Argistis** (790-765BC). The outer wall of the tomb is covered by a long cuneiform inscription, dating from 765BC. Inside, there are a number of inter-linked rock chambers with small niches in the walls which originally would have held sacrificial offerings.

The path continues up to a flat, open terrace with a stone-carved platform that was once a temple. The inner keep is directly above.

The footpath continues along the lower walls and then crosses over to the south side of the outcrop to the **tomb of King Sardur II** (765-733BC), carved in the rock. The main chamber is roughly 6m (20ft) by 9m (30ft) and has smaller chambers leading off each side. The chamber on the right has a carved ceiling which gives the effect of a timber roof. There is another **royal mausoleum** complex further along the path, belonging to King Ispuini (815-807BC) and King Menua (804-790BC).

The main part of the **castle** is at the tip of the spur, recognised by the outline of Atatürk and the minaret which sit on the end. The castle served as an important stronghold when Van became Ottoman territory in 1534. Most of the building is Ottoman apart from the large basalt blocks at the base which are Urartian and the smaller, cut stones which are Armenian. The castle summit is the best point from which to see the deserted city spread across the plain below.

Cavustepe is a Urartian citadel, marked by signposts off highway 975, the road to Hakkari. The road climbs up into the Erek mountains, south of Van, to the Kurabas Pass (2,225m/7,298ft). After 23km (14.3 miles) the road forks left at Gürpinar where there is a very well-preserved Urartian waterway, the **Menua Canal**, now known as the Samran Kanal. It used to supply water to *Tusba*, on the Rock of Van.

The Urartian fortress of Cavustepe is a further 2km (1.24 miles) along highway 975, on top of a rocky hill to the right of the road. A small road leads up the hillside to a hollow between the two hilltops where there is a parking area. The castle dates from the reign of King Sardur II (765-733BC) and has lain deserted ever since the collapse of the Urartian empire, around the fifth century BC.

From the car-park follow the signposts to Üçkale. The footpath passes the remains of the original stone stairway and enters the castle through the main gate. Inside the gate are a series of excavated chambers, and a little further on lie the remains of a **temple**. It has a rock-hewn platform and a perfectly preserved cuneiform inscription carved in smooth black basalt. A stone-carved roadway leads to the end of the outcrop where the palace once stood. The hilltop on the opposite side of the car-park has never been excavated and nothing can be seen apart from a rock-carved platform of a temple.

Highway 975 continues across the plateau for a further 32km (20 miles) to the village of Güzelsu. The village lies in the shadow of the high, turreted walls of **Hosap Fortress**, perched on the steep crag to the left of the road. The main road passes a few simple cafés to a left turn, signposted 'kale'. The dusty track winds around the back of the hill to the castle's main gate. Above the entrance way, which lies at the base of a large round tower, an inscription between stone-carved lions is written in Farsi. The fortress was an important Armenian stronghold in the fifteenth century, but was strengthened by the Kurdish chief of the Mahmudi tribe, Sari Süleyman, in 1643. The outer walls are impressive but very little remains inside.

A well-preserved Armenian church stands on the island of **Akdamar**, 43km (26.6 miles) from Van. It is a pleasant excursion, and can be combined with some swimming in the lake. There are picnic facilities on the island, but nowhere to buy food or drink.

The road follows the shore of Lake Van passing through the small resort of Gümüsdere, before heading overland to the town of Gevas. On the edge of the lake, near Gevas, ferries depart regularly to Akdamar Island. There is no schedule, the boats leave whenever they are full. There is a camp-site and restaurant near the jetty.

King Gagik I, a local Armenian ruler of the Artsuni family, built a palace, monastery and church on Akdamar Island in 915-921. Monks continued to inhabit the monastery up until 1890 when it was abandoned. Nothing much remains of the monastery, but the church, known as the **Church of the Holy Cross** is in excellent condition. It is not very large, but the 20m- (65ft-) high conical roof in the centre makes it appear quite tall. The outer walls are decorated with numerous bold reliefs which illustrate scenes from the Bible. Inside the church very little remains of the blue-coloured frescoes, and apart from the tiny chapels either side of the altar the church is quite derelict.

Route 8e — Van to Diyarbakir
(map B, p178, then map A, p175)

A ferry runs across the lake from Van to Tatvan, and the crossing takes 6 hours. The same journey by road takes only 2 hours but there is little of interest to see on the way. Highway 300, signposted to Elazig, follows the lake edge for 60km (37 miles), passing through Edremit, a small resort with a couple of restaurants and a small beach. The cultivated shores of the lake with their stands of poplar trees make a striking contrast to the barren mountains that rise behind. The road climbs into these mountains to the Kusgunkum Pass (2235m/7,331ft) before descending to Tatvan.

Tatvan is an unattractive town on the western edge of the lake with a poor selection of hotels and restaurants. Unfortunately visitors who wish to visit the north-west shore of the lake are faced with the prospect of staying overnight here. The Denizcilik Hotel on the lake edge is the best on offer. Alternatively visitors can travel inland to the more colourful town of Bitlis, but it has an equally poor selection of ac-commodation.

Nemrut Dag is a dormant volcano, 25km (15 miles) north of

Tree clearing near Van

Tatvan. It is one of the largest volcanic craters in the world, measuring 7km (4 miles) from one side to the other. The volcano is only accessible in the summer months and even then the track is barely passable. The soft volcanic ash covering the surface is easily gullied and eroded, and the sides of the track have a tendency to collapse.

The track begins 6km (3.7 miles) from Tatvan, left off highway 965, and heads steeply up the slope. There are no signposts along the way and visitors should bear left wherever there is a choice. At the summit, which is 3,000m (9,840ft) above sea-level, the road climbs over the lip of the crater, from where there are spectacular views down to Lake Van on one side and the crater lake on the other. The track continues for a further 3km (1.8 miles) inside the crater to the edge of the lake, passing by nomadic camps. Care should be taken not to leave vehicles unlocked, or valuables unattended, and no-madic camps should not be approached unless visitors are invited. The nomads keep fierce dogs to guard their flocks and are not accustomed to receiving strangers in their homes.

The volcano last erupted in 1441 and today the ground is covered by ash, pumice stone and a shiny black volcanic rock. The u-shaped lake in the centre is a sparkling blue and patches of snow lie on the steep surrounding slopes all year round. A complete circuit of the lake

Akdamar Island, Lake Van

can be made in about 4 hours, but a tour of the crater rim takes much longer as it is over 22km (13.6 miles). Hikers should protect themselves against the sun, which is very strong although the air is cool.

Ahlat is on the north-west shore of the lake, 39km (24 miles) from Tatvan, on highway 965. Ahlat was an Armenian town that suffered frequent attacks and was ruled by Moslems from the ninth century onwards. The monumental tombs, known as *kümbet*, are the most impressive remains here, but there is also an extensive Seljuk cemetery and the ruins of a castle on the lake shore.

The **Seljuk cemetery** extends for some 2km (1.3 miles) along the highway on the left. The tall, rectangular gravestones date from between the twelfth and fifteenth centuries. The first *kümbet*, **Hasan Padisah Türbesi**, is on the right after the cemetery. Built for a Seljuk leader in 1275, it is typical of the Ahlat *kümbet* with its crypt set beneath a chamber covered by a conical roof. A little further on, 300m (328yd) from the main road on the right, stands the largest *kümbet* in Ahlat, **Seyh Necmettin Kümbeti**. A small museum with a modest collection of locally found pottery and artefacts, dating from the Urartian era up to Seljuk and Ottoman times, lies on the opposite side of the road.

The ruins of the **castle** can be reached by following a dusty track

Carved relief showing Jonah and the Whale *on the south wall of Akdamar church*

on the right to the lake shore. The Ottoman sultan, Süleyman II, started building the castle in 1554, and it was finished by Selim II in 1568. The ruined mosque just inside the main gateway, Iskender Pasa Cami, was built in 1564-70. There is little else to see inside the castle walls but it is pleasant to wander through the grassy courtyards in the shade of the walnut trees.

Continuing along highway 965, an Ottoman cemetery is passed on the right where a track leads off left to a pair of thirteenth-century *kümbet*, known as the **Iki Kümbet**. Another left turn takes visitors along an earthen road to **Kesis Kümbet**. Two more *kümbet* are passed on the right before reaching the mosque, Yeni Cami. One of the most decorative *kümbet* in Ahlat, **Bayindir Kümbet** stands on the corner of the left fork just after the mosque. It has attractive colonnaded windows around its drum and was built in the fifteenth century for a local ruler, Bayindir. The track continues past Bayindir Kümbet back to the main road where the modern town of Ahlat lies straight ahead.

Bitlis is 25km (15 miles) south-west of Tatvan on highway 965. Just before the turning to Mus, 14km (8.7 miles) from Tatvan, there is a large Ottoman caravanserai, **Elaman Han**. It is built of a warm-coloured stone and has open summer quarters as well as closed winter ones and is now inhabited by large numbers of tortoises. There is another caravanserai at **Bashan**, dating from the fourteenth century, but it is usually kept locked. Approaching Bitlis, the Seljuk caravanserai, **Babsin Han**, is passed on the right. It was built in 1291 and has a very attractive carved portal.

Bitlis, the centre of a tobacco-growing region, is built between two river valleys and lies at an altitude of 1,550m (5,084ft). A **citadel**, built by Batlis, one of Alexander the Great's generals, stands on a high rock between the two rivers which converge at the opposite end of the town, to form the Bitlis Suyu, a tributary of the Tigris. **Serefiye Cami**, built in 1528 by a local Kurdish ruler, stands on the banks of the Bitlis Suyu in the middle of the lively bazaar. **Ulu Cami**, built by the Artukids in 1126, is nearby and can be distinguished by its squat minaret.

The road follows the Bitlis Suyu river to the south, passing tobacco factories, before climbing up between the Züpser and Kavussahap mountains. The road follows picturesque valleys to Baykan. At Catakköprü, a left turn leads to Batman where there are several oil wells. Beyond the turning the road passes the **Malaabadi Bridge**, built in 1146 with a single broad arch, 37m (121ft) wide.

Silvan is built on the site of the Byzantine city of *Martyropolis*, of which there are no remains. Outside Diyarbakir the road crosses the Tigris, the Dicle in Turkish, and the dark basalt walls come into view.

9

THE SOUTH-EAST

The Mesopotamian plain, often referred to as the cradle of civilisation, lies between the Euphrates and the Tigris. The influence of Mesopotamia on the early civilisations in south-east Turkey was considerable and the area is dotted with ancient settlements, called *tell*. Cuneiform tablets record the existence of sophisticated trading settlements in the region as far back as 3300BC. Later known as Chaldea in the Bible, the area is believed to be the birthplace of Abraham. This ancient landscape, now barren and virtually uninhabited, will soon become a wealthy agricultural region. The Atatürk Baraj, a huge dam across the Euphrates, will flood the land between Adiyaman and Urfa and provide irrigation for a vast area.

The distances between the towns in the south-east are large and a tour of the region involves a lot of travelling. Most visitors only come to see Nemrut Dag, but those who spend more time in the region will notice many distinct cultural differences and styles of architecture. Most of the population in the south-east is Kurdish, but there are also Arabs living close to the Syrian border. The government has tried to mix the population, by re-settling Turks and moving Kurds to other regions in Turkey. The Kurds are very sensitive about the way they are treated by the Turks and the PKK, a Kurdish revolutionary group, makes regular attacks on the towns and villages along the border. Visitors should check the current situation with the local authorities before visiting the more remote areas close to the Syrian border.

Route 9 is a circular tour that starts and finishes in Adana. It is divided into five stages each of which can be covered in a day, although it is best to allow 2 days for a visit to Nemrut Dag. Information about Adana is to be found in Route 6a.

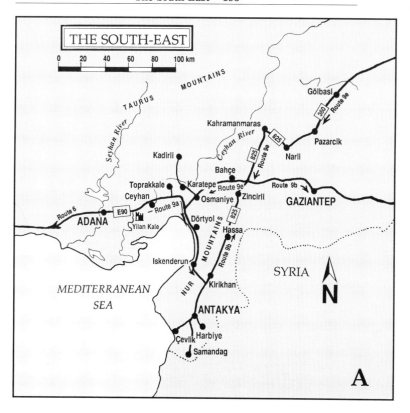

Route 9a — Adana to Antakya (map A)

The E90 to Gaziantep and Ceyhan crosses the Seyhan river into the cotton-growing plain of the Çukurova. The road is flat and well surfaced, and there are numerous fuel stations catering for the convoys of slow diesel trucks and oil tankers that use the highway. Snack bars line the road serving the local *ayran*, yoghurt drink, and *sikma*, thin sheets of unleavened bread.

Forty-one kilometres (25.4 miles) east of Adana the fairy-tale turrets of **Yilankale** come into sight. It is a well-preserved fortress thought to have been built by Leo II, King of Cilician Armenia, at the end of the twelfth century. A turning on the right leads up to a small parking area at the foot of the castle walls. From here a steep footpath climbs to the first gate. The walls tower overhead and visitors must scramble up the rocks to the second and third gateways above.

Inside the upper walls there is a large vaulted hall, partly hewn from the natural rock. The remains of a small church lie to the east and another vaulted hall can be seen to the north. The towers on either side of the upper gate are in particularly good condition. Stairs lead up to the parapets from where there are good views across the plain to the river and town of Ceyhan.

The E90 crosses the Ceyhan river, and on a clear day Dumlu Castle can be seen in the distance to the left. The road continues across the plain to **Toprakkale**, an Armenian fortress built to defend the plain of Issus which lies to the south. The dark stone fortress is not as well preserved as Yilankale, but it is easily accessible. A small road leads up to a car-park just below the main gate.

Toprakkale is in the middle of a large road junction where the E98 heads south to Iskenderun and Antakya. The road crosses the plain of Issus where Alexander the Great defeated the Persian King Darius III in 333BC. The scant remains scattered over the plain are all that remain of the ancient Seleucid city, *Epiphania*.

At **Payas**, 21km (13 miles) before Iskenderun, a fortified caravanserai lies 2km (1.2 miles) from the main road. This huge complex, with its two large courtyards, was built in 1574. It has been well restored and there is an impressive arcade of twenty-five shops and a double baths along one side, with stables, kitchens, and dining halls around the two courtyards. A *medrese* with twenty student cells, and an attractive mosque, stand nearby. The castle, **Çin Kalesi**, stands opposite the main entrance to the caravanserai. It was built by the Venetians and is surrounded by a moat.

The road continues along the coast with the Nur mountains rising steeply on the left and citrus orchards and mimosa trees growing at the roadside.

Iskenderun is named after Alexander. It stands on the site of *Alexandretta*, which was built in 333BC following the Persian defeat, but there are no remains of the ancient city. The town is dominated by a large commercial port, and there is a good selection of hotels and restaurants close to the sea-front.

A good highway zig-zags up the Nur mountains for 8km (5 miles) to Sarimazi, a small mountain village where there is a handful of good hotels and restaurants. The road continues up past the village of Belen to the Belen Pass, 740m (2,427ft) at the summit. The highway descends to a junction at the foot of the mountains, from where the 825 heads south towards Antakya. Shortly after the junction, a small road leads off right to **Batras Kalesi** near the village of Örençay, 4km (2.5 miles) from the main road. The castle stands on the Seleucid site of *Pagrae* and was built during the crusades, when it was the main crusader stronghold in the region. A footpath leads up the castle slope from the village square. Inside the walls there is a large hall with three arched windows and a well-preserved chapel.

Antakya is the capital of Turkey's most southerly province, the Hatay. The city is only 50km (31 miles) from the Syrian border and has something of an Arabic atmosphere. Many of the inhabitants of the Hatay speak Arabic rather than Turkish and television programmes are broadcast with Arabic subtitles.

A reasonable selection of restaurants and hotels can be found on either side of the river, the ancient *Orontes*, which flows through the centre of the city. Many of the local dishes in Antakya are influenced by Syrian cuisine. *Peynirli künefe*, a finely shredded pastry filled with white cheese and honey is worth sampling.

The ancient city of Antakya, *Antioch*, was founded by Seleucus Nicator in 300BC. The region was annexed to the Roman empire in 67BC by Pompey, and the **Hatay Mosaic Museum**, on the round- about near the river, contains some of the finest Roman mosaics in Asia Minor. They were mostly found during the excavations of ancient *Daphne* and date from the second and third centuries. On the opposite side of the river there is an interesting bazaar.

Two kilometres (1.2 miles) to the east of the bazaar, on the road to Reyhanli, a yellow sign points right to **St Peter's Grotto**. A church was built by the crusaders around the cave where St Peter is believed to have preached to some of the earliest Christian converts. A service is still held on the first Sunday of every month.

The main part of the church is hewn from natural rock and water drips from the cavern roof into a baptismal font. In the left corner there is a tunnel, down which worshippers could escape if the church was raided. It is now blocked off, but it originally led 200m (218yd) away to **Haron**, the site of an ancient sanctuary. *Haron* can be reached by following the path below the church, along the rock face. The sanctuary is thought to be a Hellenistic shrine dedicated to Haron, the god of fire.

Harbiye, 9km (5.6 miles) south of Antakya, was originally named *Daphne*, after the nymph who, according to legend, escaped Apollo by transforming herself into a bay tree. During Roman times it was the site of a temple to Apollo, numerous palaces, and had a reputation for decadence throughout the Roman world. The mosaics from the palaces are now in the Hatay Mosaic Museum. Harbiye is now a popular picnic area and at weekends family outings are made to the waterfalls in the valley. The air is cool and fresh and there is a good selection of hotels and restaurants built along the edge of the valley.

The road from Antakya to Samandag follows the ancient *Orontes* valley to Üzünbagi where a yellow sign points left down a track to the remains of the monastery of Stylite Simeon the Minor, 7km (4 miles)

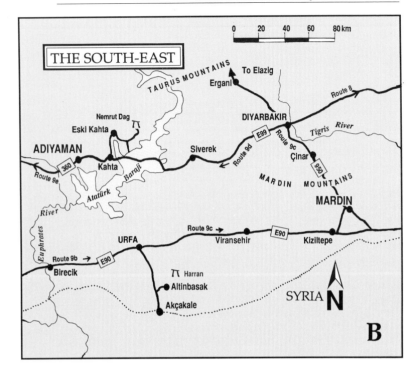

from the main road.

Samandag is just inland from the coast and Çevlik is the nearest beach. There are camp-sites and *pansiyon* built along the beach and the ancient site of *Seleucia-ad-Pieria* lies nearby. The site can be reached by following the signposts to Magaracik. The footpath leads behind a *pansiyon* and then heads right to the **Titas ve Vespasiyanus Tuneli**, an immense rock-hewn tunnel. It was built by the emperor Vespasian in the first century AD to divert the river away from the harbour which was in danger of silting up. The 8m- (26ft-) tall tunnel is just a small section of the channel, 1.3km (0.8miles) long, that directed the river to the coast.

At the tunnel entrance, a small white sign points right to Magaracik, the ancient necropolis. The most impressive of the tombs is the royal crypt, a vast rock-hewn chamber with shell and flower motifs carved on the ceiling and open graves covering the floor.

Decorating brassware with a traditional design, Gaziantep

Route 9b — Antakya to Urfa

(map A, p195 and map B, p198)

Follow highway 825 north, across the junction with the E98, to Kirikhan. The road follows the Syrian border along the east slopes of the Nur mountains, past the eleventh-century castle, **Darb-i Sak Kalesi** on the left. After the village of Hassa a yellow signpost points right to the prehistoric mounds of **Tilmenhöyük** (10km/6 miles), and **Yesemek** (30km/18 miles). At Fevzipasa another sign indicates a Hittite site, 3km (1.8 miles) from the main road at **Zincirli**. Shortly after the turning to Zincirli the road joins the E90 to Gaziantep.

Gaziantep is a wealthy city, renowned for its pistachio nuts and tradition in metal crafts. There are few buildings of any historical interest and the city is rarely visited by tourists, but it is worth stopping by to see the bazaar and to taste the top-class *baklava*. There are a number of reasonable hotels, but nothing luxurious, and plenty of restaurants.

The bazaar is located at the western end of the city and covers a maze of narrow streets. It has many interesting areas and in the copper section craftsmen can be seen working the metal by hand. An eleventh-century Seljuk fortress stands on a mound to the south of the bazaar, but it is not open to the public.

The E90 heads east towards Urfa, climbing over low hills dotted with pistachio plantations and vineyards. **Birecik** is built on the steep banks of the Euphrates river where a twelfth-century crusader castle sprawls along the bank. After Birecik the road cuts through the Arat mountains (800m/2,642ft) and the land gradually becomes increasingly barren. At Onbirnisan, 40km (25 miles) before Urfa, the road passes the Çarmelik Kervansaray.

Urfa was renamed Sanliurfa (Glorious Urfa) after the declaration of the Turkish republic. It lies on the north Mesopotamian plain, 55km (34 miles) from the Syrian border, at an altitude of 580m (1,902ft). The city has a strong middle-eastern character and although Turkish is spoken by everyone, Arabic and Kurdish are commonly heard on the streets. The old quarter around the bazaar has kept much of its original atmosphere and many of its old buildings. Known as Ur-of-Chaldees in the Bible, the city is also an important stopping place for the 85,000 Moslem pilgrims on their way to Mecca, who stop every year in Urfa to visit the shrine of Abraham.

There is a good selection of hotels and restaurants in the town, centred around the area of Köprü Basi. Urfa cuisine is well known throughout Turkey and the Urfa kebab, and *patlican* kebab, are well worth trying. *Mirra*, a strong black coffee made with ground berries, is another speciality local to the region.

The old city quarter and other places of interest are reached by heading south along Sarayönü Caddesi. **Ulu Cami** is a good starting point for a tour of the city. The tall octagonal tower in the graveyard used to be the bell tower of a Byzantine church, known as Kizil Kilise, which was built in AD457. The mosque is one of the oldest in Urfa and dates from 1170-75.

The **bazaar** lies just beyond Ulu Cami. In the centre the *bedesten* sells attractive hand-printed silks and embroidered cloths, as well as *sumak*, a type of embroidered *kilim*. **Gümrük Han**, built as a customs house in 1562, is nearby. The inner courtyard contains a busy tea-gardens, while tailors work in the small vaulted ateliers on the upper floors. **Hüseyin Pasa Carsisi**, a double arcade, is lined with copper workshops and is close to Gümrük Han.

West of the bazaar is a series of religious complexes and a number of pleasant tea-gardens. **Mevlid Halil Cami** stands next to the grotto which is identified as Abraham's birthplace. It is well attended by Moslems and has separate entrances for men and women. The large modern mosque to the west, Yeni Cami, is decorated with blue and white tiles. The most important mosque complex is built around a long rectangular fish pool, known as **Abraham's Pool**. **Rizvaniye Vakfi Cami**, built in 1716, is on the left side of the pool and has an attractive portal decorated with black and white stone. **Halil-Urrahman Cami** lies directly next to it and is believed by Moslems to be the place where Abraham landed after being catapulted from the castle by King Nimrud. By a miracle the fire in which he landed turned to water and the burning wood to fish. This offers an explanation as to why the pool is kept brimming with carp. The building at the very end of the pool, near the toilets, is a *Koran* school.

Anzilhat Parki is a pleasant shady garden built along one side of the pool. There are numerous tea-houses and restaurants in the park and it is a good place to rest before climbing up to the **citadel**. Steps lead from the behind the gardens up to the gate in the citadel walls. The citadel stands on the site of ancient *Edessa*, but the remains seen today date from the time of the crusades. The two tall columns at the summit are said to mark the point from which Nimrud threw Abraham.

Harran lies at the crossroads of the ancient Mesopotamian trade routes, 44km (27 miles) south of Urfa and daily tours are organised from Urfa. The road is signposted to Akçakale and a left turn is marked to the village of Altinbasak. The road passes through Altinbasak to **Eski Harran** where the villagers live in peculiar bee-hive shaped houses. The road leads through the **Aleppo Gate** down to a parking space in front of the eleventh-century **castle**. The castle walls are quite well preserved and there are good views across the

Abraham's pool, Urfa

 humped roofs of Eski Harran to the Mesopotamian plain which stretches into the distance beyond.

A path leads through the village towards a ruined **minaret** about 500m (546yd) away. This is all that remains of the twelfth-century mosque, originally part of a vast complex which included one of the earliest universities in Islam. However nothing much remains apart from the base of a fountain which stands in the centre of a large courtyard covered in broken columns and stones.

Route 9c — Urfa to Diyarbakir (map B, p198)

The E90, signposted to Viransehir and Mardin from Urfa, crosses a flat and monotonous plain on a reasonably well-surfaced but busy road. A caravanserai, **Hanel Bagur**, is marked by a signpost on the right 40km (25 miles) from Urfa. The ruins of an ancient city, *Sualp*, and an ancient shrine, **Sogmatar Haberi** can be reached by following this road in the direction of Eski Harran.

Viransehir, a small oasis in the barren plain, is built on the site of

Metalware shop,
Urfa

ancient *Constantina*. From here the road heads towards the Mardin mountains, and at Kiziltepe the road forks left and begins the climb up to Mardin.

Mardin is situated on the steep slopes of Mazi Dag, overlooking the Mesopotamian plain, 1,083m (3,552ft) above sea-level. It has the air of a place that has seen better times; crumbling palatial houses and large mosques are surrounded by narrow back-streets of poverty and squalor. The population is an odd mixture of Christians and Moslems, and many languages, including Arabic, Aramaic, Syrian, Turkish and Kurdish are spoken. There are eleven Syrian Orthodox churches in the town, but the Christian population is on the decline and there are only ninety households left. There is one reasonable hotel with a restaurant in the town, the few *lokanta* along the main street are only open during the day.

Sultan Isa Medrese is one of Mardin's finest monuments. It can be reached by climbing the steps which lead up the hill, half-way along the main street, Birinci Caddesi. The *medrese* is entered through a beautiful, stone-carved portal on the right. Inside, the building is still very much in use as a girls' *Koran* school, but visitors are welcome to look around. The courtyard at the far end of the building contains the tomb of the Artukid Sultan Isa, who built the *medrese* in 1385. A stairway leads up onto the flat roof that surrounds the distinctive, fluted dome of the mosque. Up above the *medrese*, the hilltop castle marks the Roman site of *Marida*. Below the *medrese*, in the centre of town, is the enormous minaret of Ulu Cami.

Ulu Cami is in the middle of the bazaar, downhill from Birinci Caddesi. It was built in the eleventh century by the Seljuks and has a large, fluted dome. **Latifiye Cami**, slightly west of Ulu Cami, dates from 1371 and has a beautifully carved façade. It is well worth spending some time wandering around the bazaar area which surrounds these two mosques. The atmosphere is very lively and there is plenty of local colour.

Sehirediye Cami is further east along Birinci Caddesi. Built in the thirteenth century during the Artukid dynasty it has a finely decorated minaret.

Kasim Pasa Medrese lies in the plain below and is a 45-minute walk from the town. From the road which runs along the bottom of the town, head west to the **Seyh Hammed Zirar Cami**. From here a rough track leads towards **Mehail Kilisesi**, an isolated church on the slopes below. A well-used path leads west from the church for about a kilometre before the fluted domes of Kasim Pasa Medrese come into sight on the slope ahead. The complex was built in the fifteenth century by Kasim Pasa, the leader of the Ak Koyunlu (White Sheep) tribe. He is buried in the tomb which lies on one side of the courtyard. There is an attractive fountain in the middle of the courtyard, but the door to the *medrese* is usually locked.

Deygrulzaferan is one of the many beautiful Syrian Orthodox monasteries that are built in the area around Mardin. It lies 4km (2.5 miles) from the town, on a small road marked by signposts, off the main highway to Nusaybin. It is set in the middle of the countryside, at the foot of a steep mountain, overlooking the Mesopotamian plain. The monastery is still used by a small Syrian Orthodox community, which is made up of a bishop, four men, four women and twenty-five students, but the monastery has greatly dwindled in importance since its foundation in the fifth century. The services are conducted in Aramaic and many Aramaic stone-carved inscriptions can be seen on the walls of the building.

Visitors are welcome to look around inside and will be shown around by a member of the monastery staff. The building surrounds a central courtyard and is built on two storeys. The **crypt**, on the ground floor, contains the sarcophagi of the former bishops who are buried in a seated position and next to it is the **church**. Both buildings date from the fifth century and have beautifully carved doors and niches. The **baptistry** is the next building round the courtyard. It doesn't see much use these days and is used as a store room for redundant items such as the two antique bishop's litters. The **dormitories** are on the upper floor where there is a small stone **belfry** and a flat stone roof built around the fluted dome of the church.

On the mountainside above Deygrulzaferan there are two deserted monasteries, partly built into the natural rock. They can be reached by a steep 45-minute climb up the path behind the monastery. **St Jacob's Monastery** is on the right and **Mary's Monastery** is to the left, near a large cave.

Highway 950 from Mardin to Diyarbakir is a poorly-surfaced, narrow road. It climbs over a range of hills to a rolling plain, which gradually becomes less undulating as it approaches Diyarbakir. The road follows the course of the Tigris river where tobacco and watermelons grow on the sandy banks. Diyarbakir is famous for its giant water-melons and holds the national record of 50kg (110lb).

Diyarbakir has a predominantly Kurdish population and Kurdish is the language heard most often on the streets. Despite the irrigation potential of the Tigris the city has an impoverished appearance, and hoards of scruffy children play in streets which can only be described as filthy and squalid. The summer heat brings sanitation problems and gastro-enteritis is rife. Despite this the city has a bustle and excitement that make it worth stopping here, especially as there is a good selection of hotels and restaurants.

The most striking feature of Diyarbakir is the dark basalt wall that surrounds the city. It is an impressive 5.5km (3.4 miles) long and has seventy-two towers and four main gates. The **citadel**, in the northeast corner, is a good point from which to start a tour of the city. It is reached by walking east along Izzet Pasa Caddesi to the fortified gateway, known as **Saray Kapi**. **Hazretti Süleyman Cami**, inside the citadel wall, has an unusual square minaret, decorated with black and white stonework. It was built during the Artukid dynasty, in 1160. The ruins of the **Church of St George** also stand inside the citadel, but at present they are in a military zone and cannot be visited. A walk-way leads along the top of the citadel walls from where there is a panoramic view over the Tigris river.

The Ottoman mosque, **Fatih Pasa Cami**, lies to the south of the citadel. It was built in 1522 and is decorated with the local black and white stone, but is only open during prayer times. In the side streets to the west of the mosque there is an Armenian church, **Sürp Giragöz**, which is best found by looking for its distinctive belfry. The church is enclosed within a courtyard that contains a number of

Villagers making dung patties, Eski Harran

Armenian homes. A few Armenian families still live here and someone usually has the key to the church.

Ulu Cami is one of Diyarbakir's finest monuments and can be easily identified by its tall, square tower. It was originally built as the Syriac cathedral of Mar-Toma, St Thomas, but was converted to a mosque in 639 when the Baqr dynasty invaded and gave the city its present name 'place of the Baqr'. It was rebuilt by the Seljuk sultan, Malik Shah, in 1091, but many of the original stones can be seen along the elegant colonnades that surround the courtyard. Two finely patterned relief carvings decorate the upper walls. One is composed of acanthus and vine leaves, the other of stylised kufic lettering. A *Koran* school forms one side of the courtyard and two ablution fountains with conical roofs stand in the centre. Inside the mosque there is a beautiful wood-carved ceiling dating from the Ottoman period. The mosque is one of the five holiest places in the Islamic world, and visitors should take care to dress appropriately. Two *medrese* stand in the back streets near the mosque, **Mesüdiye**

Mardin: Ulu Cami minaret and view over the Mesopotamian plain

Medrese and **Zinarli Medrese**, but both are closed for restoration.

There are two museums in the city and both are in traditional local houses. The **Ziya Gökalp Müzesi** is to the south-west of Ulu Cami and was the home of a philosopher and doctor in 1876-1924. The house surrounds a courtyard and is built of the local basalt stone. **Safa Cami** is in the alley opposite the museum and is worth visiting if only to see its minaret and fine tiles. The **Kültür Müzesi** is housed in the home of a nineteenth-century poet, Cahit Sitki Taranca. The building is attractively decorated with black and white patterned stonework.

The **bazaar** lies in the area surrounding Ulu Cami. It is quite extensive and colourful and is a good place to look for traditional textiles. Carpets and *kilim* can be found in **Hasan Pasa Han**, a sixteenth-century building surrounding an open courtyard.

Melek Ahmet Caddesi leads to the west city gate, Urfa Kapi. **Mereyemana Kilisesi**, a Syrian Orthodox church, stands near here in the small street opposite Melek Ahmet Cami. The church was built on the site of a seventh-century monastery and the buildings around the courtyard are the homes of local Syrian Orthodox families. Inside the church there is a row of private chapels, each separated by an intricately fretted wooden screen.

 One of the best-preserved stretches of the city wall lies between Urfa Kapi and Mardin Kapi and has a footpath running along the top. The **Ulu Badan**, the great wall, and the large tower, **Yedi Kardes**, are passed on the way. The outer faces of the walls are decorated with the Seljuk motifs of lions and eagles. Tea-houses can be found along the base of the walls and near Mardin Kapi there is a seventeenth-century black and white patterned caravanserai called **Delliler Han**. From here the main road leads back to the town centre.

Route 9d — Diyarbakir to Adiyaman

(map B, p198)
The E99 heads across the dry undulating plain due west of Diyarbakir and crosses the Euphrates before climbing over gentle hills to the Kahta river valley.

Kahta is a small town with a selection of hotels and camp-sites which cater for the large number of tourists who visit the tumulus of Nemrut Dag. Adiyaman, a larger town, is 25km (15 miles) further along the highway. The road passes a selection of comfortable hotels as it approaches the town.

Adiyaman has a mediocre selection of hotels and restaurants, and a few shops which sell copper and *kilim* to the passing tourists. There is a small museum on the main highway west of the town which houses some of the relics of Samsat, the former Byzantine *Samosata*, which is now beneath the waters of the Atatürk Baraj.

Kahta and Adiyaman both provide convenient bases for touring the land of the Commagene, the smallest kingdom in the ancient world, which was founded by King Mithridates in the first century BC. The kingdom reached its peak between 69-43BC under the rule of Antiochus I, who built the large tumulus, under which he is believed to be buried, on the summit of Nemrut Dag.

Due to its remote location **Nemrut Dag** is only accessible between May and October when the roads are free of snow. The ascent is not easy even in summer, as the road is narrow, poorly surfaced and very steep. Most visitors join a group tour organised by their hotel, and at 2am convoys of minibuses and jeeps set out to reach the site in time for the sunrise. The ruins are much less crowded during the day and just as impressive at sunset.

Most of the traffic follows the 70km (43.4 miles) road 9km (6 miles) east of Kahta up to Nemrut Dag, returning through Eski Kahta on the road that leads directly to Kahta. There are a number of motels and camp-sites along the roadside near the summit where the tours stop for tea on the way up, and breakfast on the way down.

The road ends at a car-park, where there is a cafeteria and some souvenir stalls. The tumulus is a 20-minute climb up the footpath behind the cafeteria. At the summit, a lonely peak 2,150m (7,052ft) above sea-level, a vast heap of stones 50m (164ft) high is piled up on a rock-cut platform. It is believed that the tomb of Antiochus I lies somewhere beneath the mound of limestone, but although many attempts have been made to find it none have been successful. The last attempt to force a way in, using dynamite to clear the stones, resulted in the partial destruction of the tumulus which used to be 75m (246ft) tall.

A ceremonial way runs around the base of the tumulus and links the two terraces which lie either side, one facing the sunrise, the other the sunset. The terraces were originally lined with giant statues of weather gods. Only the heads now remain, but their size, some 10m (32ft) high, gives an indication of the monumental scale of the original statues. The vast thrones on which the gods were seated also remain and are carved from blocks of limestone thought to weigh about 5 tons a piece.

Antiochus I wished to be deified after his death and so built his tomb in this high remote spot to be as near the gods as possible. On the east terrace his statue is even placed amongst the gods. The heads of Apollo, Fortuna and Zeus lie to his left and Heracles to his right. Smaller statues were made of the royal family and originally stood on the plinths at either end of the terraces, while the platform at the front of the east terrace served as an altar. The statues on the west terrace are more weathered but larger than those on the east terrace. The head of Fortuna on the west terrace is particularly grand, and a fine stone-carved relief shows King Antiochus I shaking hands with the gods.

The road winds down from Nemrut Dag through the villages of Tutanocak and Kustepe to the Cenderes river valley. **Arsemia**, the ancient Commagene capital, sits on a square-topped hill just after the village of Damlacik. A rough track leads to a car-park, from where a footpath climbs steeply up, past a carved relief of Mithras, the sun god, who points the way to the temple. Further along the path, fourteen stone-cut steps lead down to a burial chamber, 9m (29ft) deep. An excellent, carved relief shows Antiochus I shaking hands with Hercules, who is holding a club in one hand. It stands above and to the right of the burial chamber. Below the relief is the entrance to a steep tunnel, thought to have led down to the river 158m (518ft) below. On the summit of the hill, all that remains of the palace and temple dedicated to Mithridates is a flat terrace scattered with stones.

The fortress of Eski Kâhta can be seen on the other side of the valley.

The thirteenth-century fortress at **Eski Kâhta**, also known as Yeni Kale, is built on the side of a sheer gorge, 300m (984ft) above the Kahta Cay river. The castle was built by the Mamelukes on the site of an earlier Commagene palace. It is in excellent condition and has impressive battlements along the outer walls and a maze of stairways and corridors surrounding the inner keep.

The road leads from Eski Kâhta to a Roman bridge crossing the Cenderes river, known as the **Cenderes Köprüsü**. It was built by Septimus Severus (193-211) and has a single arch which stretches for 92m (301ft) from one side of the river to the other.

Karakus tumulus, signposted off the road that leads back to Kahta, is the burial place of the Commagene women. The mound is made up of loose stones, similar to Nemrut Dag, but only stands 21m (69ft) high. Four columns surround the mound each with a different carving on top. The site takes its name, Black Bird, from the eagle carved on the column to the east of the mound.

Route 9e — Adiyaman to Adana

(map B, p198, then map A, p195)

Highway 360 crosses a wide plain before climbing over undulating hills planted with vineyards and orchards. From the small lakeside town of Gölbasi the road follows the Aksu Çay river valley to Narli, where it joins highway 835. Follow the road to the right through fields of cotton for 30km (18 miles) to Kahramanmaras.

Kahramanmaras lies at an altitude of 568m (1,863ft) on the edge of the Taurus mountain range. There are a few good hotels in the town and a number of restaurants, although many close in the evenings. It is worth trying the local *baklava* and ice-cream. The ice-cream is known as *maras*, and although it can be found all over Turkey, the original recipe, which includes mastic, comes from Kahramanmaras.

The **bazaar** area runs alongside the main square, Meydan. The small streets are lined with workshops where craftsmen beat out copper bowls or make saddles for donkeys. The atmosphere is rural, friendly and unspoilt. The bazaar mosque, the sixteenth-century **Ulu Cami** is at the far end of the bazaar. **Tas Medrese** stands across the main road at the corner of an underground shopping precinct. The *medrese* still functions as a boys' *Koran* school and contains the Seljuk tomb of Ama Mehmet Bey and his wives.

The main road heads uphill, past the post office where a yellow signpost indicates the turning on the left to the castle, **Kale**. Very little remains of the castle which was built during the reign of Süleyman I (1520-1566), but the hilltop is covered by shady tea-gardens and is a pleasant resting spot.

Saddle maker,
Kahramanmaras

The small **museum** is at the opposite end of town, on 12 Eylül Bulvari, near the bus station. It has a mixed collection of local artefacts which range from prehistoric to Ottoman times.

Highway 825 heads south of Kahramanmaras across fields of cotton, passing the town of Türkoglu before joining the E90 to Adana. The E90 climbs up the Aslanli Beli Pass (970m/3,181ft), which is often congested with lorries, and continues past Bahçe to Osmaniye. Yellow signposts point right to the sites of *Karatepe* and *Hieropolis*, along the road to Kadirli.

Hieropolis was the capital of a small independent kingdom in 52BC. The ruins of the city are 15km (9.3 miles) from the E90, at the foot of the prominent fortress, *Castabala*. A footpath leads across the cotton fields and up into the fortress, from where most of *Hieropolis* can be seen spread out below. The overgrown **theatre** and the roadway lined with Corinthian columns are the only substantial remains of the city.

The Kadirli road continues for a further 10km (6 miles) over a range of rocky hills before *Karatepe* is signposted up an unsurfaced track on the left. **Karatepe**, a neo-Hittite citadel, lies on the edge of Ceyhan Lake, inside a national park area. There are basic camping facilities and a picnic area inside the park, but there is nowhere to buy food or drink. Excavation is still underway at Karatepe and it is necessary to tour the site under the supervision of the guardian; photography is forbidden.

The citadel stands on a mound, enclosed by a wall that has monumental gateways on the north and south sides. It was built as a summer palace in the eighth century BC for Asitawandas, King of Hittite Cilicia. The gates have been the main focus of the excavation work and carved reliefs on large slabs of basalt have been restored to their original positions around the entrances.

The footpath leads across the citadel mound to the second gate where vast stone-carved sphinxes with ivory eyes guard the entrance. The relief carvings lining the walls of the second gate are even better preserved than those in the first gate. Pagan gods, including a sun god and a monkey god, are carved alongside scenes of hunting and merrymaking in the palace. In one panel a woman is depicted suckling her child, and as in the first gate, hieroglyphic inscriptions are accompanied by Phoenician translations.

Osmaniye caters for the enormous number of oil tankers and transport lorries that pass through and there are countless service stations along the road. The highway crosses the plain past the castle of Toprakkale and joins the E5 to Adana, details of which can be found in Route 9a.

10
CENTRAL ANATOLIA
AND CAPPADOCIA

Central Anatolia has a rich selection of historical remains and one of the most fascinating landscapes in Turkey. The scenery in Cappadocia, at the southern edge of Central Anatolia, is unique. The land is covered in a thick bed of volcanic ash, originating from Erciyes, a 3,916m-high (12,845ft-) volcano, just south of Kayseri. Over the centuries the ash has become a soft tufa rock, worn by weather and time into weird shapes and formations, while the land has developed fertile soils and is one of the major grape-growing regions in Turkey. To the west of the region, around Aksaray, the land couldn't be more different. The earth is dry and barren and can barely support the small flocks of sheep that graze there. The area between Aksaray and Ankara, the capital city of Turkey, is covered by the salt lake of Tuz Gölü and is equally bare.

The route is planned as a circular tour which starts and finishes in Samsun (see Route 7d) on the Black Sea coast. There are five stages to the tour. Two or three days are required to see Cappadocia, and Route 10a could easily be spread over 2 days, staying overnight in Amasya. Other stages of the route can be completed in 1 day.

Route 10a — Samsun to Sivas (map A, p214)

Highway 795 to Ankara leads from Samsun up over the Canik mountains to Havza, a small town built over hot springs. The left turn to Amasya on highway 180 follows a tributary of the Yesilirmak river. Peach orchards and poplar trees line the valley and mountains rise steeply on either side. A couple of kilometres before reaching Amasya, a yellow sign points to the rock-cut tomb, **Ayna Magara**, on the left of the road.

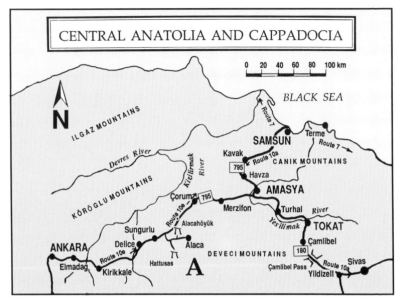

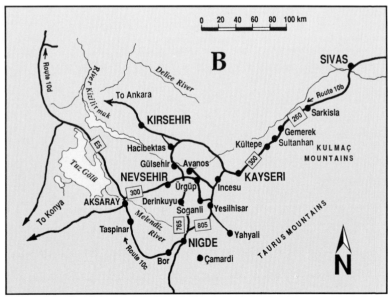

Amasya lies along the bottom of the Yesilirmak river valley. That the town has declined since the end of the eighteenth century is evident by the astonishing number of important monuments for its present size. It takes a full afternoon to see all the main sites which are spread over 3km (1.8 miles) along the banks of the Yesilirmak. The Turban Hotel on the far bank of the river provides comfortable accommodation for visitors who wish to spend longer in the town.

Toruntay Türbesi, a Seljuk tomb, stands at the western end of Atatürk Caddesi, the main street. It was built in 1278 for Emir Toruntay, a governor of Amasya. The mosque next to it, originally built as a school, was also commissioned by Toruntay, in 1266-67. The town **museum** lies further along the street, east of the tomb, and contains a good collection of locally found Bronze Age tools, Hittite pottery, Urartian metalware as well as a selection of ceramics from antiquity.

The equestrian statue of Atatürk marks the town centre. The right fork to the river passes **Gümüslu Cami** on the left, which was built in 1485, and can be recognised by its octagonal-shaped roof. To the right is a medical institution, known as the **Lunatic Asylum**. It was built in 1309 and has a finely carved portal. The mosque nearby, **Mehmet Pasa Cami**, is part of a complex built in 1486 by Mehmet Pasa, tutor of Sultan Beyazit II's son, Prince Ahmet. **Beyazit Pasa Cami** (1419) is the small Ottoman mosque next to the bridge over the Yesilirmak river. On the other side of the river, to the right of the bridge, stands **Büyük Aga Medrese**. Built in 1488 by Hüseyin Aga, one of Sultan Beyazit II's eunuchs, it has a unique octagonal ground plan and is still in use today.

The bazaar is centred around the fifteenth-century *bedesten* on Atatürk Caddesi. **Sultan Beyazit II Cami**, one of Amasya's grandest monuments, lies to the south a little further along the street. It is built on a terrace overlooking the river and was commissioned by Beyazit II in 1486. The complex surrounding it includes a *medrese*, a public kitchens and a monumental tomb. The tombs seen carved in the rock face on the opposite side of the river can be reached by following the signposts across the bridge to **Kral Kaya Mesarlar**, the royal Pontic tombs. A finely preserved, traditional timbered house, **Hazeranlar Konagi**, which is open as a museum, is passed on the way.

The path to the tombs leads up steep steps to a terrace, which was originally the site of a palace. In the rock face above there are two main groups of tombs. The largest and grandest are to the west, and are approached up an impressive stone-carved stairway, complete with a bannister. The tombs to the east have rock-cut platforms in front and the middle tomb stands completely detached from the natural rock.

A **castle** stands on the high summit above the tombs and can be reached along a rough 2km (1.3 miles) track that leads up from the Turban Hotel.

Highway 180 follows the picturesque valley of the Yesilirmak river south of Amasya. The road is well surfaced and climbs gently up and down low hills, passing the small town of Turhal, to **Tokat**. The town lies in a rocky valley at the foot of a ruined castle and has several fine

Seljuk and Ottoman monuments. The road enters the town over a **Seljuk bridge**, built in 1250, with five pointed arches, and passes the tomb of **Nürettin Bini** (1314) on the left. **Sunbul Baba Zaviyesi**, is a small mosque on the right of the road and was built in 1291-2. The museum, housed in the red-stone theological school, **Gök Medrese** (1275), has a fine collection of tombstones.

Highway 180 climbs over red-earthed hills to the Kiziliniz Pass (1,150m/3,772ft). The road passes a ruined Seljuk caravanserai and crosses a plateau to a range of mountains. After climbing over the Camlibel Pass (1,646m/5,399ft), the road winds down to Yildizeli. Shortly after the road passes the Ilica dam and a thermal baths, Sicak Carmik Kaplica is signposted on the right. As the road approaches Sivas, it passes the airport and a stone bridge which has seventeen arches.

Sivas is a wealthy agricultural town in the middle of a large fertile plateau. The town attracts few tourists, but there is a good selection of accommodation and a wealth of Seljuk monuments to visit, of which most are within easy walking distance of the main square, Hükümet Meydani. Most of the Seljuk monuments were built during the thirteenth century when Sivas was an important town under the Sultanate of Rum who ruled from Konya.

Cifte Minare, built in 1271, takes its name from the twin minarets which flank the exquisitely carved portal. Sadly, only the façade of this building remains. However, **Sifaiye Medrese**, opposite, is complete and was the largest medical institution in the Seljuk empire. It is built around a courtyard with an *eyvan* along one side, and was commissioned by Sultan Izzeddin Keykavuz in 1217, whose remains are buried in the conical-roofed tomb on the right. **Buruçiye Medrese** nearby was built in 1271 and has two minarets on either side of an intricately carved portal. A tomb stands on one side of the courtyard and an open lecture hall on the other. The mosque, **Kale Cami**, which

stands opposite the *medrese*, was built much later, in 1580 by Mahmut Pasa, Sultan Murad III's vizier.

The citadel mound, now covered in tea-gardens, is passed on the way to **Gök Medrese**, 1km (0.6 miles) south of the town centre. Gök Medrese, yet another of the fine buildings constructed in 1271, has a magnificent portal inlaid with coloured marbles. The two brick minarets have the remnants of turquoise ceramic tile decoration, and the central courtyard is surrounded by a colonnaded arcade. **Ulu Cami**, passed on the road back into town, is one of the oldest mosques in Sivas and dates from 1196. Its appearance is not enhanced by the corrugated iron roof but the interior is filled with attractive columns and vaulted arcades.

The **Inkilap Müzesi** and the **Inönü Müzesi** are marked by yellow signposts from Hükümet Meydani. The latter was President Inönü's home which is now open as a museum. Inkilap Müzesi is the congress building on the main square where Atatürk held his first successful referendum.

Route 10b — Sivas to Kayseri (map B, p214)

Highway 850 heads south of Sivas and crosses over the Kizilirmak river on the Egri Köprü bridge. Highway 260 is signposted on the right to Sarkisla and Kayseri. The road follows an ancient caravan route along the Kizilirmak river valley that originally led from Konya to Sivas. A number of derelict caravanserais stand at the road side along the route, but **Sultanhani**, 50km (31 miles) before Kayseri, is the largest and best preserved. It was built in 1236 by Alaeddin Keykubad.

Fourteen kilometres (8.7 miles) past Sultanhani the road joins highway 300 where the carpet-making town of Bunyan is signposted on the left. Continuing along highway 300 to Kayseri, a yellow signpost points right to **Kültepe**, the site of an Assyrian settlement, known as *Kanesh*. The site was founded in the third millennium BC, but little remains to be seen as the major discoveries have been transferred to the museums at Ankara and Kayseri.

Kayseri lies at the foot of Mount Erciyes (3,916m 12,844ft), ancient *Mount Argeus*. In Roman times the city was known as *Caesareia* and was the capital of the province of Cappadocia. Today, the best remaining monuments date from the Seljuk period when, during the thirteenth century, a profusion of mosques, schools and tombs were built under Sultan Alaeddin Keykubad. The main sights can be toured in an afternoon, including a visit to the bazaar. A wide selection of hotels and restaurants can be found in the main streets radiating from Cumhuriyet Meydani, the central square. *Sucuk* and *pastirma* are two local specialities worth sampling. They can be found in shops throughout the city as well as in the better restaurants.

The ancient **citadel**, built of the local dark basalt, stands in the centre of the city. It has recently been restored and has nineteen fortified towers which are linked by a walk-way around the top of the crenellated walls. The earliest fortress on the site was built by the

Yesilirmak river and rock tombs, Amasya

Byzantine emperor Justinian in the sixth century, but it has been rebuilt many times since then. The Seljuk royal symbol, the double-headed lion, can be seen carved over the main gate.

The **bazaar** lies in the small streets to the west of the citadel. It has recently been excellently restored and is one of the most attractive bazaars in Turkey. The vaulted arcades are centred around the *bedesten* which was built in 1497 and is covered by nine domes. Nowadays it is the main carpet market in the city. Kayseri is famous for its carpets, and dealers pride themselves on their sales techniques. There are two main types of carpets sold, wool carpets made in the outlying villages such as Yahyali, and silk or imitation silk carpets from Bunyan and other Kayseri villages. More carpet shops can be found in **Vezir Han**, built in 1723 by Damat Ibrahim Pasa. **Ulu Cami**, the largest mosque in the bazaar area, is next to Vezir Han. It was built between 1135 and 1205 and is easily recognised by its chunky minaret. The washing fountains stand beneath an arcade built along the outside wall of Vezir Han and on the other side of the courtyard is the library, **Rasik Efendi Kütüphanesi**.

A fine mosque complex built for Mahperi Huant Hunat, wife of Alaeddin Keykubad, stands opposite the citadel on the east side of Talas Caddesi. The **Hunat complex** consists of a large mosque, a

Ulu Cami washing fountains, Kayseri

school, a public bath and the Sultana's mausoleum. The school, known as the **Hunat Medrese**, was built in 1236 and now houses the ethnographical museum which contains nomadic Turcoman exhibits, Seljuk ceramic tiles and a diverse collection of Ottoman objects. The Sultana's tomb is joined to one side of the museum and contains a simple stone sarcophagus decorated with calligraphic carving.

The **Döner Kümbet** is one of the best examples of the many Seljuk tombs left standing in the city. It is located on the roadside due south of the Hunat complex and was built in 1276. The twelve sides of the building are beautifully carved with Seljuk eagles, the tree of life and stylised plant motifs.

The **Archaeological Museum** is in a modern building about 1km (0.6 miles) beyond Döner Kümbet. It is worth visiting to see the artefacts found during the excavation of Kültepe.

Route 10c — Kayseri to Cappadocia

(map B, p214)

Highway 805 heads 30km (18 miles) west of Kayseri to the **Kara Mustafa Kervansaray** at Incesu. This large Ottoman caravanserai was built in 1660 and remains in good condition. The road climbs up the hill through the village along a series of ridges to a plateau scattered with loose volcanic stones and boulders. At Aksalar, road signs mark a left fork to Ürgüp and the road climbs up to a summit, from where there are panormic views across the whole of Cappadocia.

Ürgüp is a popular tourist resort town, filled with shops selling handmade jewellery, onyx, carpets and antiques. It has a good selection of simple but clean accommodation, some pleasant rooftop restaurants and a few small bars. Livelier night-life can be found in the big motel complexes outside Ürgüp.

As its name suggests, **Ortahisar** stands midway between Ürgüp and Nevsehir. The rocky needle which stands in the centre of the village is covered with troglodytic cave dwellings. The towering rock at **Üçhisar** is also riddled with passages and dwellings and from the summit, which is one of the highest points in the region, there are panoramic views.

Nevsehir, at an altitude of 1,260m (4,133ft), is an important agricultural town as well as a convenient point from which to tour Cappadocia. A wide range of organised excursions is available, including pony trekking, bicycle hire and hiking. The selection of accommodation and restaurants is quite good, but the constant flow of traffic makes the centre of town rather noisy.

The small village of **Göreme** is just 2km (1.3 miles) from the popular Göreme open-air museum. The village has remained relatively undeveloped despite the large number of tourists who pass through here and there is a simple range of accommodation. Some *pansiyon* are built in genuine troglodyte caves and many offer home-cooked food.

A large area of the Göreme valley is preserved as an open-air museum and attracts more tourists than any other part of Cappadocia. The site was established as a monastic centre by St Basil the Bishop of *Caesareia* (Kayseri) in the fourth century. It continued to expand until the Arab invasions in the seventh century when the population took refuge underground. After 200 years the Byzantines made the region secure and life in Cappadocia returned to normal. Up to thirty rock-carved churches have been discovered in the Göreme valley alone. Many of the churches are decorated on the inside with frescoes which date from the mid-ninth to the eleventh centuries. Other churches lie in the less-explored valleys of **El Nazar** and **Kiliclar** which are on either side of the Göreme valley. **Sakli**

Kilise, one of the principal churches of the El Nazar valley, is marked by a yellow sign on the road to the Göreme valley museum.

Tokali Kilise stands on the left of the road, 200m (218yd) before the museum car-park. It is one of the largest and most impressive churches in the region and was originally part of a monastery complex. The interior is decorated with beautiful frescoes from the reign of Nicephorus Phocas in 963-9. They have been recently restored and are the most complete in the valley. Numerous scenes from the life of Christ, as well as portraits of saints, including that of St Basil, are depicted on the walls and ceilings of the church.

The **Göreme Valley Open-Air Museum** is laid out with concrete paths and arrows which lead visitors around the main churches. **Çarikli Kilise, Karanlik Kilise** and **Elmali Kilise** were all constructed in the mid-eleventh century and have deep cupolas and rock-hewn columns. The **Kizlar Manastiri**, a nun's convent, is entered up vertical shafts cut in the rock. Next to the convent there is a **refectory** with a long stone-carved table where the nuns, who numbered up to 300 at any one time, would come to eat. **Yilanli Kilise**, nearby, is decorated in simple ochre-coloured frescoes dating from the eleventh century. St George is shown fighting the dragon, and the Emperor Constantine and St Theodosius are depicted together with Christ.

The valley below the main cluster of churches is richly cultivated and although there are no significant churches to see, there are numerous troglodytic dwellings and a complicated system of tunnels built to direct water to Göreme. There is a well-used footpath through the centre of the valley and it is a pleasant walk beneath the fruit trees, away from the crowds at the museum.

Road signs point from Göreme to **Çavusin Kilise**, a rock-cut church set high in the cliff-face to the right of the road. A long metal staircase leads up to the entrance where the archangels Gabriel and Michael are painted on either side of the door. The interior walls are richly painted in red and yellow with frescoes showing the Nativity and the life of Christ.

Yellow road signs are marked on the right 2km (1.3 miles) beyond Çavusin to **Zelve**, a monastic centre, 3km (1.8 miles) from the highway, with churches carved along the sides of three beautiful valleys. People lived here until 30 years ago when there were a number of incidents of people being killed by falling stone. The area was deemed unsafe for habitation and the inhabitants were moved to a new village, Yeni Zelve.

The small **mosque**, originally a church, is one of the best- preserved buildings in the first valley. This is no doubt due to the fact that it was in constant use by the villagers who converted the

Rock formations in Cappadocia

columned belfry to a minaret and built a mihrab in the apse. Further along the valley are the remains of an extensive **monastery** carved in the rock-face on the left. The monastery has four different levels, and its considerable size indicates the large monastic community that must have lived here. The monks provided themselves with a hidden escape route into the second valley, by carving a tunnel 150m (164yd) through the rock. It emerges high in the rock-face on the other side, where a precarious ladder descends into the bottom of the second valley. Visitors should bring a torch as the passage through the rock is unlit.

The second valley is dominated by a large **castle** which has suffered badly from erosion. The outer wall has been worn away, exposing the maze of passages inside. From the look-out point at the top of the castle there are excellent views across the Zelve valleys. The **baptistry** is further up the valley and has a carved font at the altar.

At the entrance to the third valley, the building on the left is a **mill-house**, complete with a large grinding stone turned by a wooden beam. Further up the valley are two interesting churches, **Balikli Kilise** and **Üzümlu Kilise**. The latter, the Grape Church, is unique in that it has a grape press in the main apse. The side chapel is decorated with vine motifs, thought to be the earliest fresco work in the region.

Avanos, 7km (4.3 miles) north of Zelve, lies on the Roman site of *Venasa*, of which nothing remains. The town makes traditional earthenware pottery, which is sold in small workshops along the main street where the potters can be seen at work. The Kizilirmak river, the ancient *Halys*, flows through the centre of town and is the same colour as the local red clay. There are several *pansiyon* and restaurants along the main street, which runs parallel to the river, and some of them even serve locally produced wine. The main hotels, however, are generally block-booked by French tour groups and it may be difficult to find a room in peak season.

Sarihan, a thirteenth-century caravanserai, is 7km (4.3 miles) east of Avanos, and makes a pleasant excursion.

Gülsehir is best reached from Avanos by following the small road west of the town for 20km (12.4 miles), along the banks of the Kizilirmak river. Previously known as *Arapsun*, Gülsehir was divided between Greeks and Turks and many of the attractive Greek houses can still be seen in the village. An Ottoman mosque and *medrese* stand in the centre of the village at the foot of a ruined citadel. There are a couple of simple hotels along the main street, and a new luxury hotel has just been built on the citadel mound.

Signposts point to **Açik Palas**, a rock-carved church a few kilo- metres south-east of the village. The church, while containing no frescoes, is surrounded by unique rock formations. The **Mantar Kaya** is well known and resembles a huge mushroom.

The village of **Hacibektas** is named after the founder of the Bektasi order of dervishes, Veli Hacibektasi, who lived during the thirteenth century. The town is 20km (12.4 miles) north of Gülsehir, on the road to Kirsehir.

The dervish monastery is visited by people from all over Turkey who regard it as a shrine. The Bektasi dervish order was banned in 1926 at the same time as the Mevlana. The monastery is now open as a museum and has been recently restored. It is built around three courtyards and contains a library, a mosque and Hacibektasi's tomb. As well as being something of a shrine, his mausoleum also contains a small display of objects used by the dervish sect. There is an annual dervish festival held here every year on 14 August.

The Cappadocians had a long history of persecution, and frequent raids swept across the area, so it is perhaps not surprising that they sought shelter below ground. Throughout Cappadocia there are vast, warren-like underground cities, thought to number as many as thirty-six in total. Two of the most extensive are open to the public at Kaymakli and Derinkuyu. Both sites are located south of Nevsehir on highway 765.

※ **Kaymakli** is 19km (12 miles) from Nevsehir and reaches down 40m (131ft) below ground level. Four of the original eight storeys are open and visitors can freely wander through the maze of passages which connect the different levels.

※ **Derinkuyu**, a further 9km (6 miles) to the south, is far more extensive. The underground city here is thought to have been inhabited by up to 20,000 people at any one time and is built on at least twenty floors, eight of which are open to the public. From an insignificant hole in the ground the path leads down through the city, past kitchens, store houses and wine-cellars on the upper floors, to churches and burial chambers on the lowest levels. Large air shafts provided ventilation for the city, while heavy circular stone doors could be rolled across the narrow passages to protect the city against invaders. The main thoroughfares are clearly lit and marked with arrows, but in places the tunnels are steep and narrow and should not be visited by people who suffer from claustrophobia.

The road between Ürgüp and Yesilhisar is lined with rock-hewn churches and is one of the most scenic drives in Cappadocia. Yellow road signs from Ürgüp indicate the turning to Pancarlik Kilise and Keslik Manistiri.

The turning to the first site is 2km (1.3 miles) from Ürgüp on the right. A rough track winds up to the **Kepez and Sarica churches**. A footpath leads past the Sarica Kilise with its red frescoes, down to a cluster of smaller churches, carved in cones along the floor of the valley. The track continues on for a further 1km (0.6 miles) to the **Pancarlik Kilise** which has well-preserved frescoes. A group of smaller rock-carved chapels lie in the bottom of the valley.

The main highway continues along a lush river valley through the village of Cemil to the **Keslik Manistiri** on the right. The footpath leads to the main church, known as **Kara Kilise**, due to the black smoke that covers its frescoes. At one end of the church there is a conical belfry and at the other a narrow tunnel, closed by a rolling stone door, leads to the refectory next door. In front of the church there is an underground **baptistry** with a carved cupola above the font. The **refectory**, also used as a school, is a long rectangular room with stone-hewn tables which could seat about fifty people. The path returns to the road past a wine cellar to a smaller **church** which has crypts carved in the floor and plant motifs painted on the ceiling.

The highway continues through **Mustafapasa**, former Greek *Sinasos*, which was populated by Greeks until the 1920s. The Greek buildings, constructed from carved blocks of the local tufa, lend the village an attractive air, and a nineteenth-century monastery at the centre of the village has been converted to a hotel.

Altiparmak Kilise is another cluster of churches carved in rock cones just before the village of Sahinefendi. The road then climbs onto a plateau, from where Mount Erciyes can be seen on the left and the Taurus mountain range straight ahead. Further churches are signposted at Güzelöz, before the road descends to the Akköy dam where a yellow sign points right to **Soganli**. The road passes through the village to a magnificent valley lined with rock-carved churches and hundreds of pigeon coops. The valley divides about midway along and there are a number of restaurants and a small camp-site at the fork. A map of the valleys marks the main churches: **Yilani Kilise**, **Sakli Kilise**, **Meryemana Kilise**, **Karanlik Kilise** and **Kübbeli Kilise**. Good footpaths lead along both valleys to the churches.

Nigde is a rural town set on a high plateau (1,200m/3,936ft) on the southern edge of Cappadocia, 83km (52 miles) south of Nevsehir. There is a limited selection of hotels and restaurants in the town, but the attractive Seljuk monuments and the nearby monastery of Gümüsler make it worth visiting.

A **Seljuk fortress** stands on the ancient citadel mound above the town and is surrounded by a small park and tea-gardens. It was originally built by Sultan Alaeddin Keykubad I in the thirteenth century, and restored in 1470 by Isak Pasa; the octagonal clock tower next to it is fourteenth century. Alaeddin Keykubad also built the mosque at the far end of the citadel terrace, **Alaeddin Cami**. It was constructed in 1233 and has a beautifully carved portal. The *bedesten*, seen below the mosque, is a rectangular market building, 50m (164ft) long, built in the sixteenth century by Sokollu Mehmet Pasa, and is now used as a fruit and vegetable market.

Sungurbey Cami (1335) and **Ak Medrese** (1409) stand near the local **museum** on the west side of the town, just off Vali Konagi Caddesi. The prime exhibit at the museum is a fifth-century mummified woman found in the Ihlara valley. There is also a well-displayed collection of Christian artefacts, and pottery dating from the neolithic age through to the Byzantine era.

The two monumental tombs, **Hudavend Hatun Türbesi** and the **Gündogu Türbesi**, lie 500m (546yd) due north of the museum. The tomb built for the Seljuk princess, Hudavend Hatun in 1312, has beautiful carved reliefs on each of its eight sides of birds, animals and plants.

The Taurus mountains are close to Nigde, and the Aladag range is popular with hikers and mountaineers. Mountain trails can be followed from Camardi, 71km (44 miles) east of Nigde, a small town where guides can be hired. There is a simple mountain lodge at Demirkazak (3,756m/12,320ft), one of the highest peaks in the

Rock-cut church in the Soganli valley

Central Anatolian villagers

Peppers drying in the sun in a central Anatolian village

Aladag range, and a ski-lift operates from here in the winter.

Gümüsler is one of the best-preserved monasteries in Cappodocia. It lies concealed behind a rock face at **Eski Gümüs**, a small village 8km (5 miles) east of Nigde, marked by a yellow sign off highway 805. The entrance to the monastery leads into a deep, rock-hewn courtyard, the only one of its type in Cappadocia, which is surrounded by a series of rooms. The main church, built on a cross plan, lies on the far side of the courtyard. It is beautifully decorated with very well-preserved frescoes painted in rich blues and golds. The central dome is supported by four rock-carved columns, decorated with gold stars and red flowers. The other rooms around the courtyard, which include a crypt, have long tunnels leading off into the solid rock in all directions, but they can only be explored with a good torch as they are completely unlit.

Aksaray lies in a flat plain on the Byzantine site of *Archelais*. It was taken by the Seljuks in the eleventh century and **Ulu Cami**, a large Seljuk mosque built in 1115-56, marks the centre of the town. There is little else of historic interest as it is essentially an agricultural market town, but there is a handful of reasonable hotels which provide a convenient base from which to visit the churches along the Ihlara valley, although basic accommodation and camping facilities are also available at Ihlara itself.

Ihlara, formerly known as *Peristrema*, is a dramatic gorge, 150m (492ft) deep and 14km (8.7 miles) long, lined with rock-carved churches. The site, which lies 40km (25 miles) from Aksaray, is clearly signposted. The road crosses a high plateau dominated by the volcanic peak Hasan Dagi (3,268m/10,719ft).

At Ihlara, steps lead down into the gorge from the restaurant and souvenir shop near the car-park. At the foot of the steps a map shows the location of fifteen of the principal churches; there are supposed to be some one hundred in total.

The Melendiz river flows along the valley bed and waters the lush banks on either side, while jagged red rocks rise steeply all round. Sandy footpaths lead along both sides of the river and there are two bridges at either end of the valley, one near the steps and the other at the far end near the village of Belisirma. Many of the churches have simple but attractive frescoes, such as **Agaçli Kilise** which is at the bottom of the steps and **Yilanli Kilise** on the opposite side of the river.

Agzikarahan is a Seljuk caravanserai on highway 300, and can be visited as a short detour off the road from Ihlara to Aksaray. It was built in 1231-39 by Sultan Alaeddin Keykubad I and has an elaborately carved portal, summer and winter sleeping quarters and a small mosque in the main courtyard.

Sultanhani is the largest and best-preserved Seljuk caravanserai in Turkey. It lies 39km (24 miles) east of Aksaray on the ancient caravan route to Konya. It was built in 1229 by Alaeddin Keykubad I. A vast intricately carved marble portal leads into a spacious courtyard with a small mosque at the centre and stables, kitchens, store rooms, and sleeping quarters around the outside. A second carved portal leads to a large enclosed hall, used during the winter, which is lit by narrow slits cut in the walls and an opening in the dome.

Route 10d — Aksaray to Ankara

(map B, then A, p214)

The E90 crosses the central Anatolian plateau, passing the huge salt lake of Tuz Gölü. The landscape is gently undulating and the road is good. After Gölbasi, the road climbs a long hill from where Ankara can be seen spread below.

Ankara was made the Turkish capital in 1923 when Atatürk founded the republic. He severed all ties with the former capital, Istanbul, and didn't visit it again until 1927. Ankara, a sleepy Anatolian town, was gradually transformed by European town planners into the administrative capital of the country. Today, the city is a mixture of anonymous high-rise blocks housing the governmental departments, and an ever-growing shanty town which sprawls on the steep slopes surrounding the city.

Despite its historical background the city has few buildings of interest, and the main attraction of a visit to Ankara is the Anatolian Civilisations Museum. It is also a convenient base from which to visit ancient *Gordion* and the Hittite sites. There is a wide selection of hotels and a number of restaurants serving international cuisine, and after a long hike around rural Turkey Ankara can feel a haven of civilisation.

The old city is centred around the citadel mound which was founded in the second millennium BC as *Ankuwash*. A road leads from Ulus to a long flight of steps up through the park to the citadel wall which dates from the seventh century. The Anatolian Civilisations Museum is on the right and to the north-west stands a thirteenth-century Seljuk mosque, **Arslanhane Cami** built with columns, capitals and stones originating from the Roman city.

The **Anatolian Civilisations Museum** is housed in a fifteenth-century Ottoman *bedesten*, used at one time as a trading centre for 'angora' goats' hair. It now contains the richest collection of Urartian and Hittite finds in the world. These are excellently displayed in four main galleries which surround a large central hall filled with Hittite stone carvings and friezes. The galleries are set out in chronological order, starting at the palaeolithic age and finishing up in the Urartian period. The labels are translated into English and a comprehensive

A view down an Ankara street towards the Kocatepe Cami

guide to the museum is available at the foyer.

The first-century **Temple of Augustus** lies to the north-west of the citadel. The outer walls are covered in Latin and Greek inscriptions describing Augustus' will and his good deeds. The temple was converted to a Byzantine church in the sixth century and an apse was built at the east end. **Haci Bayram Cami** was built on the west wall of the temple in the fifteenth century. The mosque was originally a dervish school, founded by Haci Bayram, whose remains are buried in the tomb next to the mosque.

A solitary column, known as **St Julian's Column**, stands downhill from the temple. It was erected in AD362 and is now surrounded by a car-park. The remains of a third-century **Roman baths** are marked by signposts north along Atatürk Bulvari but are similarly unimpressive.

The government building at Ulus, **Kurtulus Savas Müzesi** was where Atatürk held his first national assembly, and is now a museum. The **Ethnographical Museum** south of Ulus, between Atatürk

Anit Kabir, the mausoleum of Atatürk, Ankara

Bulvari and Talat Pasa Caddesi, was purpose-built in 1928 under the direction of Atatürk to preserve and record local Anatolian culture. A **Fine Arts Museum** is next door, and from the museum gardens there are views to the fun fair and railway station which is built on the site of a Phrygian necropolis.

Atatürk's mausoleum crowns the hilltop, **Anit Tepe**. The vast scale of the building alone is impressive. Constructed with limestone and modelled on a classical temple, it covers an area of 1 sq km and took 9 years to build. The entrance is approached along a 300m (328yd) avenue, lined with Hittite-style lions and uniformed guards. Atatürk is buried in a huge sarcophagus weighing 40,000kg (88,000lb), and the mausoleum walls that surround it are inscribed with his doctrines. Atatürk's successor and first Prime Minister, Ismet Inönü (1884-1973), is also buried here.

Gordion, the ancient Phrygian capital, is situated near the Sakarya river, 96km (60 miles) west of Ankara on the E23. A turning is marked 16km (10 miles) west of the small town of Polatli and the site lies 11km (6.8 miles) from the main road, just past the village of Beylikköprü.

The site is named after Gordios, King of the Phrygian empire in the eighth century BC. It was here that Alexander the Great solved the riddle of the Gordion knot. It was said that whoever could untie the knot would rule Asia. Alexander sliced it in two with his sword and then went on to fulfil the prophecy.

The 53m- (174ft-) high tumulus is believed to belong to Gordios' son, King Midas of the legendary golden touch. A 25m (82ft) tunnel leads from the base of the tumulus into the burial chamber, built of great cedar logs now petrified. It is thought to date from the seventh century BC and is one of the largest tumuli in Turkey.

 The museum on the opposite side of the road contains some of the burial treasures, but the best exhibits are in Ankara. Outside the museum there is an eighth-century BC pebble mosaic, which is one of the earliest of its kind and probably originated from the Phrygian Palace.

Route 10e — Ankara to Samsun (map A, p214)

The E23 to Samsun leaves Ankara along a wide, well-surfaced road and passes through Elmadag and Kirikkale before climbing up onto a plateau. Sungurlu is the nearest town to the Hittite sites and has a reasonable motel which provides a convenient base for touring the region. A turning right, 8km (5 miles) beyond Sungurlu, leads across a cultivated plain for 22km (13.6 miles) to the Hittite sites at Bogazkale.

 Bogazkale is a small village built on the edge of one of the most extensive Hittite sites in Turkey, *Hattusas*. There is a small museum in the village, housing some of the local Hittite discoveries, and the restaurant at the side of the main road has a simple camp-site. Taxis can be hired from the main square in the village to visit the ruins, which are spread over a wide area. The site takes about 1$^1/_2$ hours to tour by car and 3-4 hours on foot.

Hattusas was the capital of the Hittite kingdom in the seventeenth century BC. The defensive wall that surrounded the city stretched for 6.5km (4 miles) and had up to 200 defensive towers. The city was protected on two sides by deep ravines and covered an area of 3sq km. From Bogazkale follow the signs to **Büyük Mabet**, the site of a fourteenth-century BC temple. A paved road leads into the temple precinct through a processional gate. The road is remarkably preserved and its central drainage channel remains intact. The temple base, built of granite, is surrounded by small storerooms. The vast storage jars found in these rooms have been left *in situ* by the excavators.

 Continue uphill to **Büyükkale**, the site of a royal palace dating from the thirteenth century BC. There is nothing much to see in the way of remains, but there are good views of the temple below and the surrounding countryside. The rocky outcrop, **Nisantasi**, marks the site of a thirteenth-century BC castle, but nothing remains to be seen today.

At the highest point of the city there is a well-preserved section of the original defence wall, with three monumental gateways. The first, **Kral Kapi**, the King's Gate, is built of monolithic stones and has a carved relief of a war-god guarding the entrance, the original of which is in Ankara. The next gate, **Yer Kapi** stands at the highest point of the city. The gate, originally flanked by a pair of stone sphinx, now in Berlin and Istanbul, leads into a triangular-shaped tunnel, 70m (230ft) long, which emerges the other side, outside the city wall. A stone-carved sentry's seat can be seen to one side of the gate and the outer faces of the walls either side are clad with cyclopean stone. It is worth walking along the walls to the west to see the vast stone stairway. The last gate, **Aslan Kapi**, is named after the typically Hittite-style lions carved on the stone jambs on either side of the door. The road continues along the wall and then heads back down to the village.

Yazilikaya, 3km (1.8 miles) north-east of Bogazkale, is an open-air temple dedicated to the Hittite weather gods. Well-preserved reliefs are carved on the natural rock and date from the thirteenth century BC. The sanctuary is situated in a cleft, between high rocks, and consists of two chambers. The first is for the royal cult and has four large carved relief scenes. The second chamber is smaller and the main relief shows forty-two gods walking in procession, wearing pointed head-dresses.

Alacahöyük is another Hittite site dating from the fourteenth century BC, 35km (21.7 miles) north of Bogazkale. A small museum stands on the edge of the site and contains some of the artefacts found in the excavations. The earliest finds date back to the Bronze Age, but most of the collection consists of Hittite pottery, including some attractive drinking vessels.

The **Sphinx Gate**, the original gateway into the city, lies to the right of the museum. The gate is made of finely carved blocks of stone, but the sphinx statues either side are only plaster copies. A paved road leads from the gate into the city, which is considerably smaller than *Hattusas*. The ruined foundations of buildings lie on either side of the road and a wide drainage channel runs down the centre. The buildings to the left of the road are thought to have been storehouses, and at the end of the road, also on the left, hollows can be seen in the ground. These mark the site of **royal tombs**, said to date back to the early Bronze Age.

Highway 785 heads north to the capital of the province, Çorum. It is only a small town, but there are a few simple hotels which could

The Kale district of Ankara

provide a base from which to visit the Hittite sites. After Çorum the road joins highway 795 and runs along the foot of the Black Sea mountains to Havza. Route 10a can be followed in reverse order from Havza to Samsun.

USEFUL INFORMATION
FOR VISITORS

Acropolis	ancient hilltop citadel
Agora	market-place
Arabesque	Arabic floral motif
Arasta	Ottoman shopping arcade
Architrave	lintel resing on columns
Baraj	dam
Bedesten	Ottoman building used as a stronghold in the centre of a bazaar
Belediye	council
Benzin	fuel
Börek	savoury pastry
Bouleuterion	council chamber
Caddesi	street
Cami	mosque
Cavea	seating area of a Greek or Roman theatre
Cella	central chamber in a temple
Centrum	town centre
Cirit	javelin contest on horseback
Çarsi	market
Çesme	fountain
Deniz	sea
Dolmus	shared taxi
Eyvan	open chamber at the side of a courtyard
Geceköndü	shanty town
Gulet	wooden schooner
Hamam	Turkish bath
Han	commercial building in a bazaar, built around acourtyard
Harem	women's quarters
Heroon	shrine to a dead person
Heykel	statue
Ihram	shroud worn by Islamic women
Jandarma	security police
Kale	castle
Kapi	gate or door
Kaplica	thermal spa
Kara	black
Kayak	barge
Kilim	flat-weave rug
Kilise	church
Koran	Islamic holy book
Kösk	kiosk

Kümbet	monumental tombs
Lokanta	simple restaurant
Lokum	Turkish Delight
Lunette	arch above a window
Manastiri	monastery
Mangal	barbecue
Medrese	theological school
Merkez	city centre
Mescit	small mosque
Meydan	town square
Meze	a salad or side dish
Müezzin	prayer caller in mosques
Mihrab	prayer niche in mosque
Mimber	pulpit in mosque
Müdür	director
Müze	museum
Narthex	hall between nave and west door of a church
Necropolis	graveyard
Nymphaion	ornamental fountain
Odeion	small concrete theatre
Orchestra	semi-circular area in front of a stage in a theatre
Orman	forest
Osmanli	Ottoman
Pansiyon	small family hotel
Pastane	pastry shop
Pediment	triangular wall at the end of the roof
Pronaos	porch in front of a temple
Sadirvan	ablutions fountain in mosque courtyard
Salvar	baggy trousers worn by peasants
Sarap	wine
Saray	palace
Selamlik	men's quarters
Semahane	hall for dervish rituals
Sinif	class
Sokak	street
Sumak	flat-weave with embroidery

Tekke	dervish convent
Turistik	touristic
Yali	waterside mansion
Yilan	snake

MISCELLANEOUS INFORMATION

EMERGENCIES
Emergency numbers are listed in the front of the regional yellow pages. The following numbers are for Istanbul.

Tourist Police	**528 53 69**
Emergency Police	**055**
Fire	**000**
Emergency Ambulance	**077**
American Hospital	**131 40 50**

FESTIVALS AND HOLIDAYS
Religious Holidays
The dates of the two major religious festivals are determined by the lunar calendar. The first, Seker Bayram, or sweet holiday, marks the end of the month long fast of Ramazan. All shops, banks and bazaars close for the 3 or 4 day period and many people leave the cities for the coasts.

The second, Kurban Bayram, or sacrifice holiday, celebrates Abraham's sacrifice of the ram. Families get together at this time and the festival has an atmosphere similar to that of Christmas. Shops, offices, bazaars and banks are closed for the 3 day period.

National Holidays
During the national public holidays

some shops and bazaars stay open, but banks and post offices are shut.

1 Jan —	New Year's Day
23 April —	National Independence and Children's Day
19 May —	Atatürk's Youth and Sports Day
30 August —	Victory Day
29 Sept —	Republic Day

Iyi bayramlar is the expression used to wish people a good holiday on any occasion.

Festivals

15-16 Jan —	Camel Wrestling Festival, Selçuk
1-7 May —	Epheseus Arts and Culture Festival
18-30 May —	Istanbul International Jazz Festival
June —	Çesme Pop Festival
29 May-6 June —	Kirkpinar Oiled Wrestling, Edirne
20 June-15 Jul —	International Istanbul Festival
1 July —	Sailor's Day (no ferries)
1-30 August —	Black Sea Festival, Samsun
15 August —	Special mass at Mereyemana, Selçuk
20 Aug-20 Sept —	Izmir International Trade Fair
1-9 September —	Bodrum Art and Culture Festival
20-25 Sept —	Çorum Hittite Festival
1-9 October —	Antalya Film and Art Festival
10 November —	Atatürk's Commemoration Day
6-8 December —	Festival of St Nicholas, Demre
14-17 December —	Mevlana Festival, Konya

LANGUAGE

A few words in Turkish can make all the difference to a holiday in Turkey. In the more rural areas, it brings people great pleasure to see at least an effort has been made to learn some of their language. The Turkish language is easy in that the letter sounds never change, so having learnt all the basic sounds one can pronounce any word. There are a number of good phrase books which cover a wide range of situations in detail.

MAPS

Lascelles 1:800,000 scale maps of west and east Turkey have a lot of useful detail and show the main sites of interest. The Turkish Highways Department road map is on a 1:1,225,000 scale and marks the filling stations.

NEWSPAPERS AND JOURNALS

There are three English language newspapers printed in Turkey: *Dateline* (weekly), *Turkish Daily News* (daily) and *Turkish Times* (daily). They are available in all cities and resorts. Subscriptions should be made to the following:

Turkish Daily News, 49/7 Tünüs Caddesi, Kavaklidere, Ankara

Dateline, Hürriyet Holding A.S. 17-19 Piyerloti Caddesi, Çemberlitas, Istanbul

Turkish Times, 14 Atakan Sokak, Mecidiye Köy
Istanbul

There is also a quarterly magazine about Turkey and northern Cyprus called *Turquoise*. Subscriptions can be made to the following address:

24 Berkeley Square
Mayfair
London W1X 5HB

TELEPHONES AND POST OFFICES

International calls can be made from a post office, or from a public phone booth which has an international phone sign. Public telephones are operated by tokens or phone cards, both of which can be bought from the post office. To make an international call lift the receiver, put the *jeton* in the correct slot, wait for the dialling tone and then dial 9. Wait for a second dialling tone, then dial 44 for Britain, or 1 for USA, followed by the city code and the number. The same procedure is followed for internal calls, but it is necessary to dial 9 before the city code.

Central post offices are open from 8am to midnight every day, but after 6pm only telephone and letter posting services are available. General post offices are open from 8am to12.30pm and 1.30 to 5.30pm.

Mail can be sent to any post office, addressed Poste Restante, Merkez Postane, followed by the name of the town or city. It is necessary to show some form of identification and pay a nominal charge on collecting the mail.

PLACES OF INTEREST

The following section contains practical information about museums, archaeological sites, monuments and other places mentioned in the text. It is set out chapter by chapter, with the headings in each chapter listed alphabetically. Opening times do vary, especially during public holidays and festivals, and times should be checked from local sources.

Chapter 1 — Istanbul
Archaeological Museum
Sarayiçi
Osman Hamdi Yokusu
Sultanahmet
☎ (1) 520 77 40
Open: every day except Monday 9.30am-5.30pm

Atatürk Kültür Merkezi
Taksim Meydani
Taksim
☎ (1) 143 54 00
Open: every day. From October to May classical concerts are held each Friday at 7pm and Saturday at 11am. Also contains an exhibition centre and theatre.

Aya Sofia Basilica Museum
At Meydani
Sultanahmet
☎ (1) 522 17 50
Open: every day except Monday 9.30am-5pm

Belgrade Forest
Atatürk Arboretum
Atatürk Orman Isletmeleri
Kemerburgaz Yolu
Bahçeköy
☎ (1) 162 13 94
Open: every day sunrise to sunset

Beylerbeyi Palace
Abdullah Aga Caddesi
Beylerbeyi
☎ (1) 333 69 40

Open: every day except Monday
and Thursday 9am-12.30pm and
1.30-5pm

Çinili Kösk
Sarayiçi
Osman Hamdi Yokusu
Sultanahmet
☎ (1) 520 77 41
Open: Tuesdays only 9.30am-
5.30pm

Covered Bazaar
Kapali Çarsi
Open: Monday to Saturday 9am-
6pm

Dolmabahçe Palace
Dolmabahçe
☎ (1) 161 02 25
Open: every day except Monday
and Thursday 9am-5pm
Café

Emirgan Park
The Yellow Pavilion
Emirgan
☎ (1) 165 60 39
Open: every day 8am-sunset
Ottoman summer pavilion, café

Galata Tower
Sishane
☎ (1) 145 11 60
Open: every day 9am-midnight
Nightclub, restaurant, café, shops

Haseki Hamami
Ayasofia Camii Karsisi
Sultanahmet
☎ (1) 511 81 92
Open: every day except Tuesday
9.30am-5.30pm

Hidiv Kasri
Çubuklu
☎ (1) 331 26 51

Open: all year round
Café, restaurant, hotel

Kariye Cami
28 Kariye Cami Sokak
Edirnekapi
☎ (1) 523 30 09
Open: every day except Tuesday
9.30am-4.30pm
Outdoor café, shop

Kilim and Carpet Museum
Sultanahmet Cami
☎ (1) 528 53 32
Open: every day except Monday
and Sunday 9.30am-5.30pm

Küçüksu Palace
Küçüksu Caddesi
Küçüksu
☎ (1) 332 02 37
Open: every day except Monday
and Thursday 9am-4pm

Maritime Museum
Besiktas
☎ (1) 161 00 40
Open: every day except Monday
and Tuesday 9am-5pm

Mevelevihane Museum
15 Galip Dede Caddesi
Tünel
Beyoglu
☎ (1) 145 41 41
Open: every day except Monday
9.30am-5pm
Whirling Dervish performances
held in December

Military Museum
Harbiye
☎ (1) 140 62 55
Open: every day except Monday
and Tuesday 9am-1pm and 2-5pm
Ottoman janissary band performances 3pm

Monastery of St George
Yücetepe Restaurant
Büyükada
Open: May to October
Simple outdoor restaurant serving
the local monastery wine.

Mosaic Museum
Arasta Carsisi
Sultanahmet
☎ (1) 511 97 00
Open: every day except Tuesday
9am-5pm

Museum of Ancient Orient
Sarayiçi
Osman Hamdi Yokusu
Sultanahmet
☎ (1) 520 77 42
Open: every day except Monday
8.30am-12noon and 1-5pm

Museum of Calligraphy
Beyazit Medrese
Beyazit Meydani
☎ (1) 527 58 51
Open: every day except Monday
9.30am-4pm

Museum of Turkish and Islamic Arts
Ibrahim Pasa Sarayi
At Meydani
Sultanahmet
☎ (1) 522 18 88
Open: every day except Monday
9am-5pm
Turkish coffee house, shop

Piyer Loti Kahvehanesi
1 Gümüssuyu Balmumcu Sokak
Eyup
☎ (1) 581 26 96
Open: every day 8am-6pm
Traditional coffee house overlooking the Golden Horn

Rumeli Hisar Castle
42 Yahya Kemal Caddesi
Rumeli Hisar
☎ (1) 165 04 10
Open: every day except Monday
9.30am-4.30pm

Sultanahmet Cami
Sultanahmet
Open: every day from first to last
prayer call

Süleymaniye Cami
Süleymaniye
Open: every day from first to last
prayer call

Topkapi Palace
Sarayiçi
Sultanahmet
☎ (1) 512 04 80
Open: every day except Tuesday
9am-5pm.
Harem open: 10am-4pm
Restaurant, café, shop

Yedikule Museum
Yedikule
☎ (1) 585 89 33
Open: every day except Monday
9.30am-5pm

Yerebatan Saray
Yerebatan Caddesi
Sultanahmet
☎ (1) 522 12 59
Open: every day 9am-5pm
Café

Yildiz Palace
Besiktas Barbaros Yokusu
Besiktas
☎ (1) 158 30 80
Open: every day except Monday
and Thursday 9.30am-5pm
Ottoman summer pavilion, café

Chapter 2 — Thrace and Marmara
Bursa Archaeological Museum
Kültür Park
Bursa
☎ (24) 36 77 28
Open: every day except Monday
8.30am-12noon and 1-5pm

Bursa Turkish Islamic Arts Museum
Yesil Medrese
Bursa
☎ (24) 31 24 27
Open: every day except Monday
8am-12noon and 1-5pm

Çanakkale Archaeological Museum
4 Zafer Meydani
Çanakkale
☎ (196) 32 52
Open: every day except Monday
10am-5pm

Edirne Archaeological Museum
Edirne
☎ (181) 11625
Open: every day except Monday
8am-12noon and 1-5pm

Eski Kaplica
Kervansaray Hotel
Çekirge, Bursa
☎ (24) 36 71 00
Open: every day
Public thermal baths connected to luxury hotel. Separate facilities for men and women, towel hire and refreshments available

Iznik Museum
Nilufer Hatun Imaret
Yesil Cami Karsisi
Iznik
☎ (2527) 1933
Open: every day except Monday
8.30am-12noon and 1-5pm

Termal Kaplica
Turban Çamlik Hotel
Yalova
☎ (1931) 4905 23
Open: every day
Thermal bath complex. Separate facilities for men and women. Private cubicles and outdoor hot spring pool. Towel hire and refreshments available

Yeni Kaplica
Çekirge Sokak
Bursa
☎ (24) 36 69 68
Open: every day
Public thermal baths, separate facilities for men and women, private cubicles for families, towel hire and refreshments available

Chapter 3 — North Aegean
Acropolis Archaeological Site
Bergama
☎ (5411) 96363
Open: every day 8.30am-5.30pm
Refreshments available

Aesklepion Archaeological Site
Bergama
☎ (5411) 96163
Open: every day 8.30am-5.30pm

Bergama Archaeological Museum
6 Cumhuriyet Caddesi
Bergama
☎ (5411) 11096
Open: every day 8.30am-12noon and 1-5.30pm
Refreshments available

Epheseus Archaeological Museum
5 Kusadasi Caddesi
Selçuk
☎ (5451) 1011

Open: every day 8.30am-6pm
Café

Epheseus Archaeological Site
Near Selçuk
Open: every day 8am-7pm
Café, restaurant, shop, post office

Izmir Archaeological Museum
Bahribaba Parki
Izmir
☎ (51) 14 83 24
Open: every day except Monday
8.30am-5.30pm
Museum shop

Mereyemana
(House of the Virgin Mary)
Selcuk
Open: every day 8am-7.30pm

*Chapter 4 — West Mediterranean
Coast*
Antalya Archaeological Museum
Konyaalti Caddesi
Antalya
☎ (31) 14528
Open: every day 8am-5pm

Castle of St Peter
Iskele Meydani
Bodrum
☎ (6141)1095
Open: every day except Monday
8.30am-12noon and 1-5pm

Didyma Temple
Yenihisar
Open: every day 8am-5pm

Miletos Archaeological Site
Balat
☎ (6351) 38
Open: every day 8am-5.30pm
Café, museum

Priene Archaeological Site
Güllübahçe
Open: every day 8am-7pm

Chapter 5 — Trans-Anatolia
Afyon Museum
96 Kurtulus Caddesi
Afyon
☎ (491) 11191
Open: every day 8.30am-12noon
and 1-5.30pm

**Karaman Archaeological
Museum**
Hastane Caddesi
Karaman
☎ (3431) 1536
Open: every day except Monday
8.30am-12noon and 1-5pm

Karatay Medrese Museum
Alaettin Bulvari
Konya
☎ (33) 11 19 14
Open: every day except Monday
8.30am-12noon and 1-5pm

Konya Archaeological Museum
Larende Caddesi
Konya
☎ (33) 11 12 15
Open: every day except Monday
8.30am-12noon and 1-5pm

Konya Köyünoglu Müzesi
Topraklik Caddesi
Konya
☎ (33) 15 46 00
Open: every day except Monday
8.30am-12noon and 1-5pm

Kossuth House
Kale Sokak
Kütahya
☎ (231) 14641
Open: every day except Monday
8.30am-12noon and 1-5pm

Kütahya Museum
Vacidiye Medrese
Ulu Cami Yani
Kütahya
☎ (231) 11551
Open: every day except Monday
8.30am-12noon and 1-5pm

Mevlana Museum
Mevlana Meydani
Konya
☎ (33) 11 11 40
Open: every day 8.30am-12noon
and 1-5pm

Chapter 6 — East Mediterranean Coast
Adana Regional Museum
Seyhan Caddesi
Adana
☎ (71) 14 38 55
Open: every day except Monday
8.30am-12noon and 1-5pm

Alanya Museum
5 Müze Meydani
Alanya
☎ (3231) 1228
Open: every day 9am-12noon and
1.30-6.30pm

Red Tower Museum
Kizil Kule
Alanya
Open: every day except Monday
8am-12noon and 1.30-5.30pm

Side Archaeological Museum
Selimiye Köyu
Side
☎ (3211) 1006
Open: every day 8.30-11.45am
and 1.30-5.15pm

Silifke Archaeological Museum
Inönü Caddesi
Silifke

☎ (7591) 1019
Open: every day except Monday
8.30am-12noon and 1-5pm

Chapter 7 — Black Sea Coast
Amasra Archaeological Museum
Liman Caddesi
Amasra
☎ (3895) 1006
Open: every day 8am-12.30pm
and 1.30-5.30pm

Atatürk Köskü
Soguksu
Trabzon
Open: every day 8am-5pm

Aya Sofya Church
Fatih Mahallesi
Trabzon
☎ (031) 33043
Open: every day 8am-6pm

Sinop Archaeological Museum
Deniz Sehitleri Park
Sinop
☎ (3761) 1975
Open: Monday to Friday 8.30am-
12noon and 1-5pm

Chapter 8 — The East
Isak Pasa Palace
Near Dogubeyazit
Open: every day except Friday
8am-4pm

Kars Archaeological Museum
Tasliharman Caddesi
Kars
☎ (0211) 1536
Open: every day except Monday
8.30am-12noon and 1.30-5.30pm

Sumela Monastery
Open: every day 8.30am-5pm
Café, restaurant

Van Archaeological Museum
Vani Mehmet Efendi Sokak
Van
☎ (061) 11139
Open: every day except Monday
8.30am-12noon and 1.30-5.30pm

Chapter 9 — The South-East
Hatay Mosaic Museum
1 Gündüz Sokak
Antakya
☎ (891) 11055
Open: every day except Monday
8.30am-12noon and 1.30-5.30pm

Kültür Müzesi
Cahit Sitki Taranci Evi
Diyarbakir
☎ (831) 17013
Open: every day except Monday
8.30am-12noon and 1-5pm

Mardin Museum
Sultan Isa Medrese
Mardin
☎ (841) 11664
Open: every day except Monday
8.30am-12noon and 1-5pm

Ziya Gökalp Müzesi
Melek Ahmet Caddesi
Diyarbakir
☎ (831) 12755
Open: every day 8am-12noon and
1.30-5pm

*Chapter 10 — Central Anatolia and
Cappadocia*
**Alacahöyük Museum and Ar-
chaeological Site**
Alaca
Open: every day 8.30am-12noon
and 1.30-5.30pm

**Amasya Archaeological
Museum**
Atatürk Caddesi

Amasya
☎ (3781) 4513
Open: every day except Monday
8.30am-12noon and 1.30-6pm

Anatolian Civilisations Museum
Kadife Sokak
Hisarlar
☎ (4) 324 31 60
Open: every day except Monday
8.30am-12.30pm and 1.30-5.30pm
Café, shop

Atatürk's Mausoleum
Anit Tepe
Gençlik Caddesi
Tandogan
Ankara
☎ (4) 229 55 53
Open: every day except Monday
9am-12noon and 1-5pm

**Bogazköy Museum
and Archaeological Site**
Bogazköy
Open: 8am-12noon and 1.30-6pm

Çavusin Church
Near Göreme
Open: every day 8.30am-6pm

Derinkuyu Underground City
Derinkuyu
Open: every day 8am-5pm

Ethnographical Museum
Talatpasa Bulvari
Opera
Ankara
☎ (4) 311 30 07
Open: every day except Monday
8.30am-12.30 pm and 1.30-5pm

Gök Medrese
Cemal Gürsel Caddesi
Sivas

Open: every day 8.30am-12noon
and 1.30-6pm

**Gordion Museum and
Archaeological Site**
Yassi Höyük Köyu
Open: every day except Monday
8.30am-5.30pm

**Göreme Valley Open-Air
Museum**
Göreme
☎ (4868) 2
Open: every day 8am-5pm
Café, shop, refreshments

Gümüsler Monastery
Eski Gümüsler
Open: every day except Monday
8.30am-12noon and 1-5pm

Hacibektas Dervish Museum
Hacibektas
☎ (4867) 1022
Open: every day except Monday
8.30am-12noon and 1.30-6pm

Kayseri Archaeological Museum
Kisla Caddesi, Kayseri
☎ (351) 11131
Open: every day except Monday
8.30am-12noon and 1-5pm

Kurtulus Savas Müzesi
Cumhuriyet Bulvari
Ulus
Ankara
☎(4) 310 53 61
Open: every day except Monday
8.30am-5pm

Nigde Archaeological Museum
Ögretmen Okullu Caddesi
Nigde
☎ (483) 11128
Open: every day except Monday

8.30am-12noon and 1-5pm

Sivas Museum
Buruçiye Medrese
Sivas
☎ (477) 12568
Open: every day except Monday
8.30am-12noon and 1-5pm

Temple of Augustus
Hükümet Caddesi
Ankara
Open: every day 8.30am-5pm

Tokat Gök Medrese
148 GDP Bulvari
Tokat
☎ (4751) 1509
Open: every day except Monday
8.30am-12noon and 1-5pm

Yazilikaya Hittite Open Temple
Yazilikaya
Open: 8.30am-12noon and 1.30-6pm

Zelve Monastic Centre
Zelve
Open: every day 8.30am-5.30pm

USEFUL ADDRESSES

Tourist Information Offices
Adana
13 Atatürk Caddesi
☎ (71) 11 13 23

Adiyaman
Atatürk Bulvari
PTT Yani
☎ (8781) 2478

Aksaray
Hükümet Konagi
☎ (4811) 24 74

Alanya
56 Iskele Caddesi
☎ (3231) 12 40

Ankara
33 Gazi Mustafa Kemal Bulv
☎ (4) 230 19 11

4 Istanbul Caddesi
Ulus
☎ (4) 311 22 47

Antakya
41 Atatürk Caddesi
☎ (891) 12636

Antalya
91 Cumhuriyet Caddesi
☎ (31) 11 17 47

Ayvalik
Yat Liman Karsisi
☎ (6631) 21 21

Bergama
54 Izmir Yolu Üzeri
☎ (5411) 1862

Bodrum
12 Eylül Meydani
☎ (6141) 1091

Bursa
7 Ulu Cami Park
☎ (24) 22 80 05

Çanakkale
67 Iskele Meydani
☎ (196) 23 71

Çesme
8 Iskele Meydani
☎ (5492) 66 53

Çorum
Sehir Is Han
☎ (469) 18502

Diyarbakir
24/A Lise Caddesi
☎ (831) 12173

Edirne
76/A Hürriyet Meydani
☎ (181) 15260

Erdek
54/B Hükümet Caddesi
☎ (1989) 11 69

Erzurum
Cemal Gürsel Caddesi
☎ (011) 15697

Fethiye
1 Iskele Meydani
☎ (6151) 15 27

Istanbul
3 Divanyolu Caddesi
☎ (1) 513 34 28

Izmir
Gaziosmanpasa Bulvari
☎ (51) 19 92 78

Iznik
168 Kiliçarslan Caddesi
☎ (2527) 21593

Kars
4 Lise Caddesi
☎ (0211) 12912

Kas
6 Cumhuriyet Meydani
☎ (3226) 12 38

Kayseri
61 Kagni Pazari
☎ (351) 19295

Konya
21 Mevlana Caddesi
☎ (33) 11 10 74

Kusadasi
Iskele Meydani
☎ (636) 11 03

Marmaris
39 Iskele Meydani
☎ (612) 10 35

Mersin
Inönü Bulv Liman Girisi Sahasi
☎ (741) 11265

Nevsehir
20/A Lale Caddesi
☎ (4851) 36 59

Samsun
Irmak Caddesi
☎ (361) 11228

Selçuk
23 Efes Müzesi Karsisi
☎ (5451) 13 28

Silifke
1/2 Atatürk Caddesi
☎(7591) 151

Sinop
10 Iskele Meydani
☎ (3761) 5837

Sivas
18 Osmanpasa Caddesi
☎ (477) 13535

Tasucu
18/A Gümrük Meydani
☎ (7593) 234

Trabzon
31 Taksim Caddesi
☎ (031) 35833

Ürgüp
37 Kayseri Caddesi
☎ (4868) 10 59

Urfa
3/D Asfaltyolu
☎ (8711) 2467

Van
127 Cumhuriyet Caddesi
☎ (061) 12018

Information and Advice
Turkish Embassy
Camelot House
76 Brompton Road
London SW3
☎ (071) 584 4062

Turkish Tourism Office
49 Conduit Street
London W1
☎ (071) 734 8681

Turkish Information Center
821 United Nations Plaza
New York NY 10017
☎ (212) 687 2194

Turkish Information Center
2010 Massachusetts Avenue NW
Washington DC 20036
☎ (202) 429 94 09

British Consulate
34 Mesrutiyet Caddesi
Tepebasi
Istanbul
☎ (1) 144 75 40

British Embassy
46/A Sehit Ersan Caddesi
Cankaya
Ankara
☎ (4) 127 43 10

British Consulate
1442 Sokak 49
Alsancak
Izmir
☎ (51) 21 17 95

British Council
Örs Türistik Is Merkezi
251/153 Istiklal Caddesi
Beyoglu
Istanbul
☎ (1) 152 74 74

United States Consulate
Mesrutiyet Caddesi No 104
Tepebasi
Istanbul
☎ (1) 151 36 02

United States Consulate
110 Atatürk Bulvari
Kavaklidere
Ankara
☎ (4) 126 54 65

United States Consulate
92 Atatürk Caddesi
Alsancak
Izmir
☎ (51) 14 94 26

Travel
By Air
British Airways
10 Cumhuriyet Caddesi
Elmadag
Istanbul
☎ (1) 148 42 35

Air France
1 Cumhuriyet Caddesi
Taksim
Istanbul
☎ (1) 155 30 50

Alitalia
14 Cumhuriyet Caddesi
Taksim
Istanbul
☎ (1) 131 33 91

PIA Pakistani International Airlines
Hilton Hotel Arcade

Taksim
Istanbul
☎ (1) 131 23 39

THY Turkish Airlines
199-201 Cumhuriyet Caddesi
Harbiye
Istanbul
☎ (1) 146 20 50

THY Turkish Airlines
Hippodrum Caddesi
Gar Yani
Ankara
☎ (4) 312 62 00

THY Turkish Airlines
Hastane Caddesi
Özel Idare Ishani Alti
Antalya
☎ (311) 11 28 30

THY Türk Hava Yollari
11/12 Hanover Street
London W1
☎ (071) 499 9249

THY Turkish Airlines
Turkish Centre 821
United Nations Plaza
New York
☎ (1212) 212 986 5050

Toros Air
c/o Sunquest Holidays
Aldine House
9-15 Aldine Street
London W12 8AW
☎ (081) 749 9911

By Sea
Turkish Maritime Lines
Rihtim Caddesi
Karaköy
Istanbul
☎ (1) 144 02 07

Turkish Maritime Lines
Denizyollari Acenteligi
Yeni Liman
Alsancak
Izmir
☎ (51) 21 00 77

Turkish Maritime Line Agent
c/o Sunquest Holiday
Aldine House
9-15 Aldine Street
London W12 8AW
☎ (081) 749 9911

Libra Maritime
Plateia Loudovicou No 4
Piraeus
Greece
☎ 411 7864

By Rail
Orient Express
Suite 200
Hudson's Place
Victoria Station
London SW1 1JL
☎ (071) 928 6000

Orient Express
Suite 2565
One World Trade Center
New York
NY 10048

Haydarpasa Rail Station
Haydarpasa
Istanbul
☎ (1) 336 20 63

Sirkeci Rail Station
Sirkeci
Istanbul
☎ (1) 520 65 75

By Coach
Anadolu Coach Station
Harem

Istanbul
☎ (1) 582 10 10

Trakya Coach Station
Topkapi
Istanbul
☎ (1) 333 37 63

By Car
Turkish Touring and Automobile
Association
364 Halaskargazi Caddesi
Sisli
Istanbul
☎ (1) 131 46 31

Turkish Touring and Automobile
Association
4/11 Adakale Sokak
Yenisehir
Ankara
☎ (4) 131 76 48

Turkish Touring and Automobile
Association
370 Atatürk Bulvari
Alsancak
Izmir
☎ (51) 21 71 49

Avis International
4/A Yedikuyular Caddesi
Elmadag
Istanbul
☎ (1) 141 78 96

Budget Car
33/1 Inönü Caddesi
Gümüssuyu
Istanbul
☎ (1) 145 75 62

Europcar
47/2 Cumhuriyet Caddesi
Taksim
Istanbul
☎ (1) 150 88 88

Hertz
9/5 Çim Apartment
Meyva Sokak
Cumhuriyet Caddesi
Harbiye
Istanbul
☎ (1) 141 69 66

Inter Rent
23/2 Recep Pasa Caddesi
Taksim
Istanbul
☎ (1) 155 06 90

Special Interest Holidays
Trek Travel
10 Aydede Caddesi
Taksim
Istanbul
☎ (1) 155 16 24

Trans Orient Tourism and Travel
223/2 Cumhuriyet Caddesi
Harbiye
Istanbul
☎ (1) 148 68 22

Explore Worldwide Ltd
7 High Street
Aldershot
Hants GU11 1BH
☎ (0252) 319448

Goulette Cruising Specialists
Frances McCulloch
60 Fordwych Road

London NW2 3TH
☎ (081) 452 7509

Exodus Expeditions
All Saints Passage
100 Wandsworth High Street
London SW18 4LE
☎ (081) 870 0151

Ramblers Holidays Ltd
Box 43
Welwyn Garden City
Herts AL8 6PQ
☎ (0707) 331133

HF Holidays Ltd
142-144 Great North Way
London NW4 1EG
☎ (081) 203 0433

Adventure Center
5540 College Avenue
Oakland
California CA 94618
☎ (415) 654 1879

Sobek Expeditions
PO Box 1089
Angels Camp
California CA 95222

Mountain Travel Inc
1398 Solano Avenue
Albany
California CA 94706

INDEX

251